齐鲁传统体育文化

李丽　主编

山东大学出版社
SHANDONG UNIVERSITY PRESS
·济南·

图书在版编目(CIP)数据

齐鲁传统体育文化/李丽主编.—济南:山东大学出版社,2022.11

ISBN 978-7-5607-7680-4

Ⅰ.①齐…　Ⅱ.①李…　Ⅲ.①民族形式体育—体育文化—研究—山东　Ⅳ.①G852.9

中国版本图书馆 CIP 数据核字(2022)第 248595 号

策划编辑　徐　翔
责任编辑　蔡梦阳　孙艳凤
封面设计　王秋忆

齐鲁传统体育文化
QILU CHUANTONG TIYU WENHUA

出版发行　山东大学出版社
社　　址　山东省济南市山大南路 20 号
邮政编码　250100
发行热线　(0531)88363008
经　　销　新华书店
印　　刷　济南乾丰云印刷科技有限公司
规　　格　720 毫米×1000 毫米　1/16
　　　　　14 印张　272 千字
版　　次　2022 年 11 月第 1 版
印　　次　2022 年 11 月第 1 次印刷
定　　价　76.00 元

《齐鲁传统体育文化》编委会

主　编　李　丽

副主编　沙芮伊　韩　庆　屈媛媛　袁　宏　文治芳

编　委　麻梦然　张苗苗　刘秋景　田恩来

张玲玉　袁凤超　朱　阁　付　帅

前言

山东是先秦时期齐、鲁两国的旧地，史称“齐鲁之邦”。其东靠大海，西傍中原，北邻京津，南依江淮，自古为中华形胜之地。齐鲁文化有着深厚的历史积淀，这里是中华文明最重要的发源地之一。同时，齐鲁体育文化是中国体育文化的来源之一，也是中国体育文化必不可少的一部分。齐鲁文化中的体育文化深深扎根于齐鲁本土文化之中，被齐鲁大地的自然、地理、民族和文化等因素影响，经过千百年发展，逐渐形成了独特的以齐鲁文化为根基的体育文化，并在中国传统体育文化中扮演着重要的角色。

齐鲁体育文化呈现出的文化性格深受齐鲁农耕文化中辛勤、简朴、安土重迁和慎终追远等因素的影响，具有稳妥和坚韧的独特特点。同时，齐国的霸主文化，鲁国的追求仁义和宗法礼仪等级的儒家文化使齐鲁体育文化具有尚武、尚礼的内涵。因此，我们不能只追溯历史让其留在过去，而应充分保护、继承和传播齐鲁体育文化。20世纪80年代以来，山东地区的竞技体育和群众体育都发展迅速，而传统体育文化发展现状却不容乐观。究其原因，是因为齐鲁体育文化的传承与传播主要在省内或国内，受众群体有限，缺少对海外受众的传播。海外传播的首要条件是语言的沟通，这也正是本书撰写的初衷，希望本书能为齐鲁传统体育项目走出国门打下良好的语言基础，同时也能够为中西方的体育文化碰撞提供更多的可能性，提升海外群体对中国传统文化的认知和喜爱程度。

本书包含两个章节的内容：第一章对目前齐鲁体育文化进行了综合概述，包含齐鲁体育文化的历史、齐鲁传统体育项目传播现状和对外传播的重要意义，为后面的论述和项目介绍打下坚实的基础，让读者对齐鲁体育文化有一个基本的了解。第二章紧紧切合本书主题，选取了山东地区国家非物质文化遗产项目或极具地域特色的项目进行中英文的分析和说明，并从项目文化、历史起源、项目器械、项目动作、传承现状等多方面介绍了十六项传统体育项目，如蹴鞠、孙膑拳、徐家拳、青州花毽、潍坊风筝、肘捶等。

《齐鲁体育文化》一书内容翔实，在介绍每个项目的同时，还配以图片以丰富读者的视觉感受，便于读者能够更为清晰全面地了解每个项目的特点。本书用朴素且客观的语言去描述项目的发展和现状，适合不同类型的读者去阅读和接受。相信本书的出版会为齐鲁传统体育文化的研究和发展带来一定的启示。

在成书的过程中，作者得到了很多专家、学者的建议，在此表示诚挚的谢意。由于编者水平有限，成书时间仓促，书中难免出现疏漏之处，恳请广大读者批评指正。

编者

2022年8月

目录

第1章 齐鲁传统体育文化概况

1.齐鲁文化源远流长

中国体育的现代化是20世纪80年代后期发展起来的中国现代文化研究之一，它准确定位了中国体育文化在体育现代化中的地位。古代体育文化作为体育文化研究的重点，在体育文化的转型发展中没有得到足够的重视，体育文化、社会和文化的研究者之间缺乏深度的联系，很大一部分的体育文化研究仅限于奥林匹克文化研究。冲突是文化发展的动力，是文化发展的源泉，体育和文化的共同规律也是如此。在申奥成功之前，我们对传统体育文化多进行批评性研究，有建设意义的分析很少。在2008年北京奥林匹克运动会的举办过程中，有一小部分专家认为西方体育文化存在的内部矛盾可以被中国传统文化弥补。这些倾向对于传承传统文化的精神是毫无益处的，对于中国体育文化的发展也是毫无价值的。从社会环境和传承传统文化精神的角度研究体育文化的蜕变，将会为体育运动的发展提供一条较为可行的道路。

齐鲁体育文化具有独特的个性和与众不同的风格。它的形成过程深受农耕文化中稳妥、中庸、辛勤、简朴、自我守成、安土重迁与慎终追远的宗法文化影响，形成尚和的体育文化特点。齐国的霸主文化，鲁国的追求仁义、内外兼修，以及宗法礼仪等级的儒家文化，使齐鲁体育文化具有尚勇武、尚礼的特点。面对这些优秀的传统体育文化，我们不能仅仅追溯历史让其留在过去，而应充分继承并发扬齐鲁体育文化。

齐鲁传统体育文化研究不仅进一步丰富了齐鲁文化、体育文化和地域体育文化，而且有助于改善山东传统体育文化传承面临的困境，有助于推动群众体育活动的开展，为体育文化产业提供发展的动力，具有极高的社会价值。首先，齐鲁体育传统文化的研究有助于山东传统体育文化的传承与发展。传统体育文化作为传统文化的组成部分，历史悠久且内容丰富。近代以来，西方体育文化的传播对传统体育文化的生存与传承产生了一定的负面影响。虽然20世纪30年代发生的“土洋体育之争”展示了传统武术的文化内涵和发展的优势，国术馆的建立也极大地促进了武术的传播，但同时可以看出，传统体育文化发展的模式受到了严重冲击。如何解决中西体育文化的对立与冲突一直是体育界的热点问题。20世纪80年代以来，山东体育事业发展迅猛，尤其是在竞技体育领域，无论是竞技成绩还是运动训练场地设施的建设，在全国一直位于前列。与竞技体育的大发展相比，传统体育的传承与发展却不容乐观：传统武术拳种后继乏人，民间民俗健身项目在城镇化的进程中逐渐失去生存的土壤，传统养生项目的参与群体主要局限于老年群体，民间体育游戏在青少年中缺乏普及推广等。齐鲁传统体育文化研究有助于解决目前传统体育文化发展面临的困境。该研究针对传统体育文化传承与发展中面临的困境及具体问题，进行深入调研分析，提出具有可操作性的解决方法及路径；通过分析产生传统体育文化的土壤，探讨其文化特征及发展困境的深层次原因，为中西方体育文化的碰撞、融合及多元并存提供策略；通过对传统体育文化历史的梳理，丰富传统体育文化传播的内容，营造传统体育文化发展的氛围，提高人们对传统体育文化的认知水平，进而激发民众参与健身活动的热情。因此，加强齐鲁传统体育文化的研究，将为当今传统体育文化的发展提供一定的理论资源和实践对策。

综上所述，齐鲁传统体育文化是世代生活在齐鲁大地上的人们在生产劳动、娱乐休闲、修身养性、民俗节庆以及为自身的权益进行积极抗争中创造、积累起来的。齐鲁传统体育文化发展到新时代，需要我们结合时代的需求，赋予其更丰富的内涵，并为其发展做出应有的贡献。

2.齐鲁文化与齐鲁传统体育文化

齐鲁文化是集地域和文化于一体的概念。秦汉时期，齐鲁文化中作为学术思想文化代表的儒家思想和作为民族宗教的道教，融入中华民族的主流文化并成为其主体部分。从此齐鲁文化由地域文化上升为主流文化，同时齐鲁文化的概念与内涵也发生了重大变化。纵观历史发展进程中的齐鲁文化，其内涵可以概括为两个方面：一是地域文化，即以齐国、鲁国领地的范围为依托的文化，包括该地域的政治、经济、文化思想和风土人情等；二是主流文化，这需要从中国传统文化的层面分析，其内涵主要涉及学术思想、宗教信仰等价值观念层面。

儒家伦理思想是儒家学说的核心内容，孕育于齐鲁大地，影响着齐鲁传统体育文化的发展和演变。在儒家礼制的影响下，齐鲁传统体育活动带有明显的礼仪性，如齐鲁武术的拜师礼、蹴鞠的社规、射礼和齐鲁秧歌等，形成了注重礼仪的体育价值观。儒家尚仁的伦理思想使齐鲁传统体育项目规则的制定都十分注重道德的作用，如蹴鞠和传统武术等。“中庸平和”是儒家伦理思想理性原则的集中体现，在齐鲁传统武术的技击特点上和蹴鞠的发展脉络中都体现出了这个特点。在齐鲁大地上开展的丰富多彩的娱乐活动，也充分体现了儒家伦理中的“义利观”对道德与利益关系的论证。但我们也应该认识到，儒家伦理思想具有两面性。在封建社会上升时期，儒家伦理思想具有稳定社会秩序的特性，对齐鲁传统体育活动的开展起到了积极的作用；到了封建社会末期，儒家伦理思想则阻碍了齐鲁传统体育活动的发展。

齐鲁文化以儒家文化为基础，在漫长的历史进程中不断地吸收其他各种文化的精髓，形成了博大精深、极其丰厚的思想内涵。齐鲁文化的精神内涵在本质上是以“仁”“礼”为核心的人文主义精神、崇尚国家的爱国主义精神、崇尚民族的自强不息的奋斗精神、崇尚民本的厚德仁民精神、崇尚群体的大公无私精神等。齐鲁文化和齐鲁民间体育游戏同时出现在历史的长河中，又都随着历史的车轮前进和繁荣壮大。无论在历史上还是在现在，无论哪一种齐鲁民间体育游戏，都体现和宣扬了齐鲁文化所表达的精神内涵。也就是说，博大精深的齐鲁文化在齐鲁民间体育游戏运动的发展中占据着主导地位，有着至关重要的作用，支配着齐鲁民间体育游戏未来的发展趋向。同时，两者之间又有着相辅相成的作用，勤劳朴实的齐鲁人民通过民间体育游戏演绎着齐鲁文化，不断地充实着齐鲁文化，并向世界传播宣扬了齐鲁文化。

3.齐鲁传统体育项目国际传播

3.1　齐鲁传统体育项目国际传播的意义

3.1.1　齐鲁传统体育项目是丰富世界体育文化的新资源

纵观近现代世界体育发展，西方因其经济优势和国际地位使得世界体育成为西方体育的天下。以体育最大盛事奥运会为例，源于西方的运动项目比比皆是。在夏季奥运会中，除了柔道、跆拳道等个别项目外，其他项目都为西方体育项目。世界体育文化的展现也往往依托于西方体育赛事，如美国职业篮球赛（NBA）、FIFA 国际足联世界杯、超级碗（美国职业橄榄球大联盟年度冠军赛）

等。随着我国由体育大国向体育强国的迈进，有着五千年历史积淀的中国体育文化正在向世界吹响号角，以太极等项目为代表的中国传统体育项目已走进西方校园。而齐鲁传统体育文化所包含的人性关怀、身心并重、积极进取、追求和谐、维护和平的思想与奥林匹克精神有着高度的相似之处，并且以儒家思想为基础、以道德至上的齐鲁传统体育文化也是中华传统体育文化的精华。所以齐鲁传统体育文化符合世界体育文化主题，并具有民族文化特质，这为齐鲁传统体育文化的传播提供了有利条件。齐鲁传统体育项目是齐鲁传统体育文化的承载体，项目种类繁多、特色突出，因此向世界推广齐鲁传统体育项目，有利于丰富世界体育文化资源，促进世界体育文化的健康、和谐发展。

3.1.2　齐鲁传统体育项目的国际传播是弘扬中国传统文化的新途径

习近平总书记在纪念孔子诞辰 2565 周年国际学术研讨会上曾指出，科学对待文化传统，不忘历史才能开辟未来，善于继承才能善于创新。优秀传统文化是一个国家、一个民族传承和发展的根本，如果丢掉了，就割断了精神命脉。我们要善于把弘扬优秀传统文化和发展现实文化有机统一起来、紧密结合起来，在继承中发展，在发展中继承。齐鲁传统体育项目是历史上齐、鲁两国传统体育文化的集中体现，是齐鲁地区儒家等思想的表现形式。齐鲁传统体育项目的国际传播，实质上是对齐鲁传统体育文化的重构及以儒家思想为地区体育精神的优化。通过对外传播，使之成为世界可以接纳的中华体育文化，在一定程度上实现了齐鲁传统体育项目的创造性转化，将以齐文化的尚功利崇武勇精神、儒学的尚中贵和精神、道学的养生思想为基本文化渊源的中国传统体育观念依托传统体育项目进行推广，为弘扬中国传统文化提供了新的途径。

3.1.3　齐鲁传统体育项目是拉动区域体育产业的新动力

2018 年 12 月 21 日国务院办公厅发布《关于加快发展体育竞赛表演产业的指导意见》，指出要坚持“体育＋”和“＋体育”做法，促进体育竞赛表演产业与文化和旅游、娱乐、互联网等相关产业深度融合，拓展发展空间，为经济增长提供支撑。并以观赏性较强的运动项目为突破口，创作开发体现中华优秀文化、具有中国特色的体育竞赛表演精品。齐鲁传统体育项目的国际传播是“体育＋互联网”以及“体育＋旅游”的融合产物。以临淄蹴鞠为例，临淄建立足球博物馆，并打造了蹴鞠表演队，将蹴鞠文化真实、动态地展现在参观者面前。博物馆在 2015 年与英国足球博物馆建立合作伙伴关系，促进了蹴鞠文化及齐文化的对外传播。临淄自 2016 年起已成功举办三届世界足球文化高峰论坛，吸引了大批国内外游客前来参观旅游，拉动了临淄区域旅游业的迅速发展，使得蹴鞠成为临淄体育与旅游的城市品牌。

3.1.4　齐鲁传统体育项目的国际传播是保护传统体育项目的新方法

现如今齐鲁传统体育项目的保护传承主要针对国内传统体育爱好人士，一般通过师徒相传、短期培训表演和申报各级非物质文化遗产名录三种途径进行。而齐鲁传统体育项目的国际传播可以说是打开了对其保护及发展的另一片天空，了解、接受，甚至是习练者从国内扩展到世界范围，从师徒相传转变为远程教学，从短期表演转变为时时观看，从单一保护转变为交融与兴盛。临淄蹴鞠在经历历史的变迁与文化的兼容后，成为风靡世界的足球运动。因此，齐鲁传统体育项目的传承人、习练者及学者应向外、向前看，将齐鲁传统体育项目推广到世界，让其国际传播真正成为保护并发展项目的新方法。

3.2　齐鲁传统体育项目传播现状

3.2.1　翻译资源稀缺

齐鲁传统体育项目如何“走出去”？毫无疑问借助语言文字符号进行国际传播是最直接的方式。但国内目前体育英语的丛书或是教材主要集中于西方体育竞技项目或是奥运英语，如苏州大学出版社出版的《专门用途英语 ESP 规划教材系列·体育英语》，涉及奥运会比赛项目 25 个。即便涉及传统体育项目，也只是挑选个别项目简略介绍，如武汉大学出版社出版的《体育英语》中第九章涉及中国体育运动，但只简单介绍了功夫、跳绳、踢毽子、太极、围棋五个项目。山东文艺出版社出版的《山东省省级非物质文化遗产名录图典》是至今较为系统介绍齐鲁传统体育项目的图书，但缺少对项目文化、项目动作的深入介绍。针对齐鲁特色的传统体育项目的规范性翻译，如肘捶等，经查阅国家图书馆、高等体育院校图书馆发现目前资料显示为零。

3.2.2　国际传播途径单一

齐鲁传统体育项目中具有代表性的以娱乐为主的项目如临淄蹴鞠等，与查拳、螳螂拳等民间武术项目，已被列入国家级非物质文化遗产，但目前宣传渠道单一，大众对于这些传统项目的信息获取主要集中于电视媒体。然而随着数字技术、网络技术与移动通信技术的迅猛发展，以网络媒体、移动媒体等为主体的新媒体孕育并快速成长。2018 年 8 月中国互联网络信息中心（CNNIC）发布的第 42 次《中国互联网络发展状况统计报告》显示，截至 2018 年 6 月 30 日，我国网民规模达 8.02 亿，互联网普及率为 57.7%。新媒体因稳定而庞大的用户群，应该成为传播齐鲁传统体育项目的主要渠道。但调查发现，集中展示齐鲁传统项目及齐鲁传统体育文化的新媒体宣传平台却几乎不存在。

3.2.3 传播范围局限

绝大部分齐鲁传统体育项目都留存在山东发展相对落后、位置较为偏远的基层，受到城镇化、现代化的冲击，传承青黄不接，后继乏人的问题较为突出。例如肘捶、孙膑拳等项目传承方式主要为带徒授艺的师徒传承、家族传承，或是短期培训的群体传承、学校传承等，这些传承方式确实为齐鲁传统体育项目的保护起到了一定的作用，但是因为其大多数为点对点的传播方式，因而其传播范围存在局限性。

Overview of Qilu Traditional Sports Culture

1.Qilu culture has a long history

The modernization of sports in China is one of the modern Chinese cultural studies that developed sports in the late 1980s, which accurately positions the status of Chinese sports culture in sports modernization. As the focus of our sports culture research investment, ancient sports culture has not received enough attention during the transformation and development of sports culture. There is a lack of deep relationship context between researchers of sports culture, society, and culture. A large part of the study of sports culture is limited to the study of Olympic culture. Conflict is the driving force of cultural development, the source of cultural development, and the common law of sports and culture. Before the success of the Olympic bid, we had more critical research on traditional sports culture and there was little analysis of construction significance, especially in the process of hosting the 2008 Beijing Olympic Games. A small number of experts believed that the internal contradictions of Western sports culture could be compensated by traditional Chinese culture. These tendencies were of no benefit to inheriting the spirit of traditional culture and they were also worthless to the development of Chinese sports culture. Analyzing the sharp changes in sports culture from the perspective of social environment and inheriting the spirit of traditional culture will provide a more feasible path for the development of sports.

Qilu sports culture has a unique personality and a distinctive style. Its formation process was deeply influenced by patriarchal culture of agrarian culture, which is stable, moderate, hard-working, simple, self-observant, and relying on the land to pursue the future with caution. Therefore, the characteristics of the sports culture of advocating peace have been formed. The hegemonic culture of the State of Qi, the pursuit of benevolence and self-cultivation in the State of Lu and the Confucian culture of patriarchal etiquette have endowed Qilu sports culture with the cultural characteristics of encouraging martial and etiquette spirits. In the face of these outstanding sports cultures, we should not only trace the history and let them stay in the past but fully inherit and carry forward the Qilu sports culture.

The study of Qilu traditional sports culture not only further enriches Qilu culture, sports culture, and regional sports culture, but also helps to improve the dilemma faced by the inheritance of traditional sports culture in Shandong and promote the development of mass sports activities and provides a driving force for the development of the sports culture industry, which is of great social value. First, the study of Qilu sports culture is conducive to the inheritance and development of traditional sports culture in Shandong. Traditional sports culture has a long history and rich content as an integral part of traditional culture. The dissemination of Western sports culture has had a certain negative impact on the survival and inheritance of traditional sports culture in modern times. Although the "Traditional and Modern Methods Sports Dispute" in the 1930s shows the cultural connotation and development advantages of traditional martial arts and the establishment of the National Art Museum has also greatly promoted the spread of martial arts. However, at the same time, the traditional model of the development of traditional sports culture has been seriously impacted, and how to solve the confrontation and conflict between Chinese and Western sports culture has always been a hot issue in the sports industry. Since the 1980s, Shandong's sports industry has developed rapidly, especially in the field of competitive sports. Whether it is competitive performance, or the construction of sports training venues and facilities, it has been at the forefront of the country. Compared with the great development of competitive sports, the inheritance and development of traditional sports are not optimistic: The inheritance of traditional martial arts and fists is lacking; folk fitness projects have gradually lost the soil for survival in the process of urbanization; the participation group of traditional health care projects is mainly limited to the elderly group; folk sports games lack popularity among teenagers and so on. Qilu sports culture research helps to solve the current dilemmas facing the development of traditional sports culture. The study is aimed at the dilemmas and specific problems faced in the inheritance and development of traditional sports culture, and carries out in-depth research and analysis to propose operable solutions and paths. By analyzing the cultural soil of traditional sports culture, exploring its cultural characteristics and the deep-seated reasons for its development dilemma, we provide strategies for the collision, integration and multiple coexistence of Chinese and Western sports cultures. By sorting out the history of traditional sports culture, we enrich the content of traditional sports culture dissemination, create an atmosphere for the development of traditional sports culture, and improve people's awareness of traditional sports culture. It also creates an atmosphere for the development of traditional sports culture, raises people's awareness of traditional sports culture, and stimulates people to participate in fitness activities. Therefore, strengthening the study of Qilu sports culture will provide certain theoretical resources and practical measures for the development of today's traditional sports culture.

To sum up, Qilu sports culture is created and accumulated by people living on the land of Qilu for generations in the process of production labor, entertainment and leisure, self-cultivation, folk festivals and active struggle for their own rights and interests. As Qilu sports culture has developed into a new era, we need to combine the needs of the times, give it a richer connotation, and make our due contributions to its development.

2.Qilu culture and Qilu traditional sports culture

Qilu culture is a concept that integrates region and culture. Confucianism as the representative of academic ideology and culture and Taoism as a national religion in Qilu culture were integrated into the mainstream cultural concept of the Chinese nation and became the main part of it during the Qin and Han dynasties. Since then, Qilu culture rose from regional culture to mainstream culture and the concept and connotation of Qilu culture also underwent major changes. The connotation of Qilu culture in the process of historical development can be summarized into two aspects: First, it is the regional culture, which is based on the territory of Qi and Lu, including the politics and economy, cultural thought, customs and local conditions of the region; second, it is the mainstream culture, which needs to be analyzed from the level of traditional Chinese culture, and its content mainly involves academic thought, religious beliefs and other values.

Confucian ethical thought is the core content of Confucianism, which was conceived in the land of Qilu and influenced the development and evolution of Qilu traditional sports culture. Influenced by the Confucian etiquette system, Qilu's traditional sports activities have obvious etiquette, forming sports values that focus on etiquette. The rituals of Qilu martial arts, the social rules of Cuju, the archery ceremony, and the Qilu Yangko are all carried out in a ceremonial manner. The Confucian ethical thought of advocating righteousness has made Qilu traditional sports attach great importance to the role of morality in the formulation of the rules, such as Cuju and the traditional martial techniques. Neutralization is a concentrated embodiment of the rational principle of Confucian ethical thought and its "moderate and peaceful" characteristics are embodied in the technical characteristics of Qilu's traditional martial arts and in the development of Cuju. The argument of the "concept of righteousness and profit" in Confucian ethics for the relationship between morality and interests is reflected in Qilu's colorful entertainment activities.

However, we should also recognize the two sides of Confucian ethics. Confucian ethical thought had the characteristics of stabilizing social order and played a positive role in the development of traditional sports activities in Qilu during the period of rising feudal society. But Confucian ethical thought hindered the development of traditional sports activities in Qilu in the late feudal period.

Based on Confucian culture, Qilu culture has continuously absorbed the essence of other cultures to form a broad and profound and extremely rich ideological connotation in the long historical process. The spiritual connotation of Qilu culture is essentially expressed as the humanistic spirit with "benevolence" and "courtesy" as the core; advocating the national patriotism; advocating the national self-improvement spirit; advocating the people-oriented spirit of virtue and benevolence; advocating the selfless spirit of the group, and so on. Qilu culture and Qilu folk sports have appeared in the long river of history at the same time, and they have all advanced and prospered with the development of history. No matter in history or nowadays, any kind of Qilu folk game can reflect and promote the spiritual connotation expressed by Qilu culture. In other words, the profound Qilu culture occupies a dominant position and plays a vital role in the development of Qilu folk sports games, which dominates the future development trend of Qilu folk sports games. They are complementary to each other. The industrious people of Qilu interpret Qilu culture, enrich Qilu culture and publicize and disseminate Qilu culture to the world through folk games.

3.International dissemination of traditional sports in Qilu

3.1 Significance of the international dissemination of traditional sports in Qilu

3.1.1 It's a new resource to enrich the world's sports culture

The West has made world sports the world of Western sports because of its economic advantages and international status throughout the development of sports in the modern world. For example, in the biggest event in sports—the Olympic

Games, sports originating in the Western countries are great in number.

Except for individual sports such as judo and taekwondo, all other sports are western sports in the Summer Olympic Games. The world sports culture is also often displayed in Western sports events such as the National Basketball Association (NBA), the FIFA World Cup, the Super Bowl (the annual championship game of the National Football League) and so on. With the advancement of China from a sports country to a sports power, Chinese sports culture with a history of 5,000 years is blowing a clarion call to the world and Chinese traditional sports such as tai chi has entered Western campuses. The Qilu sports culture contains the idea of human care, equal emphasis on body and mind, positive progress, the pursuit of harmony, and the maintenance of peace and the Olympic spirit also have a striking similarity. The Qilu traditional sports culture based on Confucianism and the supremacy of morality is also the essence of traditional Chinese sports culture, so Qilu sports culture is in line with the theme of world sports culture and has national cultural characteristics, which provides favorable conditions for the dissemination of Qilu sports culture. The Qilu traditional sports with a wide variety of projects and outstanding characteristics are the carrier of Qilu sports culture and the promotion of Qilu traditional sports projects to the world, which is conducive to enriching the world sports culture resources and promoting the healthy and harmonious development of world sports culture.

3.1.2　It's a new way to promote traditional Chinese culture

At the International Academic Symposium commemorating the 2565th anniversary of the Birth of Confucius, General Secretary Xi Jinping pointed out that only by treating cultural traditions scientifically and not forgetting history can we open up the future, and only by being good at inheritance can we be good at innovation. Excellent traditional culture is the foundation of the inheritance and development of a country and a nation. If it is lost, it will cut off the spiritual lifeline. We must organically be good at closely integrating the promotion of excellent traditional culture with the development of realistic culture and develop during inheritance and inherit during development. The

Qilu traditional sports project is a concentrated embodiment of the expression of Confucianism and other ideas and traditional sports culture in Qilu. The international dissemination of traditional sports in Qilu is essentially a reconstruction of Qilu sports culture and the optimization of Confucianism as the regional sportsmanship. Making it become a Chinese sports culture that the world can accept through external dissemination to realize the creative transformation of Qilu traditional sports projects. The traditional Chinese sports concepts relying on traditional sports projects promote traditional Chinese culture with the spirit of Qi culture's material gain and martial spirit, Confucian spirit of moderation and peace, and Taoist health care ideology as the basic cultural source to carry forward traditional Chinese culture.

3.1.3 It's a new driving force for the regional sports industry

The General Office of the State Council issued the *Guiding Opinions on Accelerating the Development of the Sports Competition Performance Industry* on December 21, 2018, pointing out that it is necessary to adhere to the practice of "sports +" and "+ sports" and promote the deep integration of the sports competition performance industry with related industries such as culture and tourism, entertainment, and the Internet, expand development space to provide support for economic growth. Taking sports with ornamental values as a breakthrough, we will create and develop sports competition performances that reflect China's excellent culture and have Chinese characteristics. The international dissemination of traditional sports in Qilu is the product of the integration of "sports + Internet" and "sports + tourism". Taking Linzi Cuju as an example, Linzi established a football museum and created a Cuju performance team to display Cuju culture truly and dynamically in front of visitors. The museum established a partnership with the National Football Museum of England in 2015 to promote the external dissemination of Cuju and Qi culture. Linzi has successfully held three World Football Culture Summit Forum since 2016, attracting many domestic and foreign tourists to visit and travel, which has boosted the rapid development of tourism in Linzi region, making Cuju the city brand of sports and tourism in Linzi.

3.1.4　It's a new approach to the protection of traditional sports

Nowadays, the protection and inheritance of traditional sports in Qilu are mainly aimed at domestic traditional sports enthusiasts generally through three ways: master-apprentice transmission, short-term training performances and declaration of intangible cultural heritage at all levels. The international communication of traditional sports in Qilu is different. Those who understand, accept and even practice expand from China to the world, from mentoring to distance teaching, from short-term performance to moment watching, and from single protection to integration and prosperity. Linzi Cuju has become a popular football sport in the world after experiencing historical changes and cultural compatibility. Therefore, the inheritors, practitioners, and scholars of Qilu traditional sports should look outward and forward to promote Qilu traditional sports to the world and let its international dissemination truly become a new way to protect and develop the project.

3.2　The current situation of the dissemination of traditional sports in Qilu

3.2.1　Translation resources are scarce

There is no doubt that the international communication with language and symbols is the most direct way to study how to "go out" of traditional sports in Qilu. However, the series of books or teaching materials for sports English in China at present mainly focus on Western competitive sports or Olympic English, such as Soochow University Press's *Special Purpose English ESP Planning Textbook Series* · *Sports English*, involving 25 Olympic competitions. Even if traditional sports project is mentioned, it is only a brief introduction to individual sports. For example, Chapter 9 in the *Sports English* published by Wuhan University Press involves Chinese sports but only briefly introduces five sports: kungfu, rope skipping, shuttlecock kicking, tai chi, and weiqi. *The Catalogue of the List of Intangible Cultural Heritage of Shandong Province* published by Shandong Literature and Art Publishing House is a book that systematically introduces traditional sports projects in Qilu so far but lacks an in-depth introduction to the culture and actions of the project. None of normative translation of traditional sports with Qilu characteristics, such as elbow punches, can be found in the current materials in the National Library of China and libraries of higher sports colleges and universities.

3.2.2 The international communication channel is single

Representative entertainment-based projects in Qilu traditional sports projects such as Linzi Cuju as well as folk martial arts such as Zha Boxing, Mantis boxing and other folk martial arts projects have been listed as a national intangible cultural heritage. The public's information access to these traditional projects is mainly focused on the television media and has a single publicity channel at present. However, with the rapid development of digital technology, network technology and mobile communication technology, the new media with mainly network media and mobile media tend to appear and grow rapidly. According to the 42nd *Statistical Report on the Development of China's Internet Network* released by the China Internet Network Information Center (CNNIC) in August 2018, the scale of China's Internet users reached 802 million and the Internet penetration rate was 57.7% as of June 30, 2018. The stable and large user base of the new media is the audience market for the dissemination of traditional sports in Qilu. However, the survey finds that the new media publicity platform that focuses on Qilu traditional projects and Qilu traditional sports culture is almost non-existent.

3.2.3 The scope of dissemination is limited

Most of the traditional sports projects in Qilu are retained in the relatively backward and remote areas of Shandong. Due to the impact of urbanization and modernization, there is a lack of inheritors. For example, the inheritance methods of projects such as elbow punching and Sun Bin Boxing are mainly the inheritance of apprentices, family inheritance or group inheritance of short-term training, and the inheritance in schools, etc. Although these inheritance methods have played a certain role in the protection of traditional sports in Qilu, the dissemination scope is limited because most of them are disseminated in a point-to-point manner.

第2章 齐鲁传统体育项目

第1节 蹴鞠

1.项目文化

蹴鞠又名“蹋鞠”“蹴球”“筑球”“踢圆”，是中国古代一种足球运动，距今已有2300年的历史。其历史最早可以追溯到春秋战国时期，当时它在齐国故都临淄已发展成为一种成熟的娱乐方式，在民间广为盛行。

在古代，蹴鞠因高频率地出现在社会生活中，所以使其在各种文学作品中大量显现，如东汉李尤的《鞠城铭》、唐代仲元颇的《气球赋》、唐代吕延济的《文选注》等。

考古活动发现并印证了蹴鞠活动有音乐伴奏这一特点，如汉代砖石画。宋代蹴鞠音乐伴奏乐谱在正式的文献《事林广记·续集》中的《圆社市语·中吕宫·圆里圆》中有详细记载。

根据史书和相关文学资料记载，球场礼仪制度在汉代就已相当完备，如汉代蹴鞠礼仪是朝廷阅兵大典的一部分，宋代对于参加蹴鞠表演的艺人有着具体的礼仪规定。但在此之后，蹴鞠礼仪逐渐淡化。

蹴鞠是我国古代体育书籍中出现较多的项目，早在汉代，《汉书·艺文志》中就记载了《蹴鞠二十五篇》(此书在隋唐以后失传)，现存的四本蹴鞠专业书为《事林广记·续集》《万宝全书·戏球场科苑》《蹴鞠图谱》《蹴鞠谱》。

2004年，国际足联确认中国古代的蹴鞠就是足球的起源。历史文献《战国策》和《史记》最早、最明确地记载了在临淄开展的蹴鞠活动。

2.项目起源

蹴鞠项目起源在刘向的《别录》和刘歆的《七略》中均有记载。蹴鞠起源于黄帝时代，用于军事练兵，黄帝将其作为一种训练手段来提高部队的团结协作能力，激励士兵勇猛作战。

1953年，半坡遗址中出土的石球经检测其时间与黄帝时期基本吻合。明清时期，陕西部分地区仍有踢石球的民俗可以进一步佐证这一发现。

从官方认可的文献（《资治通鉴》《史记》《战国策·齐策》）记载来看，早在2500年前的战国时代就有了蹴鞠。在战国时代的齐国临淄，蹴鞠作为一种娱乐方式，大受民众欢迎。

汉初时期，蹴鞠发展为两个方向：一个是提高娱乐性技巧，配合音乐伴奏成为有观赏性的娱乐表演；另一个作为军事训练手段成为军事检阅中军礼的一部分。

汉代蹴鞠发展的一个重要标志就是出现了蹴鞠的研究专著。汉代兵家写的《蹴鞠二十五篇》是我国最早的一部体育专业图书，也是世界上第一部有关足球的专业文献。

汉代的蹴鞠是在专门的蹴鞠城中进行的，其依照古代自然哲学中的“天圆地方”建造圆鞠方城，并且效仿一年中的12个月，每边6个人共12个人，两队直接冲击对抗，设立以“长”和“平”命名的正副裁判；建立比赛规章制度，规定裁判要公正执法，不能偏袒任何一方。蹴鞠到汉代已经发展成为一项专业化的运动，同时蹴鞠作为一种训练手段受到皇帝和军事家的重视。

在隋唐时期，蹴鞠外传到朝鲜和日本，并在当地有各自的发展。《新唐书》和《旧唐书》中均有对朝鲜蹴鞠的记载，蹴鞠在日本的发展情况在日本古籍《日本书纪》《游庭秘抄》《口传集》中有记载。日本、朝鲜的蹴鞠活动并未照搬中国古代蹴鞠，而是加入本民族的特色，有了新的发展。

唐宋时期由于国家兴盛，“寒食蹴鞠”民俗的开展使群众性蹴鞠运动得到极大的发展。寒食节是唐代的一个重要节日，日期定在清明节的前一日，也象征着告别了令人郁闷的冬天，因此一到春天民众便会到郊外活动，而亲朋好友也会聚在一起，做一些能舒展身体的娱乐游戏，当时最普遍的游戏就是蹴鞠。

到了宋代出现了全国性专门的蹴鞠组织“圆社”(即蹴鞠艺人为了维护本身的利益和提高技艺组织起来的行会,它是世界上最早的足球俱乐部)和全国性的比赛“山岳正”(类似于如今中国的足球联赛)。

同时期,蹴鞠被列于朝廷宴会节目,市井娱乐中有专业蹴鞠艺人表演,民间广泛开展“寒食蹴鞠”风俗,形成了蹴鞠发展的高潮。

元代女蹴鞠艺人的出现,拓展了蹴鞠娱乐的社交意义,在一定程度上冲击了封建社会对妇女的歧视观念。

明朝时期,商业性质的蹴鞠表演是上层贵族追求娱乐的一种方式,却为封建士大夫所不齿。随着这种趋势的发展,朝廷宴会将蹴鞠表演取消,蹴鞠也逐渐走向衰落。

清朝时期,由于统治者对汉民族传统文化的压制,汉族体育项目被打压禁止,传统蹴鞠逐渐走向衰亡,有满族特色的冰上蹴鞠开始盛行。

至近代,随着西方足球的传入,蹴鞠已经名存实亡。

3.项目规则

3.1 双球门直接竞赛(直接对抗)(汉代)

比赛时,设鞠城(即球场),周围有短墙,比赛双方都有座小房子似的球门,场上队员各 12 名,双方进行直接的身体对抗,就像打仗一样,踢鞠入对方球门多者胜。

3.2 单球门直接竞赛

此为间接对抗,比赛时中间隔着球门,球门中间有两尺多的“风流眼”,对方各在一侧,在球不落地的情况下,能使之穿越风流眼多者胜。

3.3 白打(花样踢)

白打注重的是技巧和花样,亦称“解数”。每一种解数都有一系列的踢法,讲求不同的花样。白打除了球之外不再用任何其他器械,场地也极为简单,只要一块平坦的地方即可,一般选在风景秀美的幽静之所。

4.项目器具

最初的蹴鞠项目器具据考证是石球(半坡遗址发现),随着生产力的提高和科技的进步，蹴鞠逐渐从石制球发展成皮制球。马王堆帛书《十大经》记录黄帝征蚩尤部落，将其擒捉，充其胃以为鞠，这启发了人们用动物胃或皮毛制成外壳，再填充毛发进球，最后随着时间发展，逐步演变成空心球。

从时间上看，用皮革制成的球不会晚于殷代，因为当时的“鞠”字偏旁从革，祭祀时有鞠舞，并有了鞠姓家族。汉代的鞠是“以韦为之，实以物”，开始有较为标准的制球规格。唐代是蹴鞠改革的重要时代，由于制球工艺提高，由实心球改为充气球。宋代的制球工艺在唐代的基础上有所改进，制球更加接近圆形，改成用皮制工具添气。宋代手工业发达，制球的工艺精湛而且出现品牌(《蹴鞠谱》中记载的有 41 种，如“六锭银”“八月圆”“云月台”“花虎掌”“满园春”“百花朝阳”等)，这一时期蹴鞠制球发展达到顶峰。

四片蹴鞠

Four-piece Cuju

球门

Goal

5.动作解析(《蹴鞠谱》校译版本并做整理)

踢球的基本功是拐、搭、臁、辟,其余动作都是由此产生的。上场踢球须姿势端正,腰背不曲,脚步放开。遵守球场规定,不乱走,不移位。

拐:球来偏高使拐宜,弯腰抬腿不犹豫,脚弓放平踢不脱,退步慢踢更出奇。

搭:球来正面用搭踢,眼看准确脚放低,使力轻缓能控球,踢巧踢好靠步移。

臁：须要肩头对着脚尖，身体侧倒重心微偏，挺身直腰抬起脚，小腿平踢便是臁。

辞：球来凶猛用膝挡，使力要轻不要忙，可以上前迎球踢，亦可停球踢花样。

肩：球来高处用肩顶，左肩右肩须分清，上步退步都无碍，只能两次不频仍。

桩：踢漏了用桩补，认准落处快上步，勾起脚尖趾向上，踢时筋节要硬住。

捻：凶球要用脚来挡，准备从容不慌张，按踢犹如球打脚，再踢便能花样。

6.项目传承人

马国庆，山东淄博临淄人，国家体育总局体育文化发展中心蹴鞠研究基地秘书长，临淄世界足球博物馆、中国体育博物馆临淄分馆负责人，系临淄蹴鞠列入国家首批非物质文化遗产的领导小组成员，国家首批非物质文化遗产——蹴鞠承传代表，现任齐文化博物院院长。他通过在公众面前展示蹴鞠技艺，让更多人了解蹴鞠。马国庆作为蹴鞠的非物质文化传承代表人为蹴鞠文化的传播做出了杰出的贡献。

在足球起源地论证之初，马国庆起草了基础性的论证资料《关于临淄为世界足球起源地的研究报告》和《关于确认临淄为世界足球起源地的陈述报告》，"复活"了唐宋时期的蹴鞠运动。他担任《足球起源地探索》《齐都盛典》《齐都蹴鞠》的主要编辑，为世界足球起源地的确认、蹴鞠文化的研究与传播、临淄足球博物馆的成功运营、临淄区的足球产业和文化开展做出了突出贡献。

7.项目新发展

2006 年 5 月，蹴鞠被列入首批国家非物质文化遗产名录。

2005 年 4 月 2 日，蹴鞠队在国内最高足球赛事——中国足球超级联赛开幕式上进行了仿古蹴鞠表演。

2015 年 10 月，国家主席习近平访问英国，将临淄四片仿古蹴鞠作为国礼赠送给英格兰国家博物馆，加深了两国的交流。文化特色和个性是历史文化名城独特和珍贵的标志，历史文化名城间的文化交流与合作将极大地促进城市文化可持续发展和繁荣。

2017 年 1 月，蹴鞠再次作为国礼赠予国际奥委会，这是蹴鞠作为国礼在世界上的完美亮相。

足球博物馆的蹴鞠表演

Cuju performance in the football museum

8.历史故事趣谈

汉代刘歆所著的《西京杂记》中记载了一个有趣的故事：刘邦当了皇帝之后，就把刘太公接到长安城的未央宫养老，但这位刘太公却并不满意。原来刘太公从小就离不开蹴鞠。于是，刘邦就下了一道圣旨，在长安城东百里之处，仿照原来沛县的规模，造起了一座新城，把这位刘老爷子和原来沛县丰邑的居民全部迁到新城，又开始了“斗鸡、蹴鞠为欢”，刘太公这才心满意足。

司马迁的《史记・扁鹊仓公列传》留下了世界上第一个狂热球迷的记载：西汉时临淄名医淳于意将给人看病的情况都记录在《诊籍》中，创造了世界上最早的病历册。他在《诊籍》中记录一个名为项处的人患了重病找自己诊治，他一再嘱咐项处不要从事剧烈活动，否则定会吐血而死。但项处没有遵循医嘱，外出蹴鞠，结果出现了冒冷汗、吐血等症状。项处再让他诊治的时候，他料定项处不可能活过第二天傍晚。果然，如他所言，项处第二天去世了。

Cuju

1. Project culture

Cuju (also called "Kick-ball Game" or "Tzu-Chu") is a kind of football program in ancient China. It has a history of 2,300 years which can be traced back to the Spring and Autumn Period and the Warring States Period. At that time, this game was evolved into a well-known and systematical entertainment widely popular among the folks in the ancient capital of Qi.

In ancient times, the Cuju activities had been frequent in social life, which further created many artworks in various literary works, such as Li You's *Jucheng Ming* in the Eastern Han Dynasty, Zhong Wupo's *Bestow on Cuju* in the Tang Dynasty, and Lu Yanji's *Comments of the Selected Works* in the Tang Dynasty.

Archaeological activities discovered and confirmed the musical accompaniment activities in the Cuju activity, such as brick and stone paintings in the Han Dynasty. In the Song Dynasty, the music accompaniment records were described in detail in the official document *Songs Performed on Market Places-Zhong Lv Gong-Yuan Li Yuan in Vast Record of Varied Matters-Sequel*.

According to historical books and related literary materials, the court etiquette system has been quite complete in the Han Dynasty. For example, the etiquette was part of the court parade in the Han Dynasty. The Song Dynasty had specific regulations on the etiquette of Cuju artists participating in the official performance. After that, the etiquette gradually faded.

Cuju is a popular project that published many books in ancient Chinese sports field. In the early period of the Han Dynasty, *Treatise on Literature from the Book of Han* recorded "25 Articles on Cuju" (This book was lost after the Sui and Tang dynasties.), and the existing four books are *Vast*

Record of Varied Matters-Sequel, *Wanbao Quanshu-Theatre and Court*, *A Collection of Cuju Drawings*, and *A Collection of Cuju*.

In 2004, FIFA confirmed that the ancient Chinese Cuju was the origin of football. The earliest and most explicit records of the Cuju activities conducted in Linzi can be found in historical documents *Strategies of the Warring States* and *Historical Records*.

2.Project origin

The origin of the Cuju is recorded in Liu Xiang's *Bie Lu* and Liu Xin's *Qi Lue*: Cuju originated in the Yellow Emperor's era as the Yellow Emperor used it as a military training way to improve the unity and cooperation of the troops and to motivate soldiers to fight bravely.

The stone ball unearthed in the Banpo site in 1953 was tested and proved to be originated basically in the period of Yellow Emperor period. During the Ming and Qing Dynasties, according to folklore, residents still played stone ball in parts of Shaanxi could further prove this discovery.

According to the records of the officially recognized literature (*Comprehensive Mirror in Aid of Governance*, *Historical Records*, *Strategies of the Warring States-State of Qi*), as early as 2,500 years ago, Cuju activities were popular in the Warring States Period. In State of Qi, it became a typical way of entertainment.

In the early Han Dynasty, Cuju developed in two directions: One was performance entertainment accompanied with the music which improved the entertainment skills; the other was as a military training, which means it grew into a part of the military review.

Another important sign of the prosperity of the Han Dynasty was a monograph on Cuju research. The *25 Articles on Cuju* wrote by the Han Dynasty military strategist was the book of professional earliest sports in China and the first professional literature on football in the world.

The Cuju activities of the Han Dynasty were carried out in a special square-shaped court for round Cuju, which was built according to the ancient natural philosophy "fitting between square and circle ducts". Using the 12 months in one year as a guide for the number of players, two teams confronted each other having six members for each side. For the fair of the match, chief and deputy referees (named "Zhang" and "Ping" respectively) were set up. Rules and regulations for the competition were established, stipulating that the referee should be fair in judgement without favoring any side. Cuju hacl developed into a specialized sports project by the Han Dynasty, which was valued by emperors and military strategists as a means of training.

During the Sui and Tang dynasties, Cuju activity spread to North Korea and Japan, and thus added cultural characters in their respective countries. The *New Book of Tang* and the *Old Book of Tang* have records of this sport in North Korea; and records for the development of Cuju in Japan can be found in *Japanese Book of Records*, *Secret of the Court* and *The Collection of Oral Collections* and other related ancient books in Japan. It should be mentioned that Cuju activities in these two countries have been developed by adding their own characteristics with some differences from ancient Cuju in China.

During the prosperous Tang and Song dynasties, the folklore development of "playing Cuju in Cold Food Festival" boosted the development of Cuju among the mass. The Cold Food Festival was an important holiday in the Tang Dynasty, which was on the day before the Qingming Festival, symbolizing the farewell to the depressing winter. When Spring came, people would go to the suburbs, and the relatives and friends would get together for some entertainment games to stretch their bodies. The most common game at that time was Cuju.

In the Song Dynasty, a nation-wide Cuju organization was established, called "Yuan she" (An association organized by the Cuju artists to safeguard their own interests and improve their skills. It is the earliest football club in China and the world.). In addition, the national competition "Shan Yue Zheng" (like today's China Football Super League) came into being.

During the same period, Cuju appeared on the list of loyal reception, and professional Cuju actors started showing their skills in market place. The wide-spread of "playing Cuju in Cold Food Festival" in the folk boosted the peak development of this sport.

The appearance of the female Cuju players in the Yuan Dynasty expanded the social significance of entertainment and, to a certain extent, impacted the concept of discrimination against women in feudal society.

During the Ming Dynasty, the commercial performance of Cuju was a way for the upper aristocrats to pursue pleasure, but was despised by feudal scholars. With the development of this trend, the imperial banquet canceled the Cuju performance, and Cuju gradually declined.

During the Qing Dynasty, due to the suppression of the traditional culture of the Han nationality, the governors suppressed the Han sports project, and the traditional Cuju gradually met its downturn. However, the Cuju on ice with Manchu characteristics began to prevail.

In modern times, with the introduction of Western football, Cuju has existed in name only.

3.Project rules

3.1　Dual-goal direct competition (direct confrontation) in the Han Dynasty

During the competition, the Cuju court was set up surrounded by short walls. Both sides of the game have a small house-like goal. There were 12 players on the field. The two sides conducted a direct physical confrontation. Just like snoring, the side that scored higher by kicking the ball into the opponent's door was the winner.

3.2　Single-goal direct competition

This was an indirect confrontation. During the competition, a two-foot high hole called "Fengliuyan" was set up in the middle of the goal. Two teams were at either side of the court separated by the goal, and the team that passed the ball through the Fengliuyan without falling could win the game.

3.3　Bai da (pattern kicking)

Bai da focuses on skills and tricks, also known as "Xie shu" (pattern kick). Each Xieshu has a series of kicks which are totally various. Ball is the only apparatus used in the project, and the venue is also very simple, such as a flat place where generally have tranquil surroundings.

4.Project apparatus

According to the survey, the original Cuju was a stone ball (found in the Banpo site). With productivity improvement and technology advancement, the apparatus of Cuju was developed from stone ball to leather ball. As recorded in the document in Mawangdui *Shi Dajin*, the Yellow Emperor's conquered the Chiyou tribe, catching the tribal leader and filling his stomach with air. Inspired by this, people used the animal stomach or fur to make the shell, then filled the hair to score, which gradually evolved into a hollow ball over time.

From the perspective of time, the ball made of leather was not later than the Yin Dynasty, which can be reflected by the Chinese character component of Ju at that time. In addition, there was Cuju dance during the sacrifice ceremony, and family surnamed "Ju" also appeared. The Cuju of the Han Dynasty was "knitted by Wei (a plant used for plait tool), and standard ball making specifications were prepared. The Tang Dynasty is an important era for the reform of Cuju as the ball was changed from a solid ball to an inflatable ball thanks to the improvement of the ball making process. In the Song Dynasty, the ball making technology was improved based on that in the Tang Dynasty, and the ball was closer to a circle, and filled by a leather tool. As the handicraft industry in the Song Dynasty was developed, the craftsmanship of making ball was exquisite and the brand appeared (*A Collection of Cuju Drawings* recorded 41 famous brands at that time such as Liudingyin, Bayueyuan, Yunyuetai, Huahuzhang, Manyuanchun, Baihua Chaoyang, etc.). The ball making reached its peak in this period.

5.Action parsing (Translated, corrected and sorted from *A Collection of Cuju Drawings*)

The basic skills of kicking Cuju include Guai, Da, Lian, and Ci, and the rest of the actions are evolved from these four. Playing on the court requires a correct posture without bending back and with steps separated. Game players should obey the rules of the course and should not wander and move their positions in breach of rules.

Guai: Kick the ball high to make a turn, and bend and raise the leg without hesitation. The arch of the foot should be flat, and the slow kick is desired.

Da: The ball is kicked when it comes from the front. The eyes should focus on the ball and the legs should be lowered. The ball is controlled with gentle force, and step movement is the key.

Lian: The shoulder should be aligned to the tip of the toes, the body should be slightly inclined to the center of gravity. Sit up straight and raise the foot. Kick the ball with the calf.

Ci: Receive the coming ball with knees. Apply as much force as is necessary. Kick the ball by stepping forward, or stop to kick the ball with tricks.

Jian: Head on the ball with shoulder top, and the left shoulder and the right shoulder should be distinguished. Move forward and retract backward without obstacle, or kick the ball only two times.

Zhuang: Stride forward quickly and correctly to receive the missing ball. Hook your toes without relaxing the muscles and joints when kicking the ball.

Nian: Block the fierce ball with feet. Be calm when preparing to catch the ball. Receive and kick the ball as it hits your feet, and kick it again with skills.

6.Project inheritor

Ma Guoqing (from Linzi District, Zibo City, Shandong Province) serves as the Secretary-General of the Research Base of the Project Culture

Development Center of the State General Administration, the head of the Linzi Branch of the Linzi World Football Museum and China Sports Museum, a member of the leading group for inscribing Linzi Cuju onto the first batch of National Intangible Cultural Heritage, the Cuju heritage representative for the first batch of National Intangible Cultural Heritage, and is currently the dean of the Qi Culture Museum. He shows the Cuju skills in front of the public to let more people know about it. As a representative of the intangible cultural heritage of Cuju, he has made outstanding contributions to cultural communication.

At the beginning of the demonstration of the origin of football, Ma Guoqing drafted the basic argumentation data *Research Report on Linyi as the Origin of World Football* and *Report on Confirmation of Linzi as the Origin of World Football*, and revived the Cuju activities in the Tang and Song dynasties. He is the main editor of *Exploration of the Origin of Football*, *Grand Ceremony in Capital of State of Qi*, *Cuju in Capital of State of Qi*, and has made outstanding contributions to the confirmation of the origin of the world football, the research and dissemination of the culture of Cuju, and the successful operation of the Linzi Football Museum, as well as the football industry and cultural development in Linzi District.

7.New development

In May 2006, Cuju was listed in the first batch of National Intangible Cultural Heritage List.

On April 2, 2005, the Cuju team performed an antique performance at the opening ceremony of the China Football Super League, the highest level of football event in China.

In October 2015, President Xi Jinping visited the United Kingdom and presented Linzi antique four-piece Cuju as a national gift to the National Football Museum of England. This visit strengthened the communication between China and the UK. Cultural characteristics and individuality are the unique and precious symbols of historical and cultural cities. Cultural exchanges and cooperation between historical and cultural cities will greatly promote the sustainable development and prosperity of urban culture.

In January 2017, Cuju was once again presented to the International Olympic Committee as a national gift, a perfect debut of Cuju as a national gift in the world.

8. History story

An interesting story is recorded in the *Miscellany of the Western Capital* written by Liu Xin in the Han Dynasty. After Liu Bang became an emperor, he received Liu Taigong from the Weiyang Palace to Chang'an City, but Liu Taigong was not satisfied. It turned out that Liu Taigong was inseparable from Cuju since his childhood. Therefore, Liu Bang gave a sacred decree to build a new city in the east of Chang'an City by imitating the original Peixian scale. Then, Liu Taigong and the original residents of Fengyi in Peixian all moved to the new city where they could play the cockfighting and Cuju again. So, Liu Taigong was satisfied.

Sima Qian's *Historical Records-Bianque Canggong Biography* left the record of the first fanatics in the world: In the western Han Dynasty, the famous doctor Chun Yuyi recorded the medical information in *Medical Book*, the world's first medical book. In the book, he recorded that a person with serious disease called Xiang Chu came to seek treatment, and Chun repeatedly enjoined that Xiang would not engage in strenuous activities, otherwise he would vomit blood and die. However, Xiang did not follow the doctor's advice, and went out for playing Cuju. Then, he developed symptoms such as cold sweat and vomiting blood. When Xiang Chu came to him for diagnosis again, Doctor Chun determined that he would not be alive the next evening, which was proven to be true the next day.

第 2 节　徐家拳

1.项目文化

山东省新泰市的徐家拳是由徐氏高祖徐盛才所创，历经 280 多年，汲取南北派武功之长，自成一体，世代传承不息，也逐渐从重视实战型的防身之术，发展到今天集强身健体与养生为一体的、有新时代特色的拳术。徐家拳在传承中创新，在创新中发展，打破传内不传外的族规，让徐家拳从本族到全村，入社区、进学校，从全村到全国，授徒近 20 万人。随着徐家拳的普及和广大群众的受益，其功能价值凸显，健身养生的实用性和历史文化研究的价值逐步被社会认可。2014 年 11 月，徐家拳被国务院公布为第四批国家级非物质文化遗产代表性项目，这为徐家拳的发展带来了机遇和挑战。

2.项目起源

徐家拳起源于雍正年间，由徐氏高祖徐盛才所创。徐盛才，1724 年出生（清雍正二年），卒于 1797 年。徐公自幼习武，曾走南闯北拜师学艺，练就一身绝技，创立徐家拳雏形。百余年来，世代传承不息，到第六代传人徐花葶时，徐家拳掀起了一个高潮。据老县志和徐氏家谱记载，徐花葶，字殿甲，1825 年出生（清道光五年），1900 年卒于新泰城通济村。徐花葶相貌伟岸，臂力过人，善于研究，丰富了徐家拳的内涵，发展了徐家拳法及各种兵器的使用。徐花葶武功高强，多次参加大型比武并名列前茅，在清咸丰年间封为武庠生（即武秀才），被推选为县团练团总。是年，捻军攻打新泰城，徐花葶训练的武装团严密防守，打败了来犯的捻军。因他抗敌有功，清政府赏赐他亮蓝顶藏大花翎，至今尚存。

近代，徐家拳不仅传授本族人员，还广泛传授给全村的群众进行练习。第十代传人徐勤启的爷爷徐敏德把学到的徐家拳传授给村民，让全村男女老少皆利用农闲时间习武。徐勤启自幼跟爷爷徐敏德、父亲徐志银习武，在 20 世纪 70 年代参加过新泰市武术比赛，并在部队服役时担任全团的武术教官，向官兵传授徐家拳术，培养了 300 多名武术教员。徐勤启在 2005 年 7 月获得“白马寺杯全国传统武术比赛”第一名，在 2007 年 6 月山东省传统武术比赛中，获得徐家拳术和徐家刀两个项目的冠军，徐勤启不仅获得了国家级武术五段段位称号，还充分利用节假期回村传授徐家拳。

3.动作解析

徐家拳拳术和器械独具特色，充分吸收了南北派功夫精华，既有北派功夫出拳快、发力重的特色，又具南派功夫轻灵、迅猛的特点，手法繁多，快捷实用。稳、准、狠是徐家拳的基本特征。

徐家拳主要内容体系包括拳术、拳术对练、器械、器械对练、拆手、内功、辅助功法共七大类。

3.1　拳术套路

①上势拜师；②双掌前砍；③双掌穿喉；④收拳于腰间，右腿提起，右拳高举过顶，顺势向下避挡；⑤古源步，左掌护右耳，贴步右臂拳；⑥开锤右脚向前，踮步变左马步，顶肘；⑦马步开引式；⑧目视左方，连上三步，左右弓步冲拳；⑨随步三冲拳（紧三拳）；⑩左转身，贴步开锤；⑪马步掏井；⑫左转身，踮步开锤；⑬右拳，仙人系鞋带；⑭挑锤；⑮贴脚并步，左手冲拳；⑯左转身，贴步回收，右手冲拳；⑰回转金蛟剪；⑱二起蹦；⑲金鸡独立、白鹤亮翅；⑳转身左蹬腿、右蹬腿；㉑马步打狗式；㉒拦腰斩；㉓力开弓；㉔双手系鞋带；㉕二起蹦；㉖跨虎式；㉗巧女左梳头、左打；㉘巧女右梳头、右打；㉙掼耳脚；㉚转身右蹬；㉛转身左蹬；㉜马步挂拳；㉝开拳下蹲；㉞旱地拔葱；㉟旋风腿；㊱打虎式；㊲收式。

3.2　对练套路

3.2.1　撞膀锤拳

①甲方右弓步冲拳打乙方斜肋；②乙方左虚步，左手立掌外挡，右手握拳收腰间，踮步石马步冲拳，甲方左弓步右臂避挡，随即顺臂掼耳；③乙方在马步右臂下压，左拳掼耳，甲方右转身左弓挡开；④乙方右马步出拳；⑤甲方左马步避挡；⑥乙方用掌握甲方左手腕按下同时右拳损耳；⑦甲方左马步推开，同时左拳冲乙方右肋；⑧乙方左马步臂挡，顺势右马步冲右举；⑨甲方虚步左手变立掌外挡；⑩收式。

3.2.2　十字按拳

前半部分套路与撞膀锤拳基本相同，只是在甲方左举打乙方右肋时，乙方右弓步用臂肘外磕甲方左臂腕，随冲拳打甲方面门；甲方右弓步右手挡，收式。

3.2.3　裁手拳

①甲方上右弓步冲拳打乙方斜肋；②乙方右马步臂挡；③翻手上步右手抓右手腕，左手按甲方臂肘，冲拳打甲方面门；④甲方左手变掌将乙方右手削脱，右挡开乙方冲来的面门拳，顺势变削乙方咽喉；⑤乙方左手挡开，右手冲面门拳；⑥甲方左手托住乙方右肘，并提膝，右手马步冲举打斜肋；⑦乙方右倒弓步右臂挡；⑧甲方倒插步，双手抱拳用右肘捣乙方面门（心脏）；⑨乙方虚步双手合掌托肘护挡；⑩甲方顺势右手反背拳盖乙方头顶，随即撩阴击裆；⑪乙方双手交剪避挡上下拳；⑫甲方左转身右马步冲掼耳拳；⑬乙方避挡；⑭收式。

3.2.4　小劈风拳

①甲方上势冲拳击打面门；②乙方虚步按拳；③甲方上步掼耳；④乙方右弓步接掌；⑤甲方削掌掼耳；⑥乙方上步下打撩阴；⑦甲方上步踢撩阴脚；⑧乙方双手变举避挡击打对方脚面破之，随即上步掼耳；⑨甲方挡开；⑩收式。

3.2.5　二郎拳

①甲方右弓步冲拳；②乙方右弓步右臂挡；③甲方顺臂上滚拳掼耳，双腿前后扫膛；④乙方双脚跳跃躲避；⑤甲方翻身撩阴脚，反背锤盖顶；⑥乙方右弓步，右臂上举挡拳；⑦甲方冲举打斜肋；⑧乙方缠手；⑨甲方后撩阴脚；⑩乙方双手变掌下压破之；⑪甲方反背锤盖顶；⑫乙方右手避挡，向前三冲拳；⑬甲方后退三外扒举破之；⑭收式。

3.3　项目器械（包括单练和对练）

项目器械包括疯魔棍、九龙棍、春秋刀、单刀、七节鞭、三节棍、长矛、羊角拐。

春秋刀

Chunqiu broadsword

3.4 拆手(徐家拳致命绝技)

拆手包括撮鼻梁、打斜肋、顶心、盖顶、掼耳、击裆、削喉。

3.5 内功(站桩)

站桩分技击桩和养生桩，是徐家拳提升内在功力的关键所在。

3.6 辅助功法(抓四路)

①石狮、石锁；②铁牛耕地；③铁指功(三指、二指、单指)；④掷石、春秋刀。

综合以上，拳术单练套路共 37 式，动作干脆勇猛，招招制敌，体现稳、准、狠的技术风格。拳术对练套路又分为五大类，包括撞膀锤拳、十字按拳、裁手拳、小劈风拳、二郎拳。此拳术可练习攻防的配合，接近实战的程度，行云流水，快而不乱，节奏清晰。

4.项目传承人

徐家拳的拳法因为实战性和表演性强而备受人们的喜爱。为进一步将徐家拳发扬光大，徐勤启义务教徒 1 万人次，并逐步将徐家拳推向全国，特别是 2009 年在清华大学年会表演徐家拳后受到一致好评。

随着国家对非物质文化遗产的重视和人民群众健身需求的提高，徐勤启积极发掘、整理、传承省级非物质文化遗产，建立了徐家拳网站，免费义务授徒。近年来，有来自北京、上海、天津、香港、云南、河北等地的武术爱好者前来交流、学习徐家拳，它的健身和实用价值正在被越来越多的专家和广大武术爱好者所认识。

2007 年、2008 年，徐家拳被新泰市和泰安市两级政府列入两级市级非物质文化遗产名录。2009 年，徐家拳被山东省政府列入第二批省级非物质文化遗产名录。徐勤启被三级政府公布为徐家拳代表性传承人。

2009 年 3 月，山东省新泰市燕鸣希望小学成立了徐家拳培训基地。2009 年 6 月，燕鸣希望小学被国家体育总局武术研究院和教育部体育卫生与艺术教育司授予“中国武术段位制教学实验学校”。2009 年 9 月，清华大学建立了清华大学徐家拳武术队。2011 年 8 月，徐勤启带领的徐家拳代表队在“山东省武术非物质文化遗产技艺交流大会”上荣获一等奖。2011 年 10 月，山东省新泰市青云二中建立了徐家举中学培训基地。

徐家拳动作

Xu Jia Boxing action

5.项目新发展

加强世界遗产保护已成为国际社会刻不容缓的任务，这是历史赋予我们的崇高责任，也是实现人类文明延续和可持续发展的必然要求。中国拳种流派繁多，各类拳种技艺与地域文化互相交融，随着城市社区、农村建设的发展，广大群众健身娱乐选择越来越具多样性，这为徐家拳的发展带来了机遇和挑战。为使徐家拳传承延续，记忆永存，必须在保护和传承的基础上，进行发展和创新。

5.1 研究徐家拳，推广徐家拳

2012 年，山东省新泰市泰山徐家拳研究院成立，徐勤启担任院长，共有 36 名工作人员，这为进一步丰富完善徐家拳法提供了组织保障。工作人员通过泰山徐家拳研究院这个平台，组织人力、财力，系统整理徐家拳的技术理论体系，补漏拾遗，力争保留徐家拳的原貌，并在此基础上，出版传统徐家拳的有关书籍与演练光碟。

传统的传播方式已经不能满足现代社会的需求，武术的未来发展也要紧跟时代的步伐，大众传媒是传播武术的有效途径之一。推广徐家拳要利用好报纸、期刊、广播电视台、网络等现代化的舆论宣传工具，要建立和实施合理有效的对外交流管理制度，加强交流与合作，促进与其他传统拳种的交流和切磋，排除门户之见和宗派主义，打破抱残守缺、故步自封的思想作风，通过参加全国乃至世界性的竞技比赛或擂台，让更多的人了解徐家拳、练习徐家拳。

5.2　搭建平台，发展徐家拳

5.2.1　走进学校，强化教育传承

2010 年 8 月，教育部与国家体育总局联合发文向全国中小学推广实施武术健身操。学校是最重要、最广泛的传承中国传统武术的阵地，只有将武术引入学校，通过青少年进行传承，才能更好地履行武术弘扬民族精神和传承中国传统文化的历史使命。在建立 18 处徐家拳义务传承基地的基础上，加大徐家拳义务传承基地的规模和数量，让更多的青少年接触徐家拳、练习徐家拳。同时可以会同教育有关部门，在学校的体育课中增加徐家拳的选修，这将十分有益于传承民族文化，弘扬民族精神，让传统武术后继有人。

5.2.2　走进社区，普及徐家拳

非物质文化遗产项目的功能价值和意义在于满足人们的身心健康和精神文化的需要，给人以健康体验或精神慰藉。武术在社会上传播必须具备一定的传播场所，如果没有固定的传播场所，就会限制人们接触武术的机会。小区公园空地和体育场所这些地点相对固定，容易形成习武氛围，有利于保障武术的大众化进程，增加社区义务传授点。

5.2.3　举办活动，发展徐家拳

在物质生活水平极大提高的今天，人们对精神生活有着更高的要求，所以人们对丰富多彩的健身、修身、养身、娱乐项目兴趣盎然。要通过举办徐家拳研究论文报告会、武术精神演讲、传统武术绘画展、徐家拳竞技比赛和徐家拳表演等多样形式的活动进行文化艺术传播，让人们既是参与者，又是观赏者，使人们既能健身又能提高精神生活的追求，同时也让徐家拳得到更好的普及与传播。

人文旅游，开发徐家拳。伴随着不断扩大的人文旅游市场的要求，要适时将人文旅游资源的价值挖掘出来，以满足游客的要求。南北融合的徐家拳自成体系，文化内涵和外在形式别具一格，要通过设计、编排加上声电光现代舞台手段，打造一场具有现代特色的徐家拳文化盛宴，满足来自国内外探新求异的旅游者的兴趣，加快徐家拳向全世界推广的速度。

5.3　打造文化符号，探寻产业开发模式

文化符号一般指的是一个企业、地域、民族或国家独特的体现方式，是文化

内涵的重要载体和形式，具有很强的抽象性和丰富的内涵。文化符号不仅是一种文化事物显著的特点，还是其是否被大众认知和识别的标志性对象，是凝聚着精神内核的文化元素。中国武术总是和中国其他文化形态相伴发展，这更加显现其不同于其他体育项目的价值所在。

徐勤启设计的寓意平安吉祥的莲花吉祥宝剑，成为知名的特色文化旅游产品，并获山东省旅游产品大赛铜奖，被中国武术博物馆收藏，这就是非常成功的文化符号。若要打造文化符号，则必须有一套产业模式来进行指导运作。首先，从整体上构建“资源产品品牌”的良性产业循环链条，在莲花吉祥宝剑的基础上开发出针对社区和学校的徐家拳练功服、徐家拳录像制品和书籍、徐家拳纪念品和徽章等，逐渐打造出具有地域文化品牌的徐家拳。其次，在整体构建产业循环链条的基础上，明确权责主体，发挥好在旅游资源、文化品牌拳种文化中的作用，打造集健身、竞技观赏、娱乐艺术于一体的极具现代文化特色的徐家拳。

Xu Jia Boxing

1.Project culture

Xu Jia Boxing, originated in Xintai City, Shandong Province, was created by Gaozu of the Xu family—Xu Shengcai. Over 280 years, through absorbing the strength of the northern and southern schools of martial arts, and inheriting from generation to generation, Xu Jia Boxing has developed its own style from practical self-defense to a martial art with emphasis on physical fitness and health preservation in the new era. Xu Jia Boxing innovates and develops in the process of inheritance. The breaking of the rule of only passing on the boxing within the clan has made Xu Jia Boxing spread from its own clan to the whole village, community, and school, and from urban and rural areas to the whole country, thus educating nearly 200,000 students all over the country. With its popularization and benefits of the public, the outstanding functional value, practical function of fitness, historical and cultural research value of Xu Jia Boxing have been gradually recognized by society. In November

2014, Xu Jia Boxing was listed as the fourth batch of representative items of National Intangible Cultural Heritage by the State Council, which has brought opportunities and challenges to its development.

2.Project origin

Xu Jia Boxing originated in the period of Yongzheng, and was created by Gaozu of the Xu family—Xu Shengcai, who was born in 1724 (the second year of the reign of Yongzheng in Qing Dynasty), and died in 1797. Since childhood, Xu has been practicing martial arts and travelling extensively with learning from masters, and set the embryo of Xu Jia Boxing. Over hundreds of years, Xu Jia Boxing was inherited through generations and reached its climax under the effort of its sixth successor—Xu Huating. As recorded in County Chronicles and Xu Genealogy, Xu Huating, also called Dian Jia, was born in 1825 (the fifth year in the period of Daoguang in Qing Dynasty), and died in 1990 in Tongji Village, Xintai City. Xu Huating was good-looking and had powerful arms. His assiduous study enriched and carried forward Xu Jia Boxing as well as the use of various weapons. With strong skills of the martial art, Xu Huating participated in large-scale competitions many times and ranked at the top. He was conferred the title of Wu Xiang Sheng (also called Wu Xiucai) and elected as the county's general leader of the county training group during the reign of Xianfeng of the Qing Dynasty. In the same year, the armed regiment trained by Xu Huating well defeated the invasion of Nian Jun (Anti-Qing Peasant Armed Forces) which attacked Xin Tai. Because of the success of the defense, the Qing government bestowed on Xu Huating a bright blue cap with large plumes, which still exists today.

In modern times, Xu Jia Boxing was not only taught to its family personnel, but also widely taught to the masses of the whole village for practice. The tenth-generation of inheritor Xu Minde (Xu Qinqi's grandpa) taught what he learned to villagers, who can practice martial arts in their spare time. Learning martial arts from his grandfather since his childhood, Xu Qinqi took part in martial arts competition in the 1970s. When he served in the army, he served as the martial arts instructor of the army regiment. He taught Xu Jia Boxing to the officers and soldiers and trained more than 300 martial arts trainers. In July 2005, he won the first prize in the "White Horse Temple Cup National Traditional Martial Arts Competition". In the Shandong Traditional Martial Competition in June 2007, Xu Qinqi won the first prizes in Xu Jia Boxing and Xu Jia Broadsword, and won the fifth-duan title of national martial arts. In holidays, Xu often returned to his village to teach Xu Jia Boxing.

3.Action parsing

Xu Jia Boxing, with unique boxing skills and apparatuses, has fully absorbed the essence of north and south kungfu. It has the characteristics of fast punching and heavy power of the north kungfu, and the light and swift and swift characteristics of the south kungfu. The techniques are varied, fast and practical, and the basic characteristics of Xu Jia Boxing are steady, accurate and fierce.

The main contents of Xu Jia Boxing include seven categories: boxing, boxing sparring, apparatus, apparatus sparring, sticking hands, internal skills, and auxiliary skills.

3.1 Boxing routine

(1) Raise your hands to worship the teacher; (2) Move your palms forward; (3) Pass your palms at the front of the throat; (4) Take a punch in the waist, lift right leg, and raise your right fist high over the head, and move it smoothly to elude; (5) Protect your right ear with your left palm and step on your right arm; (6) Open fist, move your right foot forward, and change step on tiptoe into left seated position with the elbow on it; (7) Stand in a seated position;(8) Look to the left and step forward for three steps with your left and right bows, and punch; (9) Punch three times with steps; (10) Turn left and step away with the fist; (11) Stand in a seated position; (12) Turn left and step on toes with opening arms; (13) Punch your right fist; (14) Raise and lower the fist; (15) Stick feet, halt and punch left hand;

(16) Turn left and step back, punch your right hand; (17) Turn around; (18) Jump two times; (19) Stand on one of your foot like a golden chicken, and open arms like the white crane spreads its wings; (20) Turn around and push off your left leg, and then right leg; (21) Squat and act like hitting the dog; (22) Lower the waist; (23) Open your arms powerfully; (24) Act as tying laces with both hands; (25) Jump twice; (26) Move like tiger steps; (27) Comb your hair with your left hand, and move the left hand; (28) Comb your hair right with your right hand and move the right hand; (29) Move the leg; (30) Turn around and push off your right leg;(31) Turn around and push off your left leg; (32) Act in seated position and move your fist; (33) Punch your fist and squat; (34) Perform the action named "Handi Bacong"; (35) Perform a whirling leg; (36) Perform the action like fighting a tiger; (37) Halt.

3.2 Fighting routine

3.2.1 Crash the shoulder and fist

(1) Party A hits Party B's ribs with a right lunge; (2) Party B steps on the left side with his left hand outside, the right hand clenches the first to close the waist, squatting and punching his fist; Party A's left bow steps right and shields with right arm, then follows the arm cross the ear; (3) Party B presses the right arm, and whips ear with left fist, and Party A turns his right and left bow to block; (4) Party B steps out right and punches; (5) Party A steps out left to shirk; (6) Party B presses Party A with the left wrist and whips his ear with right fist; (7) Party A steps left while the left punch hits the right rib of Party B; (8) Party B steps left and shirks with arm, following stepping right and punching the right fist; (9) Party A steps virtually with left hand and varies into palm to shield; (10) Halt.

3.2.2 Crossing-press fist

The first part routines of this system are similar to those of "Crash the shoulder and fist". The only difference is that when Party A raises left arm to hit Party B's right rib, Party B steps with the elbow outside to against left arm wrist of Party A, following with hitting Party A's face with punch; Party

A then blocks with right lunge.

3.2.3 Cutting styled fist

(1)Party A hits Party B's ribs with a right lunge; (2) Party B steps right with arm blocking; (3) Party B turns his hand, steps to grab the right wrist, with his left hand pressing the elbow of Party A, and punching Party A's face; (4) Party A cuts off his left hand to the right hand of Party B, and the right side blocks the face fist rushed by Party B, and the right side cuts the throat of Party B; (5) Party B's left hand blocks, and the right hand punches face; (6) Party A holds the right elbow of Party B with his left hand, and raises his knee, and then moves his right hand forward to lift the oblique rib; (7) Party B steps backward and blocks with right arm; (8) Party A thrusts upside down and punches Party B's face (heart) with his right elbow, holding his fist; (9) Party B stands steady and closes palms together to support the elbow and protect crotch; (10) Party A uses his right hand to cover the top of Party B's head; (11) Party B crosses hands to shirk fist up and down; (12) Party A turns left, steps out left and pulls ear with fist; (13) Party B shirks and blocks; (14) Halt.

3.2.4 Thick split fist

(1) Party A punches the face of Party B; (2) Party B presses the fist; (3) Party A steps forward and pulls his ear; (4) Party B takes over with right lunge; (5) Party A cuts the fist and pulls his ear; (6) Party B steps forward and attack pussy; (7) Party A steps forward to block; (8) Party B hands up to shield and fight against kick from Party A; following pulling the year; (9) Party A shirks; (10) Halt.

3.2.5 Erlang Boxing

(1) Party A steps forward with right lunge and punches; (2) Party B steps forward with right lunge and blocks with right arm; (3) Party A rolls his fists over his ears, and uses legs to attack Party B's chest one by one; (4) Party B jumps to shirk; (5) Party A turns around and kick; (6) Party B steps forward with right lunge, raises right arm and blocks fist of Party A; (7) Party A punches the oblique ribs; (8) Party B tangles hands; (9) Party A

kicks backward; (10) Party B's fists vary into palms and press down to break; (11) Party A turns around and kicks party B's head; (12) Party B shields with right arm and steps forward with three punches; (13) Party A steps back three steps and holds the fist of Party B to break; (14) Halt.

3.3 Apparatus (single practice and sparring)

The project apparatus includes "Fengmo" cudgel, "Jiulong" cudgel, Chunqiu broadsword, cutlass, seven-joint whip, three-joint cudgel, lance, and Yangjiao guai.

3.4 Chai shou (fatal stunt of Xu Jia Boxing)

Chai shou includes pinching the nose, slashing the ribs, coping, pulling the ear, hitting the crotch, and cutting the throat.

3.5 Internal skills (standing pose)

Standing pose includes skill pose and health maintenance pose, which are the key of improving internal power by Xu Jia Boxing.

3.6 Auxiliary skills (focus on four skills)

(1) Shishi, Shisuo; (2) Tieniu Gengdi; (3) Iron finger skills (three fingers, two fingers, single finger); (4) Throw stones, Chunqiu broadsword.

There are 37 types of single practice routines, whose action is simple but brave, hitting the opponent with each action. It embodies the steady ruthless technical style. Routines of sparring are divided into five categories: crash the shoulder and fist; crossing-press fist; cutting styled fist; thick split fist; and Erlang Boxing. The daily practice for this boxing is close to that of actual combat, with fast and orderly actions and clear rhythm.

4.Project inheritor

Xu Jia Boxing is popular by people because of the outstanding actual combat and performance. To further promote Xu Jia Boxing, Xu Qinqi volunteered to teach 10,000 followers and gradually promoted it to the whole country. Especially in 2009, Xu Jia Boxing received unanimous praise after Xu Qinqi performed it in the annual meeting of Tsinghua University.

The tenth inheritor Xu Qinqi has been learning martial arts from his grandfather Xu Minde and father Xu Zhiyin since childhood. In recent years, as the nation pays more attention to the intangible cultural heritage, and people have higher demand for fitness, Xu Qinqi actively excavates, organizes, and inherits the provincial intangible cultural heritage, and builds a website of Xu Jia Boxing and trains people free of charge. In recent years, martial arts enthusiasts from Beijing, Shanghai, Tianjin, Hong Kong, Yunnan, Hebei and other places have come to exchange and learn martial arts. The fitness and practical value of Xu Jia Boxing is being recognized by experts and martial arts lovers.

In 2007 and 2008, Xu Jia Boxing was listed as two municipal intangible cultural heritage by Xintai and Tai'an governments and was listed as the second batch of Provincial Protecting Material Cultural Heritage by Shandong Provincial Government. Xu Qinqi was declared as the representative inheritor of Xu Jia Boxing by the third-level government.

In March 2009, Xu Jia Boxing training base was set up in Yanming Hope Primary School in Xintai City, Shandong Province. In June 2009, Yanming Hope Primary School was awarded the "Chinese Martial Art Duan System Teaching Experimental School" by the Martial Art Research Institute of the General Administration of Sport of China and the Department of Sports Health and Art Education of the Ministry of Education. In September 2009, the Xu Jia Boxing Martial Art Team was established in Tsinghua University. In August 2011, the Xu Jiafeng team led by Xu Qinqi won the first prize in the " Shandong Province Martial Art Intangible Cultural Heritage Skilled Exchange Conference". In October 2011, the training base of Xujiaju Middle School was established in Qingyun No. 2 Middle School, Xintai City, Shandong Province.

5.New development

Strengthening the protection of world heritage has become an urgent task for the international community, which is a lofty responsibility entrusted to us by history and an inevitable requirement for the continuation and sustainable development of human civilization. There are many boxing schools in China, and all kinds of boxing skills and regional culture blend with each other. With the development of urban communities and rural constructions, the broad masses have diversified choices of fitness and entertainment, which brings both opportunities and challenges to the development of Xu Jia Boxing. In order to perpetuate the inheritance and memory of Xu Jia Boxing, it is necessary to take actions to protect and innovate based on protection and inheritance.

5.1 Study and popularize Xu Jia Boxing

In 2012, Taishan Xu Jia Boxing Research Institute was established in Xintai City, Shandong Province, and Xu Qinqi served as the president with 36 staff members, which laid an organizational guarantee for further enriching and improving Xu Jia Boxing techniques. It is necessary to organize special manpower and concentrate financial resources through the platform of Taishan Xu Jia Boxing Research Institute, systematically organize the technical and theoretical system of Xu Jia Boxing, and make sure that the original appearance of Xu Jia Boxing is preserved. Based on this, books and DVDs about traditional Xu Jia Boxing are published.

The traditional dissemination of martial arts has been unable to meet the needs of modern society, and the future development of martial arts should also keep up with the pace of the times. Mass media is one of the effective ways to spread martial arts. To popularize Xu Jia Boxing, we should make good use of modern publicity tools such as newspapers, periodicals, radio and television stations, and the Internet. It is necessary to establish and implement a reasonable and effective foreign exchange management system for modern promotion means to strengthen exchanges and cooperation.. It is necessary to promote the communication and exchange with the traditional boxing, get rid of sectarianism, break the ideological style of being a backwater, and let more people know, practice and popularize Xu Jia Boxing by participating in national and even worldwide competitive competitions or challenges.

5.2 Set up the carrier and develop Xu Jia Boxing

5.2.1 Strengthen the inheritance and education of Xu Jia Boxing by entering schools.

In August 2010, the Ministry of Education and the State General Administration of Sport jointly issued a paper to promote and implement martial arts aerobics in primary and secondary schools across the country. School is the most important and extensive position for inheriting Chinese traditional martial arts. Only by inheriting martial arts in schools and through teenagers can we better fulfill the historical mission of carrying forward the national spirit and inheriting Chinese traditional culture. Based on the establishment of 18 compulsory inheritance bases of Xu Jia Boxing, the scale and number of bases for the inheritance of Xu Jia Boxing should be increased so that more young students can get in touch with and practice Xu Jia Boxing. Meanwhile, we can cooperate with the relevant departments of education to add Xu Jia Boxing as an elective course in school physical education, which will be beneficial to the inheritance of national culture and the promotion of national spirit and traditional martial arts.

5.2.2 Popularize Xu Jia Boxing in communities.

The functional value and significance of intangible cultural heritage projects lie in meeting the needs of people's physical and mental health as well as spiritual culture, enriching people's health experience or giving people spiritual solace. To promote martial art in society, there must be a certain place for spreading. Lack of a fixed place for popularizing martial art will limit the opportunity for people to get in touch with martial art. Community parks, open spaces and sports venues are relatively fixed and easy to form a martial arts atmosphere, which is conducive to ensuring the popularization of martial arts, and adding obligatory teaching points.

5.2.3 Organize activities to develop Xu Jia Boxing.

Today, with living standard greatly improved, people have higher requirements for their spiritual life, and are interested in a variety of fitness, self-cultivation, health and entertainment projects. Various forms of communication and culture art dissemination activities should be held such as research reports on Xu Jia Boxing, speeches on martial spirit, traditional martial art exhibition, Xu Jia Boxing competitions, and performances, in which people are both participants and viewers. This boosts fitness and enriches spiritual life of people, and further popularizes and spreads Xu Jia Boxing.

Develop Xu Jia Boxing through humanistic tourism. With the demand of the expanding cultural tourism market, the value of cultural tourism resources should be excavated timely to meet the requirements of tourists. Xu Jia Boxing, which integrates the martial arts of north and south, has its own system and unique cultural connotation and external form. Through design, choreography and modern stage means of sound, electric and light, a feast with modern characteristics for Xu Jia Boxing can be created to meet the interests of domestic and foreign tourists, which will speed up the promotion of Xu Jia Boxing to the world.

5.3 Create cultural symbols to explore industrial development mode

The "cultural symbol" generally refers to the unique embodiment of an enterprise, a region, a nation, or a country, and is an important carrier and form of cultural connotation with strong abstractness and rich connotation. A cultural symbol is not only the salient characteristic of a cultural thing, but also the symbolic object of whether the culture is recognized and identified by the public. It is a cultural element that condenses the spiritual core. Chinese martial art has always developed in tandem with other forms of Chinese culture, which shows its value different from other sports.

The lotus auspicious sword designed by Xu Qinqi has become a well-known characteristic cultural tourism product, which won the bronze prize in the tourism product competition of Shandong Province and was collected by the Chinese martial arts museum. This is a very successful cultural symbol. To create cultural symbols, we need a set of industrial models to guide the operation. First, a complete industrial cycle chain of "resource product brand" should be constructed. Based on the lotus auspicious sword, Xu Jia Boxing training suit, Xu Jia Boxing video products, books, Xu Jia Boxing souvenirs, badges and so on should be developed for the society and schools to gradually create a regional culture brand of Xu Jia Boxing. Secondly, based on the overall construction of the industrial cycle chain, the main body of rights and responsibilities should be defined to play the role of tourism resources and cultural brands in boxing culture to build Xu Jia Boxing into a martial art with modern cultural characteristics that integrates fitness, competitive appreciation, and entertainment art.

第 3 节 佛汉拳

1.项目文化

佛汉拳,亦称"佛汉捶""佛拳",又称"七二三八",是传统武术中的一个拳种,主要流传于山东一带。佛汉拳主要包括套路、散手、功法三类练习方法。传说佛汉拳是从清代少林寺传出的,在山东东明已传至第六代。目前,全面掌握佛汉拳的传人寥寥无几,需要相关人员抓紧开展挖掘和整理工作。

2.项目起源

据前辈拳师口述,该拳为南北朝梁武帝大通年间(527～529 年)由天竺僧人菩提达摩所创。达摩禅师东游汉土,入住少林寺,遂将此拳传与少林寺僧。该拳为少林寺镇寺之宝,为历代少林寺武僧秘密传习。此拳创始以来,少林历代掌门、高僧对其精心研造,是少林历代高僧集体智慧的结晶,也是少林拳的精华。因不轻易外传,又极具技击特色,所以佛汉拳被少林寺视为看家护院之拳法,尊为"少林暗藏门"。有口诀可为佐证,如"佛汉本是暗藏门,大通年间留下根,绘图带到少林寺,暗藏佛法少人闻",以及"初祖外传防身法,流传少林墙壁纳,千古妙术传千古,佛汉暗藏佛汉家"等。该拳一直以来作为少林寺内高僧专练之术,秘不外传。

3.项目规则(拳理)

拳理作为对具体动作技术招式的抽象理论,虽不及具体技术在传播中的影响，但也是传播内容的重要组成部分。佛汉拳的拳理是对佛汉拳具体技术理论的概述，体现了佛汉拳的文化内涵，同时也可作为佛汉拳练习者的思想指导。每个传播者所处的社会环境和受教育的程度不同，从而导致了对佛汉拳拳理接受程度的差异，这成为影响佛汉拳传播的重要因素之一。

佛汉拳的拳理思想包括武德教育、战术要点、训练歌诀、演练要求。武德教育有佛汉拳十大戒律，包括戒私斗、戒好名、戒好胜、戒好色、戒骄横、戒浮夸逞能、戒弄虚作假、戒挑拨离间、戒为非作歹、戒恃强凌弱。战术要点的格言包括："脚是战马手是兵，脚手齐到方成功""手脚一起到，神仙跑不掉""手到脚不到，落个两不照"。佛汉拳歌诀有两首：①佛汉出手侧身站，关门蓄势身自然；身如弓形手似箭，鹰眼猫腰精神贯；不丁不八疾滑步，法闪随收回拉转；动作组合莫打散，攻守合一最当先；步步挂腿巧使绊，脚手合力方向反；手到脚到身势到，脚手齐到敌胆寒；迅猛迅捷可制胜，内外兼修是佛汉。②佛汉巧打巧为先，虚实相济身自然；练时如同敌当前，用时好似独自玩；气随力发气力达，手不空回紧相连；彼不动时我不动，彼先动时我已先；心软意软身手软，身如龙形臂如鞭；粘连随顺敌势，直出横挂任我缠；不见要害不出手，一旦出手敌难还。佛汉拳的演练要求包括：擒拿抓打手脚并用，手跟手，手随手，出手不让手，搏击上中下，拳打左中右，抓拿手法随身走，边打边破，不顶不丢，随势而化，遇机而进，见势随势，见招还招，递中见打，打中带防，随截随打，随封随进，粘连抢进，吞吐沉浮，连绵不断。

综上所述，佛汉拳的拳理体现了其良好的武德教育和严格的门规，歌诀是对佛汉拳演练中手、眼、身法、步、精神、气力、功的描述，要求是对佛汉拳演练特点的体现。

4.动作解析

佛汉拳传入东明县有近 180 年的历史，经佛汉拳六代传人的习练与融会，汲取诸拳之精华，演变成具有拳路简洁、不用器械、实战性强、近距离发力等特点的拳术。佛汉拳以基本功、散手对练及单练、功法为主要传播内容，具有技术简洁的特点和独特的功法训练，突出了其实战技击性。

佛汉拳动作一

Fohan Boxing action 1

5.项目传承人

据第六代传承人李义军老师讲，佛汉拳创建于少林寺，盛行于山东省东明县，是东明县特有的本土拳种和珍贵的文化遗产。

据东明县高村《佛汉拳续谱》纪念碑记载，佛汉拳乃如来三尊佛祖所创，兴于唐，备于宋。清道光十二年(1832 年)，少林寺佛汉拳徐修文大师，经常云游在东明县马头乡(当时称“大名府杜胜集”)一带，当时马头乡贾庄贾云路、安本屯田魁皂与大师较技不敌，一起拜徐修文为师，二人均为少林寺俗家弟子，贾公号光明，田公号永明。二人赴少林寺苦学三年归里，广收门徒，相继传东明县河防营河务都尉宋金榜、李凤海、郭秀兰、安永福，河北大名练军刘长春、张金荣等。徐修文大师赠“内、初、山、寺、团、同、胜、国、少、年、用、者、思、理、多、君、酞、民、则、安”二十个字，为佛汉拳弟子按资排辈所用，沿传至今。

6.项目新发展

6.1　佛汉拳向大众健身、养生方向发展

在现代社会，佛汉拳以人体科学、运动力学、美学及医学等现代科学理论

为指导，使技术内容简单易学，能够满足不同性别、不同年龄的人群练习。现代佛汉拳的技术动作根据人体科学及养生学等有关知识创编而成，并且采用科学合理的训练方式，故其正在向着大众化健身、养生、祛病延年等方向发展。

现代佛汉拳的健身价值主要体现在防患于未然。群众通过习练佛汉拳，可以增强人体的免疫能力，使其身体健康，少生疾病。佛汉拳强调刚柔相济、快慢相间、动静相宜、外猛内静等阴阳法则，通过肢体的运动使人体中枢神经功能得到调整，加强大脑的兴奋与抑制交换的能力，提高人体对外界环境的适应能力，这与传统医学理论在阴阳学等方面是一致的。

佛汉拳除了能加快人体的新陈代谢、增强体质、提高人的适应能力外，还有练身心和练意这一特殊作用，讲究“内外合一，形神兼备”。久练佛汉拳可以使人身心俱健、精力充沛，使人的性情变得刚柔相济，达到心理和生理的平衡，从而提高身体内部功能。这些用中国传统医学理论来解释，就是内和外的修炼能使全身的血、气、津得到流通，从而达到调节脏腑机制，使人从弱变强，这种强壮是内外整体的强壮，从而达到强身健体的作用。

佛汉拳动作二

Fohan Boxing action 2

6.2 佛汉拳向竞技观赏价值方向发展

佛汉拳作为传统武术中的稀有拳种一向秘不外传，但在竞技全球化的今天，它在保留自身特色的同时，结合现代竞技赛场的需要，对技术内容和技术动作进行改革，以其独特优美的动作演练，赢得了广大观众的赞誉和认可。在云南举行的首届中国传统武术节上，骥阳市“鸿翔武院”的 4 名习练佛汉拳的学生，在校长李凡夫的带领下，获得 2 金、4 银、5 铜的好成绩，为佛汉拳在竞技道路上的发展创造了一个良好的开端。自此，佛汉拳以一种新兴传统武术拳种叱咤于竞技赛场，成为一道亮丽的风景线。

Fohan Boxing

1.Project culture

Fohan Boxing, also known as “Fo Han Chui”, “Fo Quan”, and “7238”, is a kind of traditional martial arts, which is mainly spread in Shandong. The main content of Fohan Boxing includes three kinds of practice methods: routine, Sanshou and Gongfa. It is said that Fohan Boxing originated from Shaolin Temple in the Qing Dynasty and has been passed down to the sixth generation in Dongming County, Shandong Province. At present, there are only a handful of people who have mastered Fohan Boxing in an all-round way, so the research and collation work needs to be carried out urgently.

2.Project origin

According to oral description of the boxing predecessors, Fohan Boxing was created by Bodhidharma, a Tianzhu monk, during the reign of Emperor Wudi of the Liang Dynasty in the Northern and Southern dynasties (527-529 AD). Zen Master Bodhidharma traveled east to the Han Dynasty and lived in Shaolin Temple, and then taught the boxing to the masters and monks in Shaolin Temple. This boxing is the treasure of the Shaolin Temple, and it is a secret practice for the monks of Shaolin Temple in past dynasties. Since its inception, this boxing has been carefully developed by Shaolin masters and monks of all dynasties. It is the crystallization of collective wisdom of Shaolin monks of all dynasties and the essence of Shaolin boxing. Because it is rarely spread to those outside the temple and has the characteristics of fighting, it is regarded as the boxing method of guarding the house by Shaolin Temple and respected as "Shaolin Secrete Boxing". This can be evidenced by pithy formulas, such as "Buddhist Han was originally a secrete boxing, which was originated from the Datong period with its drawings were brought to Shaolin Temple. Therefore, it is rarely heard by people." and "The self-defense method created by the first ancestor is spread within Shaolin walls for thousands of years and is hidden in the Shaolin Temple." and so on. The boxing has always been an art specially practiced by the Shaolin Temple monks without spreading.

3.Project rules

As an abstract theory of specific movements and techniques, the theory of Fohan Boxing is not as influential as specific techniques in communication, but it is also an important part of communication content. The theory of Fohan Boxing is an overview of its specific technical theory, which reflects the cultural connotation of Fohan Boxing, and is also the ideological guidance of its practitioners. Because each disseminator's social environment and the degrees of cultural education are different, the acceptance of the theory of Fohan Boxing is also different, which becomes one of the important factors that affects the dissemination of Fohan Boxing.

The thought of Fohan Boxing includes the education of martial art morality, the main points of tactics, the training songs, and the requirements of drills. For the martial art moral education, Fohan Boxing has its ten commandments: Abstain from private fight; abstain from fame; abstain from the eagerness to win; quit lechery; quit arrogance; abstain from boasting and showing off; abstain from fraud; do not sow dissension; abstain from doing evil; and abstain from the strong bullying the weak. Its main tactical point includes: The foot is like the war horse, the hand is like the soldier, the foot and hand work together to make enemies terrified. With hands and feet together, immortals cannot run away. If the hands reach while the feet do not, neither can succeed in hitting the opponent. There are two Fohan Boxing songs. The first one is as follows: When playing Fohan Boxing, one should stand sideways, close the door and get ready naturally. The body is like a bow and the hands are like arrows; the eyes are like eagles; the waist is like a cat and the spirit is very imposing. The sliding speed is very fast, turning around with retraction and rotation quickly. Don't break up the action combination, and the combination of attack and defense is the most important. Hang legs skillfully step by step, and feet and hands work together in the opposite direction. One can win with rapidity and swiftness from hand to foot to body and from foot to hand. Fohan Boxing is about both internal and external cultivation. The second song is as follows: To play Fohan Boxing skillfully, the combination of deficiency and reality is the key, which makes the body natural. When practicing, it's like the enemy's current, and when using it, it's like playing alone. Qi develops with force. When Qi reaches, hands are connected tightly. When the opponent does not move, I do not move; when he moves first, I can move faster. The heart is soft, the body is soft too. The body is like a dragon, and the arm is like a whip. Based on the enemy's situation, go straight out, hang horizontally, and let me entangle. If you don't see the vital parts, don't hit the person. Once you do, the enemy will be difficult to return. Fohan Boxing drill requirements are as follows: Capture, grasp, and hit with hands and feet; hand follows hand without concession; fight up, down, punch left, middle and right, walk while playing grasping techniques; break while fighting; do not reach the limit and do not get relaxed, and change with the situation; attach when the opportunity arises and based on specific situation; and fight while defensing, and attack based on the opponent's actions to ensure smooth action.

The theory of Fohan Boxing embodies its good martial arts education and strict door rules. The song formula is the description of the hand, eye, body, step, spirit, strength, and skill in the practice of this boxing, while the requirement is the embodiment of the characteristics of its drills.

4.Action parsing

Fohan Boxing has been introduced into Dongming County for nearly 180 years. Through the practice and integration of six generations of its inheritors, Fohan Boxing has evolved into one with the characteristics of concise boxing path, strong actual combat, and close force without using any apparatus. The main contents of Fohan Boxing are basic skills, Sanshou practice, and single practice and Gongfa. The concise technique and unique skill training of Fohan Boxing highlight the actual combat skills.

5.Project inheritor

According to Li Yijun, the sixth-generation inheritor, Fohan Boxing was founded in Shaolin Temple and originated in Dongming County, Shandong Province. It is a unique local boxing and precious cultural heritage of Dongming County.

According to *Continued Spectrum of Fohan Boxing* monument in Gaocun Village, Dongming County, Fohan Boxing was created by three Buddhas, and developed in the Tang Dynasty, and flourished in the Song Dynasty. In the 12th year of Daoguang of the Qing Dynasty (1832), Master Xu Xiuwen of Shaolin Temple often traveled to Matou Township of Dongming County ("Damingfu dushengji" at that time). At that time, Jia Yunlu and Anben Tuntian Kuizao of Matou Township were defeated by the master. They worshipped Xu Xiuwen as their teacher. Both were secular disciples of Shaolin Temple. Jia Gong's name was Guangming and Tian Gong's name was Yongming. They went to the Shaolin Temple to study hard for three years and received a wide range of disciples, such as Song Jinbang, Li Fenghai, Guo Xiulan, An Yongfu, Liu Changchun (an officer in Daming County, Hebei Province), Zhang Jinrong and so on. Master Xu Xiuwen presented twenty characters: Nei, Chu, Shan, Si, Tuan, Tong, Sheng, Guo, Shao, Nian,

Yong, Zhe, Si, Li, Duo, Jun, Tai, Min, Ze and An. They are used by the disciples of Fohan Boxing according to their seniority and have been handed down to this day.

6.New development

6.1 Fohan Boxing develops with higher values in mass fitness and health preservation

In modern society, with the improvement of productivity and the enrichment of material life, Fohan Boxing is guided by modern scientific theories such as human science, sports mechanics, aesthetics and medicine. Its technical content is simple and easy to learn, which can meet the needs of people of different genders and ages. Its technical movements are based on human science and health preservation. And the training methods are scientific and reasonable, so the value orientation of modern Fohan Boxing is developing towards popular fitness, health preservation, disease prevention and longevity.

The fitness value of modern Fohan Boxing is mainly embodied in the prevention of accidents in the future. Practicing Fohan Boxing can enhance immunity, promote health, and reduce diseases. It emphasizes the principles of Yin and Yang, such as combining hardness with softness, alternating speed and slowness, appropriate movement and stillness, fierce outside and quiet inside. Through the movement of limbs, the function of central nervous system of human body can be adjusted, the ability of excitement and inhibition exchange of brain can be strengthened, and the adaptability of human body to external environment can be improved, which is consistent with traditional medical theory in emphasizing Yin and Yang.

In addition to promoting the metabolism of the human body, enhancing physical fitness, and improving people's adaptability, Fohan Boxing also has the special function of training body and mind, which pays attention to "the unity of inside and outside, both form and spirit". Practicing Fohan Boxing for a long time can make people physically and mentally healthy, energetic, make people's temperament become firm and gentle, achieve psychological and physiological balance, and improve the internal function of the body. When explained by the theory of traditional Chinese medicine, it achieves the circulation of blood, qi and body fluid throughout the body through internal and external cultivation, so as to regulate the mechanism of viscera. It helps make people grow from weak to strong in an all-round manner and achieves fitness.

6.2　Fohan Boxing develops with higher competitive and viewing values

As a rare boxing in traditional martial arts, Fohan Boxing has always been kept secret without spreading to external groups. However, in today's global competition, technical content and movements of Foshan Boxing are reformed while retaining its own characteristics in combination with the needs of modern competitive arena, which wins the praise and recognition of the broad audience with its unique and beautiful action drills at the first Chinese Traditional Martial Art Festival held in Yunnan Province, four students from Hongxiang Martial Art Academy in Jiyang City, under the leadership of President Li Fanfu, achieved good results of 2 gold, 4 silver and 5 copper medals, which created a good start for the development of Fohan Boxing on the competitive road. Since then, Fohan Boxing has become a beautiful scenery in the competitive arena as an emerging traditional martial art.

第 4 节　孙膑拳

1.项目文化

孙膑拳是以战国军事家孙膑的名字命名的中华古拳。孙膑拳又称“大架举”,又有“二二节腿”与“长袖拳”之称,是武技与兵家思想有机相融的结晶,是我国武术中起源较早的拳术之一,山东安丘、青岛等地是孙膑拳的主要流传地。该拳种风格古朴雄浑,尤重技击实战,所以深得历代武术家的推崇。

其技术和理论体系完整，以孙膑智慧为文化内涵，融涉孙膑兵法思想，具有中华武术特色。

2.项目起源

孟宪堂在《中国孙膑拳》一书中描述了孙膑拳的发源，并阐明研究孙膑拳首先要了解孙膑其人。孙膑出生在战国时代中期(约为公元前 386 年)，在齐国经历了“桂陵之战”(即历史上有名的“围魏救赵”“马陵之战”)后，因将相不和，田忌赴楚，遂逃遁隐居。有关孙膑的史料记载很少，而民间传说却描述得细致入微，栩栩如生。

孙膑拳到底是不是由孙膑所创，现在人们还存有异议。1972 年 4 月，在山东临沂银雀山汉墓中，发现了失传 2000 多年的《孙膑兵法》，这对孙膑拳的研究会有所帮助，但据目前现有的资料看，没有孙膑传授拳术的记载，更没有孙膑拳法的专门文献资料。所以有很多专家学者认为，孙膑拳是后人假托附会由孙膑所创，但从孙膑拳械的风格特点，以及口授心传的技法原理和技术方法来看，孙膑拳是吸取武术各派之长后，运用孙膑兵法创编组合的拳种套路，这已得到了武术界人士的公认。

3.项目规则

孙膑拳是流传于山东的主要古老拳种，也是全国稀有拳术。它在演练和击法上都独具一格，朴实无华、结构紧凑、攻防显著、弹簧劲力、发鞭梢劲、螺旋手法，采取打架统一方法，故具散手、武术精华之特点。

孙膑拳吸取武林各门派很多击技特点，运用《孙膑兵法》中“内得民心，外知敌情”“必攻不守”“出其不意，攻其无备”“静如处子，动如脱兔”等理论，加上在战略上运用“空、诓、虚、实、晃”，在战术上运用“速、巧、软、绵、小”的技法，所以孙膑拳又称“精华拳”“散手拳”等。

孙膑拳动作一

Sun Bin Boxing action 1

（资料来源：孙膑拳国家级代表性传承人刘海港提供）

4.项目器械

该项目具备枪、刀、棍、剑、双刀、双剑、棒、铁尺、钩、鞭、锏、锤、斧、叉、流星锤等 180 余套拳械。

5.动作解析

关于孙膑拳的体系与主要套路内容，至今有很多说法。有“三十二式手、六十四式手、九十六手三个套路”之说，也有“大架（九十六式）、中架（三十二式）、小架（七十四式）、四架（一百零七式）、五架（五十五式）五个套路”之说，还有“孙膑拳分八套，前二三套为拆教基本功，后五套为技击法”之说，以及“孙膑无器械套路说”等。但一般公认的孙膑拳体系及主要套路有大架、中架、小架、对练、捶谱、六十手和孙膑拐共七套。

孙膑拳动作二

Sun Bin Boxing action 2

（资料来源：孙膑拳国家级代表性传承人刘海港提供）

6.项目继承人

孙膑拳传于安丘，可推至清光绪十年（1884 年）。孙膑拳流传至今，有史可考的已历经五代，其传承谱系完整、脉络分明、可证可考，在不同时期都涌现出了精英。其中，杨明斋是一位爱国武术家，早在青岛国术馆任教期间就积极组织抗日，最终在河南省永城县罗寨战役中为国捐躯。

孟宪堂，山东济宁人，现任青岛市武术文艺研究会会长、青岛孙膑武馆馆长兼总教练、青岛市武协常委兼科教部主任、青岛市孙膑拳研究会常务副会长兼秘书长、中国艺术院东方人体文化研究中心特约研究员等，系孙膑拳第四代传人。孟宪堂 1962 年开始授徒，曾发表《孙膑拳精华》《孙膑拳 32 手》《孙膑拳 64 手》等数篇文章，著有《中国孙膑拳》《中国当代武林名人志》等专著，编辑《作家学者武术家》论文集。他为使孙膑拳发扬光大，曾先后到访波兰、美国、德国、新加坡、加拿大等国家，并与国际、国内友人在青岛切磋武术多次。1991 年，他被评为青岛市武协工作积极分子，1992 年青岛市体育总会授予他积极分子称号，先后被收入《中国民间武术家名典》《中国大百科专家传集》《中国当代武术家名典》。孟宪堂习武授徒，著书立说，几十年如一日，为弘扬中华民族传统文化，推广普及孙膑拳做出了贡献。

刘海港，山东安丘人，现任中国艺术研究院东方人体文化研究中心主任助理、特邀研究员，安丘市孙膑拳训练基地主任，安丘市武术运动协会主席，安丘市青云山武术馆馆长，安丘市八届政协委员，海峡两岸青少年风筝放飞队领队，孙膑拳代表性传承人。刘海港自幼受伯父刘峻骧影响，7 岁开始习武，师承王建国，学习少林武术。1988 年，他拜中国孙膑拳四代传人孟宪堂为师，专心学习孙膑拳术，同时分别得到孙膑拳四代传人刘峻骧、张万福、刘振厚、王玉奎的指教。刘海港是研究传承孙膑拳并做出突出贡献的后起之秀，是目前收徒最多、技术最规范、活动最频繁的第五代传人。自他创办青云山武术馆、孙膑拳训练基地以来，已有 3000 人先后参加孙膑拳基础培训，他和他的弟子多次参加全国及省市级武术比赛，获得各类奖牌百余枚，为继承发展我国的孙膑拳术和弘扬中华武术事业做出了积极贡献。

孙膑拳动作三

Sun Bin Boxing action 3

（资料来源：孙膑拳国家级代表性传承人刘海港提供）

7.项目新发展

中华武术是中华民族历经数千年创造的一份具有民族特色的优秀的文化遗产。中华武术拳派套路有数千种，名称五花八门，举凡天上人间飞禽走兽、仙佛罗汉，甚至抽象哲学名词皆可成为套路名称，如黑虎拳、金舞拳、罗汉拳、大悲拳、少林拳、子午剑、青龙剑、八仙剑、太极拳、形意拳、八卦掌等，可谓包罗万象，显示了中华武学深厚广博的文化内涵。在这些拳名中，以人名命名的拳种最少，而且以确有的历史人物命名的则可能只有孙膑拳一种。把战国时期的著名军事家孙膑冠于其拳名之上，可谓斩钉截铁，毫不含糊。孙膑拳是战国中期齐国人孙膑所创的说法并无文字记载，只有 1995 年 1 月西苑出版社出版的孟宪堂《中国孙膑拳》有较全介绍，该书是国内首部全面总结孙膑拳的著作。现在，孙膑拳在山东济南、聊城、菏泽、安丘、曲阜、明水、淄博、莱阳、莱西、烟台、青岛、德州及湖北沙市等地，以及日本、美国、德国、菲律宾、新加坡等国家已经普遍流行。孙膑拳在中国台湾尤为盛行，台湾中国文化大学专门设有武术课，由孙绍棠教授传授孙膑拳大、中、小架和其他武术套路。孙膑拳已在全国普及，并走向世界。孟宪堂在匈牙利 MTX 武术学院任总教练。新加坡著名武术家、新加坡武术总会国家教练考官严崇腾先生也拜在孟宪堂门下专心习练孙膑拳。孟宪堂不辞辛苦地在世界各地传授孙膑拳，还抽时间又主编了《中国当代武林名人志》的一、二、三卷。2005 年由中国人民体育音像出版社出版的《中国孙膑拳》(VCD 教学带，一套十个光碟)，使学习研究孙膑拳法有了参考资料。2011 年 6 月，孙膑拳被列入第三批国家级非物质文化遗产名录。

Sun Bin Boxing

1.Project culture

Sun Bin Boxing (also called "large-action boxing", "two-section leg boxing" and "long-sleeved boxing") is named after the famous militarist Sun Bin in the Warring States Period, and is an ancient boxing blended martial arts with militarists' thought. It is one of the martial arts with earlier source in Chinese martial arts, and is popular in Shandong Province. It is highly regarded by generations of martial experts for its practicability and plain, vigorous, and unique styles. Mainly spread in Anqiu and Qingdao of Shandong Province, Sun Bin Boxing has a complete technology theory reflecting the militarists' thought and wisdom of Sun Bin with the characteristics of Chinese martial arts.

2.Project origin

In *Chinese Sun Bin Boxing*, the author Meng Xiantang states the origin of Sun Bin Boxing and the necessity of knowing Sun Bin well before studying this martial art. Sun Bin was born in about 386 B.C., the Middle Warring States Period. While vividly alive in legend, Sun Bin was rarely written about in historical records. After the Battle of GuiLing (famous for the strategy of "Relieving the State of Zhao by besieging the State of Wei" and the "Battle of Maling"), Sun escaped and lived in solitude because of the conflict with General Tianji and the misunderstanding of King of Qi. While vividly alive in legend, Sun Bin was rarely written about in historical records.

It is still arguable whether Sun Bin created this kind of boxing. *The Military Science of Sun Bin* which had been lost for more than 2,000 years was discovered in April 1972 in the tomb of Han Dynasty in Linyi Yinque Mountain. Its discovery contributes a lot to the study of Sun Bin Boxing. However, there is no record on the teaching of this boxing by Sun Bin and no special documents about Sun Bin Boxing according to the existing data. Many experts believe that Sun Bin Boxing was created by the posterity in the name of Sun Bin. It is generally acknowledged among martial arts circle that this boxing has the essence of the militarists' thought and wisdom of Sun Bin and the strengths of other Chinese martial arts from its actions and theory.

3.Sports rules

Sun Bin Boxing is the major school of Shandong traditional boxing styles and a rare traditional boxing style. It is characterized by its simple, unique, coherent, flexible, hectic and practical actions and integrative attacking and defense strategies. Therefore, the boxing has the essence of Sanshou and other martial arts.

With the theories of "Win the hearts of people, and learn the enemy information", "Offense is the best defense", "Attack the unprepared", and "Deliberate in counsel, prompt in action" in the *Military Science of Sun Bin*, the strategy of "erratic exchange of real and false "and tactics of "quickness", "skillfulness", "mildness" and "perceptiveness", Sun Bin Boxing shares many common characteristics of other boxing styles, and therefore is also called "Essence Boxing" and "Sanshou Boxing".

4.Project apparatus

This martial art has over 180 kinds of apparatuses, such as: spear, broadsword, cudgel, sword, double broadsword, double sword, club, iron ruler, hook, whip, mace, hammer, axe, fork and meteor hammer, etc.

5.Action parsing

Different kinds of interpretations exist as to the content and system of Sun Bin Boxing. Some people say it has three systems: 32 actions, 64 actions and 96 actions. Other people say it has five systems: big frame (96 actions), middle frame (32 actions), small frame (74 actions), the fourth frame (107 actions) and the fifth frame (55 actions). There is another saying that it has eight systems: The first two and three systems emphasize on basic skills training and the latter five focus on combat techniques. What's more, there are people assuming that it has no system at all. Most people agree that the content and system of Sun Bin Boxing includes seven parts: large frame, middle frame, small frame, sparring, thump spectrum, 60 actions and Sunbinguai.

6.Project inheritor

Sun Bin Boxing can date all the way back to the tenth year of Guangxu

Emperor in Qing Dynasty (in 1884) in Anqiu City. It has been handed down through five generations. It is complete in system, clear in stage, and provable in evidence. Among the masters of Sun Bin Boxing, Yang Mingzhai is famous for his patriotism. As a coach in Qingdao Martial Arts School, he devoted himself to counter-Japanese campaign and gave his life for the country in the Battle of Luozhai in Yongcheng, Henan Province.

Meng Xiantang, born in Jining City of Shandong Province, is the 4th generation successor of Sun Bin Boxing. Currently, he is the President of Qingdao Martial Arts and Culture Research Association, the Director and Chief Coach of Qingdao Sun Bin Boxing School, the Standing Committee and Director of Science and Education Department of Qingdao Martial Arts Association, the Executive Vice President and Secretary-general of Qingdao Sun Bin Boxing Research Association, and the Special Researcher of the Oriental Human Body Culture Research Center of China Arts Academy. He began teaching Sun Bin Boxing in 1962. He has published several papers, such as the *Essence of Sunbin Boxing*, *32 Actions of Sun Bin Boxing*, *64 Actions of Sun Bin Boxing* and so on. He is the author of *Chinese Sun Bin Boxing* and the *Contemporary Celebrities of Chinese Martial Arts*, as well as the editor of the collected papers *Writer*, *Scholar and Martial Arts Masters*. He works at spreading Sun Bin Boxing and often exchanges the understanding of martial arts with foreign and domestic masters. He was appraised by Qingdao Martial Arts Association in 1991 and by Qingdao Sports Federation in 1992 for his initiative contribution to the spreading of Martial Arts. Being a master of Sun Bin Boxing, he has been recorded in the book *Chinese Folk Martial Arts Masters*, *The Biography of Chinese Encyclopedia Experts*, and *The Contemporary Master of Chinese Martial Arts*. With efforts in practicing and teaching the martial art, and writing books, he has made great contributions to carrying forward the traditional Chinese culture and popularizing Sun Bin Boxing for decades.

Liu Haigang, born in Anqiu City of Shandong Province, with university degree, is the assistant director and researcher of the Oriental Human Body

Culture Research Center of China Arts Academy, the director of Anqiu training center of Sun Bin Boxing, Chairman of Anqiu Martial Arts Association, President of Qingyunshan Martial Arts School, the 8th CPPCC member of Anqiu City, the leader of cross-strait youth kite team and regarded as a representative successor of Sun Bin Boxing. Under the influence of his uncle Liu Junxiang, Liu Haigang began to learn Shaolin martial arts from Wang Jianguo at the age of 7. He began to learn Sun Bin Boxing from the 4th successor Meng Xiantang in 1988 and got instructions from 4 generation successors one after another (Liu Junxiang, Zhang Wanfu, Liu Zhenhou and Wang Yukui). As the 5th generation successor of Sun Bin Boxing, Liu Haigang is acknowledged as a rising star owning to his outstanding contributions to the popularization of Sun Bin Boxing with the largest number of students, most regular skills, and most frequent activities. Qingyunshan Martial Arts School and Sun Bin Boxing Training Center created by Liu attracted more than 3,000 students for base training of Sun Bin Boxing. Liu and his students have participated in national and provincial Martial Arts Competitions for many times and won more than 100 medals. Liu has made active contributions inheriting and popularizing Sun Bin Boxing as well as Chinese Martial Arts.

7.New development

Chinese martial arts is an excellent cultural heritage with national characteristics created by the Chinese nation over thousands of years. There are thousand kinds of actions and schools with various names ranging from heaven down to the earth, from birds to animals and even from gods to demons, such as Black Tiger Boxing, Gold Dancing Boxing, Fohan Boxing, Great Grief Boxing, Shaolin Boxing, Meridian Swordsmanship, Black Dragon Swordsmanship, PaHsien Swordsmanship, Taichi boxing, Xingyi boxing, Eight Trigrams Palm, etc. Covering all kinds of things, these names show the profound and extensive cultural connotation of Chinese martial arts, with the exception that Sun Bin Boxing is the only one named after a person. There is no record for the rumor that Sun Bin Boxing was created by Sun Bin (State of Qi in the middle of the Warring States Period). Evidence of the relationship between Sun Bin and the boxing can be found in *Chinese Sun Bin Boxing* written by Meng Xiantang in January 1995, which is the first book about Sun Bin Boxing. Sun Bin Boxing is now widely popular in many cities of Shandong Province such as Jinan, Liaocheng, Heze, Anqiu, Qufu, Mingshui, Zibo, Laiyang, Laixi, Yantai, Qingdao, Dezhou and Shashi City in Hubei Province. It is also popular in Japan, the United States, Germany, the Philippines and Singapore. It is even more popular in Taiwan, China: The University of Chinese Culture in Taiwan, China has regular martial arts classes, with professor Sun Shaotang teaching the large, medium and small actions as well as others. Sun Bin Boxing has been popularized in the whole country and gone to the world. Meng is the head coach of MTX Martial Arts Academy in Hungary. A famous Singaporean martial artist, Yan Chongteng, the national coach examiner of the Singapore Martial Arts Association and the President of Singapore Jianxin Sports Association, also learned Sun Bin Boxing from Meng. In addition to the teaching of Sun Bin Boxing world widely, Meng published *The Contemporary Celebrities of Chinese Martial Arts* (Volumes I, II, and III). The publishing of *Chinese Sun Bin Boxing* (10 VCDs) in 2005 provides the basis for learning and studying this boxing. In June, 2011, Sun Bin Boxing was subscribed on the third batch of National Intangible Cultural Heritage List.

第 5 节　查拳

1.项目文化

查拳又称“插拳”或“叉拳”。该拳系因多插掌而得名(关于查拳名称的由来与说法较多,但都无法考证),是中国传统武术中影响较大的拳种之一,在武术史上有“南拳北腿山东查”之说。查拳萌发于山东冠县,盛行于山东聊城、济宁、临清、阳谷,后传至山西、河南、河北、北京和港台地区以及东南亚各国。它以崭新的姿态、高超的技艺、独特的风格得到武术界人士的公认和赞誉。

2.项目起源

关于查拳的起源有多种说法，具体如下。

2.1 唐朝说

据山东省志《体育志》和查拳拳谱记载，唐代一支东征军队路经冠县，青年将领滑宗岐负伤滞留该地，在当地群众的精心照料下，恢复了健康。留住期间，他把自己的武艺"架子拳"传授给当地村民，之后他又将旅居长安的师兄查尚义请来一同施教。查尚义又名"查密尔"，擅长"身法势"。查尚义、滑宗岐故去后，当地人把查尚义传的身法势叫"在举"，滑宗岐传的架子拳叫"滑拳"。

2.2 明末说

关于查拳的另一说法是，查尚义是明朝末年新疆地方的回民，他年轻时正值倭寇侵扰闽浙沿海一带。明朝统治者下诏征集义民从军御倭，查尚义激于义愤，请缨东来，但没有到达前线就病倒了。同行的伙伴把他留在聊城冠县休养，经过治疗后，他身体痊愈，为了报答当地百姓的关照，就把自己多年练习的查拳套路传给了他们。后来学习的人越来越多，范围也越来越广，查拳也就传播开来。

2.3 清末说

在《回族武术初探》一文中有这样的介绍，相传在八国联军入侵北京时，西域人查密尔出于义愤，东去抗敌，行到冠县附近病倒，被当地穆斯林医救。他病愈后，八国联军事已平息，查密尔无以为报，便在当地传授拳术。后来查尚信、查守义继承，为师传艺，所以后称"查拳"。

2.4 沙亮可能是查拳创编者

20世纪80年代初期，著名的武术家、学者张文广、康戈武等人在挖掘整理查拳传统套路时，曾对查拳的起源问题进行了调查、采访、研究与论证。大量的史料证明，查密尔东来传拳说与历史背景不符。据现有的资料看，查拳初盛于鲁西，之后逐渐流传到各地。

依据明代戚继光《纪效新书》、唐顺之《武编》、何良臣《阵记》等书，均未见有"查拳"这一名词，也就是说查拳的创编应晚于《纪效新书》成书。根据大量的史料分析、研究可看出，查拳架势与戚继光的《纪效新书》中的"拳经捷要"、唐顺之的《武编拳》所记相近，推测查拳是明末在山东流行拳法的基础上，吸收戚、唐的精华而创编的。它发展于清代初、中期，盛行于清末民初，山东聊城冠县人沙亮可能是查拳的创编者。

3.项目规则

查拳属长拳类拳种，在运动风格特点上与其他长拳类同，且结构紧凑、动作舒展而又严谨、技法清晰而又连贯、功架整齐而又虚实分明、节奏明快、干净利落、快速有力、刚柔相济，特别注重爆发力。

查拳的基本动作包括手型、手法、步型、步法、腿法、身法、跳跃、平衡等内容。

查拳动作一

Cha Boxing action 1

4.项目器械

查拳以弹腿为基础，还包括枪、棍、刀、剑等器械练习，主要器械有查刀、昆吾剑、锁口枪、群羊棍、查钩、拦马撅、双手带等器械。

5.动作解析

查拳体系与主要套路内容包括弹腿十路、查拳十路、滑拳二路、炮拳三路、洪拳四路、腿拳二路。

弹腿：起源于山东临清回族穆斯林（也有说出自山东临清龙潭寺），是由回族原始武术演化而来，属武术中的昆仑派，是习练查拳的基本功，也叫“入门功”。弹腿共有十路，每一路都是单一动作的左右对称联系。

十路查拳是该拳种中最基本的套路，也是流行最广泛的套路，其动作特点如下：①一路母子：属于查拳的开门拳，动作工整、舒展、严谨规范，以练习功架为主。②二路行手：以腰为轴，注重手法与身法，抡臂穿灵活多变，疾快迅猛有行手之说。③三路飞脚：步伐灵活，动作协调干净利落，明快通畅，以跳跃动作居多。④四路升平：内容丰富，结构严谨，奔打四方招法多变。⑤五路关东：动作大力，潇洒自如，势知行云流水。⑥六路埋伏：动作紧凑，变幻莫测，有六角式之称。⑦七路梅花：动作招式圆滑柔软、舒展大方。⑧八路连环：动作简洁干练，连贯不断，招招紧扣，步步连环。⑨九路龙摆尾：动作如苍龙升空，迅猛忽变，变化多端。⑩十路串拳：动作柔中有刚，刚中有柔，刚柔相济。

滑拳：滑拳套路分为一路滑拳、二路滑拳、三路滑拳，其中三路滑拳是对练套路。

炮拳：炮拳分为三路炮拳、六路炮拳、九路炮拳，共三个套路。

洪拳：洪拳分为一路洪拳、三路洪拳、四路洪拳、七路洪拳，共四个套路。

腿拳：腿拳可分为一路腿拳和二路腿拳两种。

6.项目传承人

查拳只在穆斯林民众中传授，很少外传，当时在冠县主要分布于县城西街、南街、城郊张尹庄及十里铺、沙庄、里固等十几个回族聚居的村庄，后来逐渐传播到全国各地的穆斯林民众中，在武术界素有“南拳北腿山东查”之誉。新中国成立后，民族藩篱被打破，查拳开始广泛传播，现已成为在全国拥有重要影响和众多习练者的著名武术流派之一。

沙亮（约 1701～1747 年），又名“密尔”，查拳名家，回族，山东冠县人，生于寿张县（今阳谷县）张秋镇。他自幼习武，尤擅查拳，青年时曾以“飞腿沙亮”名冠鲁西，并同郭登云被当地人誉为“武林二杰”。

张其维（1850～1934 年），清末民初的查拳大师，是继名师沙亮、张乾之后的又一代传人。他一生培养了很多高徒，对查拳的发展起到了很大的作用。冯玉祥为表扬张其维武德高尚，其奖“道德剑”一把。张其维的事迹在中国《武术大辞典》《图说中国武术史》二书中都有专条注释，他的徒弟张英键、张锡太、张风岭、何振全、何英亭都是著名的查拳师。

杨鸿修（1864～1944 年），查拳名家，山东冠县人，幼跟洪占元、马老维学查拳系拳械，擅拳摔打技法，曾以“大枪杨鸿修”“快拳杨”而闻名。他终生研习查拳，武术名家王子平、马金镖、何振江、马裕甫等，都是其门徒。

张文广，回族，河南通许人，著名武术教育家。1929 年跟张风岭、常振芳习查拳，精查、花、炮、地躺、形意、八卦等拳械，对摔跤、太极、击剑、散手也颇有造诣。他多年来培养了大批武术人才，曾获国家体委颁发的“新中国体育工作 30 年奖”“新中国体育开拓者”荣誉奖、中国国际武术节武术贡献奖。

张子英，号俊杰，查拳名师，回族，山东冠县人，出生于查拳世家，自幼跟随祖父张其维习练查拳、滑拳等器械。他 1985 年参与了《查拳》的编写，同年创办冠县查拳学校，1988 年获中国国际武术节武术贡献奖。

查拳动作二

Cha Boxing action 2

7.项目新发展

随着武术的整体衰落，完整传承查拳也变得艰难起来，对查拳的抢救、整理、保护已经是刻不容缓的事情。

作为查拳的发源地，冠县地方政府已经把查拳这一非物质文化遗产的保护、抢救、开发工作列入重要议事日程。县政府已成立“保护振兴查拳工作领导小组”，有关规划已经列入全县体育事业发展规划中。查拳文化的发掘、整理、抢救、保护工作已全面开展，并取得了初步成果。县体育局专业人员已在县城部分公办、民办学校开设了查拳课程。2005 年注册的冠县查拳协会，由沙宗朝（查拳的第十四代传人）担任会长。查拳在鲁西南地区有着广泛的群众基础，近现代以来流传到上海、江苏、河南、山西、北京、云南等地。现代发展起来的新编长拳套路及现代竞技武术采用了较多的查拳动作素材，并吸收了查拳的运动风格。查拳为中华武术发展做出了贡献，弘扬查拳对于发展民族运动、强健全民体魄具有重要意义。

Cha Boxing

1.Project culture

Cha Boxing, or Cha Style Boxing, or Fork Boxing, is named for its many palm-thrusting actions. There are many origins and arguments about the name of this school of boxing, but they are all unverifiable. It is one of the most influential Chinese traditional martial arts. In the history of Chinese martial arts, "The fist techniques of the South, the leg techniques of the North, Cha Boxing of Shandong" are ranked together as the first three important techniques. Cha Boxing was born in Guan County, Shandong Province, and was popular in the counties of Liaocheng, Jining, Linqing and Yanggu in Shandong Province. Later it spread to Shanxi, Henan, Hebei, Beijing, Hong Kong and Taiwan and Southeast Asian countries. With its brand-new look, superb techniques and unique style, it has been recognized and praised by the martial arts community.

2.Project origin

There are many stories about the origin of Cha Boxing, as follows.

2.1 Originated in the Tang Dynasty

According to *Sports Record*, a Shandong provincial journal and the records of Cha Boxing, in the Tang Dynasty, an army marching east passed through Guan County, and Hua Zongqi, a young general, was injured and had to stay in the county. Being taken precious good care of the local people, he regained his health quickly. During his stay, he taught his martial arts "Frame Boxing" to the local villagers. Later, he invited Cha Shangyi, a senior fellow disciple of his master who travelled to Chang'an to teach the villagers together. Cha Shangyi, also known as Cha Mier, was good at body techniques positioning. After the death of Cha Shang and Hua Zongqi, the locals named Cha Shangyi's body techniques "Zaiju" and the Frame Boxing of Hua Zongqi as "Hua Boxing".

2.2 Originated during the end of the Ming Dynasty

There is another statement about the origin of the boxing: During the last years of the Ming Dynasty, Cha Shangyi, a young man of Hui people in Xinjiang, learned that some Japanese pirates were invading the coastal areas of Fujian and Zhejiang and that the rulers of the Ming Dynasty were recruiting the righteous civilians to fight against the pirates. Out of indignation to the Japanese pirates, he volunteered and hurried to the east coastal areas, but he fell ill before reaching the front line. His peers left him in Guan County of Liaocheng. After being well-treated, he recovered. In order to repay the care of the local people, he taught them the practice routines of Cha Boxing which he had practiced for many years. Later, more and more people from different areas started to study Cha Boxing, and the boxing spread quickly.

2.3 Originated at the end of the Qing Dynasty

In the article "Preliminary Study of Hui People's Martial Arts", there was such an introduction: When the Eight Power Allied Forces invaded Beijing, Cha Mier of the Western Regions went to the east to fight against the enemy but he fell ill when he arrived near Guan County and was rescued by the local Muslims. When he recovered, the invasion of Eight Power Allied Forces had come to an end. Cha Mier, who had no idea how to repay the local Muslims, chose to teach boxing in the local area. Later, the boxing techniques were inherited and passed on by Cha Shangxin and Cha Shouyi, and was named as Cha Boxing.

2.4 Sha Liang, a possible creator of the boxing

In the early 1980s, when exploring the traditional routine of Cha Boxing, Zhang Wenguang and Kang Gewu, two famous martial arts masters and scholars, had done much investigation, interview, study, and discussion concerning the origin of Cha Boxing. A large amount of historical data proved that Cha Mier's story was inconsistent with the historical background. According to the existing information, Cha Boxing originated in the western Shandong and later gradually spread to various places.

In three martial arts books written during the Ming Dynasty (*New Treatise of Examples to Follow*, by Qi Jiguang; *Wubian*, by Tang Shunzhi; *Zhenji*, by He Liangchen), the name of Cha Boxing was not mentioned, which means that Cha Boxing was born later than *New Treatise of Examples to Follow*. According to the analysis and research of a large amount of historical data, the postures of Cha Boxing were like that of "the Main Points of Boxing" recorded in Qi Jiguang's *New Treatise of Examples to Follow* and *Wubian* of Tang Shunzhi. Thus, it can be inferred that Cha Boxing was formed at the end of the Ming Dynasty based on popular boxing techniques in Shandong with a combination of the essence of the boxing techniques of Qi and Tang. It developed in the early and middle period of the Qing Dynasty and prevailed in the late Qing Dynasty among the ordinary folks. It was initially believed that: Sha Liang, a native of Guan County, Liaocheng of Shandong Province, might be the founder of Cha Boxing.

3.Project rules

Cha Boxing belongs to the school of Long Boxing (Changquan) and is similar to other kinds of this school in sport style. It has compact structure, extended and rigorous movements, as well as clear and coherent techniques. Its actions are very neat with clearly demarcated emptiness and solidness, and sprightly rhythm, containing agility and power and coupling hardness with softness. The boxing also pays special attention to explosive force.

The basic movements of Cha Boxing include hand forms, hand

techniques, stance, foot techniques, leg techniques, body techniques, jumping, balance and so on.

4.Apparatus

Cha Boxing is based on the routines of leg kicking boxing, and it also includes the practice of spears, clubs, broadswords, swords, and other apparatuses.

The main apparatuses of Cha Boxing are Cha broadswords, Kunwu swords, spears, clubs, Cha hooks, short wooden stakes, long hist broadswords and other weapons.

5.Action parsing

Cha Boxing and its main routines include 22 free hand or with-weapon routines: 10 routines of leg kicking boxing, 10 routines of Cha style boxing, 2 routines of slippery boxing, 3 routines of cannon boxing, 4 routines of Hong boxing and 2 routines of leg boxing.

Leg kicking boxing: leg kicking boxing originated from Hui Muslims in Linqing, Shandong (or from Longtan Temple in Linqing, Shandong). Leg kicking boxing evolved from primitive martial arts of Hui People and belonged to Kunlun School of martial arts. It is the basic skill, or introductory skill for studying Cha Boxing. There are ten routines of leg kicking boxing, each of which is symmetrically connected by a single action.

Ten-routine Cha Boxing: Ten-routine Cha Boxing is the most basic and popular in this kind of boxing. The characteristics of its movement are as follows:

Routine 1: A series of introductory actions of Cha Boxing, which are neat, extended, and rigorous and standardized movements, mainly practicing postures.

Routine 2: This routine, with waist as axis, pays attention to hand and body techniques. Its arm-swing actions are flexible, changeable, and swift.

Routine 3: There are flexible paces and coordinated and neat movements in this routine. Most of the actions are jumping movements.

Routine 4: This routine has rich content, rigorous structure and changeable tactics.

Routine 5: The actions are vigorous, free and unrestrained and continuous.

Routine 6: This routine is known as hexagonal routine with compact, unpredictable movements.

Routine 7: The action style is smooth, soft and graceful, thus is also called Routine of Plum Blossom.

Routine 8: The actions are concise, succinct and continuous.

Routine 9: It is called dragon wags tail because the actions are like a dragon ascending into the air with movements changing rapidly.

Routine 10: The actions are a perfect combination of hardness and softness.

Slippery boxing: Slippery boxing is divided into one-routine boxing, two-routine boxing and three-routine boxing. The three-routine boxing is a two-person practice routine.

Cannon boxing is divided into three-routine boxing, six-routine boxing and nine-routine boxing.

Hong boxing: Hong boxing is divided into one-routine Hong boxing, three-routine Hong boxing, four-routine Hong boxing and seven-routine Hong boxing.

Leg boxing: Leg boxing can be divided into one-routine leg boxing and two-routine leg boxing.

6.Project inheritor

Cha Boxing was only taught among Muslims and was seldom known by other people. At that time, it was mainly distributed in West Street and South Street of Guan County, Zhang Yin Village on the edge of the county, and a dozen villages like Shilipu, Sha and Ligu villages where Muslims lived. Later, it gradually spread to Islamic disciples all over the country and was related to two famous boxing techniques as "the fist techniques of the South, the leg techniques of the North, Cha Boxing of Shandong." After the founding of the People's Republic of China, the national fence was broken, and Cha Boxing began to spread widely. Today it has become one of the famous schools of martial art with important influence and many practitioners in the country.

Sha Liang (about 1701-1747), also known as Mi'er, was a famous Cha Boxing master. He was a native Hui of Guan County, Shandong Province, and was born in Zhangqiu Town, Shouzhang County (today's Yanggu County). He had been practicing martial arts since childhood, and was especially good at Cha Boxing. When he was young, he was famous in the West of Shandong as "Sha Liang — the Flying Leg". He and Guo Dengyun were praised as "two outstanding martial heroes" by the local people.

Zhang Qiwei (1850-1934), a master of Cha Boxing in the late Qing Dynasty and the early Republic of China, was a successor to Sha Liang and Zhang Qian. He trained many high quality practitioners in his life, which played a great role in the development of Cha Boxing. General Feng Yuxiang praised his virtue and awarded him a "moral sword". There were special annotations of him in *Chinese Martial Art Dictionary* and *Illustrated History of Chinese Martial Art*. His followers Zhang Yingjian, Zhang Xitai, Zhang Fengling, He Zhenquan and He Yingting were all famous boxers.

Yang Hongxiu (1864-1944), a famous Cha Boxing master, was born in Guan County, Shandong Province. When he was young, he followed Hong Zhanyuan and Master Ma for the study of Cha Boxing and Cha Boxing weapons. He was good at boxing and wrestling techniques, and was once known as "Long Spear Yang Hongxiu" and "Fast Hands Yang". For his whole life, he had been studying and exploring Cha Boxing. Many famous martial art masters such as Wang Ziping, Ma Jinbiao, He Zhenjiang and Ma Yufu were all his disciples.

Zhang Wenguang belongs to Hui nationality of Tongxu, Henan Province. Zhang is a famous martial arts educator. In 1929, He followed Zhang Fengling and Chang Zhenfang to practice Cha Boxing. He is good at Fine Cha Boxing,

Flower Boxing, Cannon Boxing, Ground Boxing, Xingyi Boxing and Eight Trigram Boxing as well as wrestling, Shadow Boxing, swordplay, and free sparring. Over the years, he has trained a large number of martial arts talents and has won the "Award of China's 30 Years Sports Work" issued by the National Sports Commission, the "China's Sports Pioneer" honorary award issued by the National Sports Commission, and the Martial Arts contribution Award of China International Martial Arts Festival.

Zhang Ziying, also named Junjie, is a famous Cha Boxing boxer of Hui nationality from Guan County, Shandong Province. Born in the family of Cha Boxing, he practiced Cha Boxing and Slippery Boxing with his grandfather Zhang Qiwei as a child. In 1985, he participated in the compilation of *Cha Boxing* and founded Cha Boxing School at Guan County in the same year. In 1988, he won the Martial Arts Contribution Award of China International Martial Arts Festival.

7.New development

With the decline of martial arts as a whole, the complete inheritance of Cha Boxing has become difficult. It is now urgent to rescue, organize and protect Cha Boxing.

The local government of Guan County, the birthplace of Cha Boxing, has put on an important agenda the protection, rescue and development of Cha Boxing, the intangible cultural heritage. The county government has set up a leading group for the protection and revitalization of Cha Boxing, and some of its projects has been included in the county sports development plan. The excavation, sorting out, rescue and protection of Cha Boxing culture have been carried out in an all-round way, and preliminary achievements have been gained. Professional staff of the County Sports Bureau have opened Cha Boxing courses in some public and private schools in the town. In 2005, Guan County Cha Boxing Association was registered, and Sha Zongchao, was elected the president (Sha Zongchao was the fourteenth generation of Successors of Cha Boxing in Guan County). Cha Boxing is very popular among local civilians in Southwest Shandong. It has spread to Shanghai, Jiangsu, Henan, Shanxi, Beijing, Yunnan and other places since modern times. The new Long Boxing Routine and modern competitive martial arts developed in modern times have adopted many techniques from Cha Boxing, and have absorbed its sport style. Cha Boxing has greatly contributed to the development of Chinese Martial Arts. Promoting Cha Boxing is of great significance to the development of the national sport and the strengthening and perfection of the people's physiques.

第 6 节　梁山子午门功夫

1.项目文化

梁山子午门功夫，迄今已有 800 多年的历史。北宋末年，以宋江为首的 108 名英雄好汉啸聚梁山，凭借水泊天险，依靠精绝武功，仗义疏财，除暴安良，威震朝野。他们战前练功，战后休整，经常到梁山北部的六工山建福寺切磋武艺，研讨兵法。后来，鲁智深、武松、燕青、时迁、林冲等好汉到建福寺为僧，与该寺方丈圆通禅师反复研习，取长补短，探讨印证，形成了梁山子午门功夫之雏形。

梁山是中国武术四大发祥地之一，一向与河南少林、湖北武当、四川峨眉齐名。梁山人崇尚武术，习武之风甚盛，许多武术高手驰名中外，为继承和发展中华武术做出了贡献，但近些年来提及的较少。据考，梁山拳种流派很多，有梅花拳、佛汉拳、洪拳、醉拳、螳螂拳、脱铐拳、埋伏拳、查拳、猴拳、燕青拳、掌洪拳、少林拳、太极拳等十几种；器械也较多，长兵器有枪、朴刀、禅杖等，短兵器有斧、锏、钩、剑、叉拐、双圈等，软兵器有三节棍、七节鞭、流星锤、绳镖等。梁山子午门第 21 代武术掌门人宋文样在梁山创办了中国梁山功夫研究院，传授醉拳、猴拳、武松拳、燕青拳、智深拳、江拳、少林拳、刀、枪、剑、叉、斧、钩等套路。

2.项目起源

山东是中国武术的发源地之一，素有“武术之乡”的美誉。坐落在鲁西南的水泊梁山，因《水浒传》108 名梁山好汉的精湛武功、传奇故事而驰誉中外。水浒众英豪的动人故事来源于历史上一段真实的以水泊梁山为营寨的农民起义。子午门功夫(又称"梁山派")就是在当时特定的历史条件下,由梁山众英雄好汉在行侠仗义、除暴安良的生活经历中创编的,至今已有800多年的历史。子午门功夫在形成发展的过程中深受齐鲁文化的影响。

《梁山县文史资料》第4、12辑中有如下记录:六工山建福寺有个老和尚,法号圆通,收小和尚近百人,有非凡的武艺,刀、枪、剑、棍无一不精,气功法术高超,个个刀枪不入。传说花和尚鲁智深投奔梁山时,途经此处,曾与建福寺的僧人比武,胜了建福寺的师徒,被尊为师,六工山从此成了梁山寨北部的哨卡。

关于子午门功夫名称的由来,据传是因好汉们在每天的子、午两个时辰练习此功,此功练先天之躯补后天之精华,练后天之精华补先天之不足,二者相辅相成,先天为阴,后天为阳,阴为子,阳为午。功夫练到一定程度后,练功时身上就会出现一股热流和一股冷流,热流被称为"火候",冷流被称为"精华之泉"。冷为阴、阴为子,火属阳、阳为午,功夫练到这种地步,也就达到了人们所说的出神入化,炉火纯青的境界。武术界形容此功厉害,又把子定为生,午定为死,寓意出拳抬腿可决定对方生或死,故名"子午门功夫"。

梁山武术流派林立、风格迥异,据统计梁山一带流行的拳术达十余种,影响力较大的有子午门功夫、太极拳、少林拳、佛汉拳、洪拳、二门洪拳。其中,近年发展较好影响较大的当数子午门功夫。《梁山功夫》中载,子午门功夫萌生于梁山民间,是水泊梁山众好汉及历代掌门人集体智慧的结晶。它根植于齐鲁大地,是齐鲁文化的再现;流行于中国,是中华民族智慧的体现;走向世界,是世界武术之瑰宝。目前,经21世纪掌门人宋义祥先生的精心挖掘、整理,现已形成了以子午拳为核心的38种特色套路,除此以外还有36种长短软硬器械和36种内功心法。梁山子午门功夫的各套路及动作名称大都与《水浒传》中众英雄的名字及其英雄行径相结合,套路动作易于记忆的同时更能陶冶习练者的情操。

3.动作解析

子午门功夫特点:顺臂、拧腰、合胯、大开大合、气势凶猛,蹦跳擢捣、勾挂点踹、飞撩劈踢,身法忽长忽短、摔打推拿、快稳准狠,与内功浑然一体,动中有静、静中有动,变化多端,难破难防。

3.1　徒手套路

3.1.1　子午拳十二路

子午拳十二路是元通禅师与宋江等众位梁山好汉所创，它意境高远，气力通达，动静结合，极具健身和实用价值。子午拳十二路又历经数十代子午门前辈的改革和心血灌注，使其内外兼修，大开大合，刚柔相济。演练该拳讲究气贯四梢，阴阳结合，动作灵活多变，步法轻盈，亮式清澈，舒展优美。该拳法共十二路，每路风格各异，勇猛间促智慧，奔放中持清境，宛如大漠雄风剽悍凌厉，又似小桥流水缓绵轻盈。

3.1.2　子午八卦游身桩与子午八卦拳

此举与拳为入云龙公孙胜与建福寺方丈元通所创，后经子午门功夫继承人西竺禅师（1487～1523 年）研习，并命名为子午八卦游身桩。该桩法刚柔相济，内外兼修，有气吞山河之势。本桩法分四段，第一段，走正极，以小架势为主，专攻人之下盘；第二段，架势高大，气势凶猛，以左八卦为主；第三段，变换成顺时右八卦，以大架势为主；第四段，又变换成逆时左八卦，以大、小架式混合练法。

3.1.3　宋江拳

宋江拳传说为 108 将首领宋江所创，经子午门七世掌门人（1377 年）道衍禅师充实、整理后命名为“宋江拳”，子午门弟子称之为“初祖拳”。拳法特点为刚柔相济、内外兼修，招招相连、环环相扣、快慢相间，招法独特、难破难防。

3.1.4　麒麟拳

麒麟拳传说为玉麒麟卢俊义所创，经子午门五世掌门人江泓（1309～1377 年）研习充实并将该拳命名为“麒麟举”。拳法特点为大开大合、气势凶猛、招式变化多端、柔中寓刚、刚中有柔，与内功浑然一体。

3.2　器械套路

子午门功夫的器械套路中尤其以“宋江追魂刀”“卢俊义奇门棍“和“公孙胜八卦剑”较为出名。动作搭配器械，提高动作的攻击力，可以和其他的器械碰撞，以求在最短的时间达到有效攻击敌人的效果，结束战斗。器械套路快速勇猛，都以精微巧妙的武术套路为基础，刀术和拳术与棍、剑等器械都是三法一体，要求在刚猛迅疾的动作和因敌变化中，必须身法一体，身器不散，善于集进攻和防守于一体，故能用最短的时间解决战斗。

梁山子午门功夫

Liangshan Ziwumen Kungfu

梁山子午门功夫在其发展过程中，汲取百家之长，又有自身特色，自成体系，且极具开拓精神。这在演练过程中与内功浑然一体，摔打推拿，快稳准狠。其技术方法一般可分为踢、打、破、摔、拿、击、刺七大类。“踢”“打”指的是以腿法见长的上下肢进攻方法；“破”指的是防守化解之法；“摔”指的是使对方身体失去重心，让对方倒地的方法；“拿”指的是擒拿之法，包括锁、点等，一般以反屈对方关节和点穴为主要手段，锁拿之后加点法；“击”“刺”主要是指以器械击败对方的方法。这些方法特别重视实用性，比较适合当时的作战方式。

4.项目传承人

当今 21 世纪掌门人宋义祥大师，走遍大江南北，汲取众家之长，继承发扬了子午门功夫。他善用腿功，打破陈规，于 1989 年回故乡梁山，创办了水泊梁山精武学校并任该校校长；在梁山县体委的支持下，1991 年成立了中国梁山子午门功夫研究会，任该会总教练。宋义祥还在百忙中，为《少林与太极》《气功》《气功报》《武当》《拳击与格斗》《武魂》等武术报刊撰写论文百余篇，先后被聘为《气功报》顾问、浙江省永嘉县武术体育器械厂顾问、中国实战功夫促进会顾问、少林武术馆顾问等。子午门功夫历经数十代前辈的心血贯注，集天下功夫之大成，日趋精华，内功练精化气，练气生力，练力生神，气贯周身，可延年益寿，养生健体，功成后可使血肉之躯成为"钢筋铁骨"。

Liangshan Ziwumen Kungfu

1. Program culture

Liangshan Ziwumen Kungfu, has more than 800 years of history. In the late years of the Northern Song Dynasty, a group of 108 heroes headed by Song Jiang gathered on Liangshan Mountain, relying on the natural dangerous environment, especially the water area, and great martial art, fought for righteousness and spread the wealth, got rid of the cruel, pacified people, and shocked the government. They practiced before the war and rested after the war. They often went to Jianfu Temple of Liugong Mountain in the north of Liangshan to discuss martial arts and military strategies. Later, Lu Zhishen, Wu Song, Yan Qing, Shi Qian, Lin Chong and other heroes came to Jianfu Temple and became monks. They studied repeatedly with the abbot of the temple, Master Yuan Tong, to learn from each other's strengths, which formed the rudiment of Chinese Liangshan Ziwumen Kungfu through discussion and verification.

"Liangshan is one of the four birthplaces of Chinese martial arts, and has always been equally famous with Henan Shaolin, Hubei Wudang, and Sichuan Emei". Martial art is highly advocated and flourished among Liangshan people. Many martial arts masters are well known at home and abroad, who have contributed to the inheritance and development of Chinese martial art, but less has been mentioned in recent years. According to the study, Liangshan Boxing has many schools, such as Meihua Boxing, Fohan Boxing, Hong Boxing, Drunk Boxing, Mantis Boxing, Handcuffed Boxing, Ambush Boxing, Cha Boxing, Monkey Boxing, Yan Qing Boxing, Zhanghong Boxing, Shaolin Boxing, Tai Chi and so on. There are also many devices: long weapons (spear, simple knives, Zen sticks and so on), short weapons (axes, mace, hooks, swords, forks, double circles and so on) and soft weapons (three sticks, seven whips, meteor hammer, rope darts, etc.). Song Wenxiang, the 21st generation martial arts master of Liangshan Ziwumen, founded Liangshan Martial Art Academy in Liangshan, teaching routines including Drunk Boxing, Monkey Boxing, Wu Song Boxing, Yan Qing Boxing, Zhishen Boxing, Jiang Boxing, Shaolin Boxing, knives, spears, swords, forks, axes, hooks and so on.

2.Project origin

Shandong is one of the cradles of Chinese martial arts and is known as the "hometown of martial arts". Shuibo Liangshan, located in the southwest of Shandong, is well known at home and abroad for the exquisite martial arts and legends of 108 Liangshan heroes recorded in the book *All Men Are Brothers*. The story of the heroes comes from a real peasant uprising with Shuibo Liangshan. Ziwumen Kungfu (also known as "Liangshan School") was created under the specific historical conditions at that time by the Liangshan heroes in the life experience of chivalry, which has a history of more than 800 years. Ziwumen Kungfu is deeply influenced by Shandong culture in the process of formation and development.

The fourth and twelfth episodes of the *Cultural and Historical Data of Liangshan County* contain the following records: There is an old monk Yuantong received nearly 100 young monks. They have extraordinary martial arts, and have good command of knives, guns, swords and sticks, and excellent Qi Gong. Weapons can't hurt their bodies. Legend has it that when the Figured Monk Lu Zhishen went to Liangshan, he once competed with the monks of Jianfu Temple, defeating the master and disciples of Jianfu Temple and was respected as a teacher. Liugong Mountain has since become the sentinel in the northern part of Liangshan.

On the origin of the name Ziwumen Kungfu, it is said that the heroes practice this work at 23:00, 1:00, 11:00, and 13:00. This martial art practices the innate body and acquired essence, both complements each other, congenital thing as Yin, acquired one is Yang. Yin is Zi. Yang is Wu. After practicing to a certain extent, there will be a heat flow and a cold flow on the body, in which the heat flow is called the heat, and the cold flow is called "the spring of essence". Cold is Yin. Yin is Zi. Fire belongs to Yang. Yang is Wu. Practicing to this point, Kungfu reached what people say the pink of perfection. The martial arts area describes this work great and calls the Zi as life, Wu as death, meaning that the leg can determine the others' life or death, so named Ziwumen Kungfu.

Liangshan martial arts have many schools and different styles. According to statistics, there are more than a dozen popular boxing techniques in Liangshan area. There are many schools with great influence: Ziwumen Kungfu, Tai Chi, Shaolin Boxing, Fo Han Boxing, Hong Boxing and Er Men Hong Boxing. Among them, in recent years, Ziwumen Kungfu has great influence. *Liangshan Kungfu* (*China Literature and History Publishing House*) contained: "Originated in Liangshan, Ziwumen Kungfu is the crystallization of the collective wisdom of Liangshan heroes and masters, rooted in the land of Qilu. And it is the reproduction of Qilu culture and popular in China. It is the embodiment of Chinese wisdom, and the treasure of world martial arts. At present, after careful excavation and arrangement of Song Yixiang, the master of the 21st century, 38 characteristic routines have been formed with Ziwu boxing as the core. In addition, there are 36 kinds of soft and hard devices and 36 kinds of internal heart methods. The style and action names of Liangshan Ziwumen Kungfu are mostly from the names of the heroes in *All Men Are Brothers* and their heroic acts. While the action is easy to remember and can cultivate the upright attitude and not afraid of power.

3.Action parsing

The characteristics of Ziwumen Kungfu: Follow through arm move, take the advantage of waist, combining the all-over strength at the hip joints, perform great open and close actions, fierce momentum, jump, hook, point, kick, fly, split, flexible method, fast and ruthless, integration with internal martial art, unexpected movement of either quiescent or dynamic, full of changes and hard to defeat.

3.1 Bare-handed Routine

3.1.1 Ziwu Boxing 12 Styles

Ziwu Boxing 12 Styles is created by Yuantong Zen Master, Song Jiang and other Liangshan heroes. It has great artistic conception, strong access, combination of dynamic and static state, and great fitness and practical value. Ziwu Boxing 12 Styles has undergone reforms through painstaking efforts of dozens of generations of its predecessors of masters, which has developed with the combination of inside and outside, open and close, as well as rigidness and softness. The drill pays attention to the gas flirting in the body, the combination of Yin and Yang, flexible action, light footwork, bright and clear type, beautiful and unfolded. Each method of 12 styles is different, brave to promote wisdom, bold and unrestrained in the clear environment, just like the desert wind fierce, and like a small bridge and water slow and light.

3.1.2 Ziwu Bagua Youshen Zhuang and Ziwu Bagua Boxing

This was created by Gongsun Sheng, a hero of Liangshan, and the abbot of Jianfu Temple, which was studied by the heir of Ziwumen Kungfu, Chan Master Xizhu (1487-1523). The boxing was named Ziwu Bagua Youshen Zhuang. It is strong and soft, developing both inside and outside, with the potential of swallowing mountains and rivers. This martial art is divided into four sections. The first one is positive mainly with small postures, specializing in the bottom plate. In the second section, perform tall and fierce postures, mainly to the left Bagua. In the third section, it transforms into an up time right Bagua, to the large frame. In the fourth section, it transforms into the reverse time left Bagua, with a large, small frame type mixed practice method.

3.1.3 Song Jiang Boxing

Legend says that Song Jiang Boxing was created by Song Jiang, the leader of 108 heroes. The master of Ziwu Men VII (in 1377), Daoyan Zen Master enriched and named it Song Jiang Boxing, and the Ziwumen disciples called it the ancestor boxing. Characteristics: Strong and soft actions with internal and external cultivation, connected and interlocked actions with fast and slow speed; unique actions that are difficult to break or prevent.

3.1.4 Kirin (Qilin) Boxing

Kirin Boxing was created by Lu Junyi, one of the 108 heroes of Liangshan, and developed by Jiang Hong (1309-1377), the head of Ziwumen V, who named this boxing as Kirin Boxing (Qilin Ju). Characteristics: obvious movement, strong momentum, a variety of moves, softness in strong actions, strong in soft actions, and with the internal power integrated.

3.2 Apparatus routine

In the Ziwumen Kungfu, the martial arts routine is especially famous for "Song Jiang Zhuihun Broadsword", "Lu Junyi Qimen Club" and "Gongsun Sheng Bagua Sword". Actions are matched apparatus, improving the attack power of the action and can collide with other apparatuses to achieve the effect of effectively attacking the enemy in the shortest time and end the battle. The rapidity and bravery of the apparatus routines are based on subtle and ingenious martial arts routines. Broadsword and boxing, clubs, swords and other apparatuses are all matched together in one. In the fierce and swift movements and changes due to the enemy, it is necessary to be integrated in body and law, and be good at integrating attack and defense, so the battle can be solved in the shortest time.

In the process of its development, Ziwumen Kungfu draws the advantages of hundreds of schools and has its own characteristics. The process of practice and internal skills are integrated, and the actions are fast, steady and ruthless. Its technical method can be divided into seven categories, such as kicking, playing, breaking, falling, taking, hitting, and stabbing. "Kicking" and "playing" refer to the upper and lower limb attack method of leg: "Breaking" means the method of the defensive solution; "Falling" refers to the method of capture, including lock and point; "Hitting" and "stabbing" mainly mean to the ways to defeat others. These methods attach special importance to practicality and are more suitable for the fighting methods at the time. In the formation process, Ziwumen Kungfu has created a large variety of martial arts varieties, and everyone has their own characteristics.

4.Project inheritor

Today, the 21st master Song Yixiang travels around the country and absorbs the advantages of many schools to inherit and carry forward the Liangshan Ziwumen Kungfu. He makes good use of legs, and breaks the rules. He went back to his hometown Liangshan in 1989, and founded the Liangshan Jingwu School and became the principal. With the help of Liangshan County Sports Committee, Liangshan Ziwumen Kungfu Research Center was established in 1991, and Mr. Song became the head coach. He also wrote many papers for *Shaolin and Taiji*, *Qigong*, *Qigong Newspaper*, *Wudang*, *Boxing and Fighting*, *Soul of Wrestle* and other martial arts newspapers. And Song has been hired as the consultant of *Qigong Newspaper*, Zhejiang Yongjia County Martial Arts Sports Apparatus Factory consultant, China Association for the Promotion of Actual Combat, Shaolin Martial Arts, etc. Ziwumen Kungfu develops through the efforts of dozens of generations of predecessors through increasingly internal skills refinement, energetic power, energy, and body. It can prolong people's life and health fitness, and make body strong after practicing.

第 7 节　肘捶

1.项目文化

作为武术之乡的鲁西门户，临清武术历史悠久，可以追溯到五代十国的潭腿。临清民风彪悍，自古就有习文尚武的习俗，人才辈出，拥有武状元、武探花。“肘捶”就诞生于武学圣地临清。明清时期，肘捶、六步大架（大鸿拳）、梅花拳、二郎拳都是风靡一时的拳种，不过肘捶却是密门绝学。

2.项目起源

临清肘捶是中华武术的古老拳种之一，萌发于聊城临清。据省志、县志等各方史料证实，张东槐是临清肘捶的创始人。《临清县志》记载，张东槐字萌轩，人送绰号“神拳张五爷”。张东槐是临清唐元乡瑶坡村人，生于道光二十四年(1844 年)，卒于光绪二十七年(1901 年)。张公用毕生心血于 1874 年创肘捶拳理并成体系，薪火相传至今已有 140 年之久。百余年来，肘捶拳法经第六、七代弟子的传习延伸，已在鲁西、冀东等广大地域流传开来。

3.项目器械

肘锤主要的器械套路包括大枪、单刀、双捌十六法(捌子)、方天画戟(双)。由于传统的教授方式都是口授身传，大部分没有留下文字资料，再加上现在习练者已稀少，关于器械套路的名称基本已经流失，目前仅有肘捶中的大枪论。相关研究人员正在对其他套路进行深入挖掘、调研之中。

4.动作解析

临清肘捶经过近 140 年的演变和发展，已经发展成为颇具特色且内容丰富的技术体系，其内容包括肘捶基本功、肘捶徒手套路、肘捶对练套路、肘捶器械套路、肘捶论五个部分。

临清肘捶基本功以“龙光普照、虎威团聚”为主要内容，此二式叫作“两通”，俗称“众友之本，万象之根”。

临清肘捶徒手套路主要包括两通功单练，天、地、人三字号单练技法。

临清肘捶对练套路以十路捶法为主，辅以通过两通单练所成小组合对练，包括摽捶、搂挑打、四季捶、七星捶。肘捶对练讲究封打合一，封即是打，打也是封。封打结合，身体的四肢伸展，上下都可以击打对手。对练中一进一退、一守一攻，攻中有守、守中有攻。肘捶对练强调“封两通、滚车转”，拳谚曰：“对练之初，此是雏形，彼来我往，一封一攻。进在前腿，撤后是攻，首知进退，身体力行。四肢伸展，上下皆动，定步练习，打中带封。顾打合一，滚车转名，对练之先，此功先行。”

临清肘捶论讲究理法用则，内外兼修，法理合一；主张学一式得一法，得其法明其所用，学一法需知法中之理，以其理举一反三，变化多端。其核心拳理有肘捶内功说、肘捶打手说、三法归一说三种。

肘捶动作一

Elbow Punch action 1

5.项目传承人

创始人:张东槐,字荫轩,行五,生于1844年11月27日,于1874年创立肘捶,卒于1901年7月。

第二代:刘汝勤,生于1864年,州衙捕快,于1893年拜张公为师,卒于1940年。

第三代:周子岩,字松山,生于1896年,自幼习武,1911年拜刘汝勤为师,卒于1984年。

第四代:叶书瑞,生于1901年,于1934年拜周子岩为师,卒于1993年。胡世铭,生于1913年11月16日,于1932年拜周子岩为师,卒于1975年。张铎,生于1907年,于1930年拜孙景元为师(孙师系刘汝勤之大弟子,生卒年不详)。

第五代:刘振远、胡铁民、申孝生、李冬至、孟宪海、高登广等,1970年至1975年拜张铎、胡世铭为师,习练肘捶。

第六代:王解民、王振武、刘荣海、李林祥、孟昭华师承刘振远,张国庆、王怀德、宋克勇、贾生旺、薛子荣、修昆岭、孙大华、卞九华、高云峰1973年至2007年师承申孝生。

第七代：弟子主要是由申孝生的弟子张国庆进行传授，分别是马镇、宋悦宇、王东君、吴士东、孙士豪（河南平顶山）、郝卫宾（河南安阳）、李斌（湖南长沙）、温长刚。

第八代：现在有统计的仅有马镇弟子吴玉章（广东潮州）、劳劲源（广东深圳）和李斌弟子芦启祥（湖南长沙）等四人，第八代传人还在发展，在不久的将来，我们会看到肘捶的欣欣向荣。

肘捶动作二

Elbow Punch action 2

6.项目发展的意义

临清肘捶是萌发、流传于山东的一个具有百年历史的古老拳种，它源流有序，技法清晰，自成体系。对它的挖掘与整理，有益于山东传统武术文化的传承，对丰富山东的优秀传统文化体系，加强非物质文化遗产的科学保护和推动中国传统武术的发展，具有重要的社会历史文化价值和较高的开发应用价值。

Elbow Punch

1.Project culture

As the hometown of martial arts in western Shandong, Linqing, where elbow punch was born, has strong folk customs. Since ancient times, there is the custom of practicing martial arts, creating many national champions and other talents. Linqing has a long history of martial arts, which can be traced back to the Five Dynasties and Ten Kingdoms. During the Ming and Qing dynasties, ancient boxing such as elbow punch, six-step frame (Dahongquan), Meihua Boxing and Erlang Boxing were all popular, but elbow punch is a private secrecy.

2.Project origin

Linqing elbow punch is one of the ancient boxings of Chinese martial arts, which sprouted in Linqing, Liaocheng. According to the provincial annals, county annals and other historical data, Zhang Donghuai was the founder of Linqing elbow punch. According to *Linqing County Annals*, Zhang Donghuai, with the courtesy name Mengxuan, and the nickname "Shenquan Zhang Wuye", is a native of Yaopo Village, Tang Yuan Township, Linqing. He was born in the 24th year of Daoguang (1844) and died in the 27th year of Guangxu (1901). In 1874, Zhang Gong devoted his whole life to the creation and formation of the system of elbow punch, which has been passed down till today for 140 years. Over more than a hundred years, the elbow punch has been spread in western Shandong, eastern Hebei and other vast areas through the extension of the sixth and seventh generations of disciples.

3.Program apparatus

The main apparatus routines of elbow punch include big spear, single broadsword, double crutches 16 types (crutches) and Fang Tianhua Ji (double). Because of traditional oral and personal teaching methods, most of which do not leave written materials, and practitioners are relatively rare. As such, the names of most apparatus routines have been lost, apart from the theory of the big gun in the elbow. Other styles are being further explored and invested.

4.Action parsing

After nearly 140 years of evolution and development, the basic technical system of Linqing elbow punch has developed into a distinctive and rich system, which includes five parts: Elbow punch basic skills, elbow punch bare-handed routine, elbow punch sparring routine, elbow punch apparatus routine.

Linqing elbow punch basic skills take "dragon light shining, tiger power reunion" as the main content. These two types are called "two links", commonly known as "the foundation of friends, the root of all phenomena".

Linqing Elbow Punch unarmed routine mainly includes: two passes the work to practice alone; Heaven-Earth-Human Single Practice Technique.

Linqing Elbow Punch Routine is mainly composed of ten-way hammering method, supplemented by small combinations of two-way single training: hammering, cuddling, and picking, four-season hammering and seven-star hammering. The practice of elbow beating is about the combination of sealing and beating. Sealing is beating, and beating is sealing. The combination of sealing and beating, the limbs of the body stretch, up and down can hit the opponent. In practice, one advances and one retreats; one defenses and one attacks. There is the defense in attack, and there is the attack in defense. The boxing proverb says, "At the beginning of the practice, players come and go for attacking and defensing. They move forward with the front leg, retreat as attack. The first key is to know to advance and retreat, and then practice. Stretch your arms and legs, and move up and down. Practice with fixed steps. Combine attaching and defensing as a whole, and the sparring is the first step for practicing this boxing."

Linqing Elbow Punch pays attention to the principles of theory and law, both inside and outside, and the unity of theory and law. It is advocated to learn a form and get a law, to get its law and use it clearly, to learn a law needs to know the principle in the law, and to draw inferences about other cases from one instance with its principle, which is changeable. There are three core boxing theories, namely the theory of elbow punch internal skills, the theory of elbow punch hands and the theory of three methods being unified.

5.Project inheritor

Founder: Zhang Donghuai, also named Yin Xuan, are the 5th child of his family. He was born on November 27, 1844, created the elbow punch in 1874 and died in July, 1901.

The second generation: Liu Ruqin was born in 1864 and was a constable in yamen (government official in feudal China). In 1893, he began to learn skills from Zhang Gong, and died in 1940.

The third generation: Zhou Ziyan, also named Songshan, was born in 1896. He learned martial arts at an early age and began to learn skills from Liu Ruqin in 1911. He died in 1984.

The fourth generation: Ye Shurui was born in 1901. He formally acknowledged Zhou Ziyan as his teacher in 1934 and died in 1993. Hu Shiming, born on November 16, 1913, took Zhou Ziyan as his teacher in 1932 and died in 1975. Zhang Duo, born in 1907, took Sun Jingyuan as his teacher in 1930. Sun was the first disciple of Liu Ruqin, whose date of birth and death is unknown.

The fifth generation: Liu Zhenyuan, Hu Tiemin, Shen Xiaosheng, Li Dongzhi, Meng Xianhai, Gao Dengguang, etc. From 1970 to 1975, they were taught by Zhang Duo and Hu Shiming.

The sixth generation: Wang Jiemin, Wang Zhenwu, Liu Ronghai, Li Linxiang, and Meng Zhaohua are the disciples of Liu Zhenyuan. Zhang

Guoqing, Wang Huaide, Song Keyong, Jia Shengwang, Xue Zirong, Xiu Kunling, Sun Dahua, Bian Jiuhua and Gao Yunfeng are the disciples of Shen Xiaosheng from 1973 to 2007.

The seventh generation: Disciples are mainly taught by Shen Xiaosheng's disciple Zhang Guoqing. They are Ma Zhen, Song Yueyu, Wang Dongjun, Wu Shidong, Sun Shihao (from Pingdingshan, Henan), Hao Weibin (from Anyang, Henan), Li Bin (from Changsha, Hunan) and Wen Changgang.

The eighth generation: There are only four disciples of Ma Zhen, Wu Yuzhang (from Chaozhou, Guangdong), Lao Jinyuan (from Shenzhen, Guangdong) and Li Bin's disciple, Lu Qixiang (from Changsha, Hunan). The eighth generation is still developing. Soon, we will see the prosperity of elbow punch.

6.Significance of development

Linqing elbow punch is a kind of ancient boxing with a hundred years of history, which has been sprouted and spread in Shandong Province. It has an orderly origin, clear techniques and its own system. Its excavation and sorting out are beneficial to the inheritance of Shandong traditional martial arts culture, to enrich Shandong's excellent traditional cultural system, to strengthen the scientific protection of intangible cultural heritage and to promote the development of Chinese traditional martial arts, which has important social, historical and cultural values and high development and application value.

第 8 节　舞龙运动

1.项目文化

龙是中华民族的图腾，是一种精神、一种寄托、一种祝福，是中华民族勤劳、勇敢、奋进、坚毅、拼搏精神的象征。在中国文化中，龙扮演着重要的角色，已经渗透到中国社会的各个方面，成为一种文化的凝聚和积淀。中国是舞龙运动的发源地，千余年来，象征着吉祥喜庆、欢乐幸福的舞龙运动已经成为我国广大城乡喜庆佳节最具代表性的民俗活动，同时也是目前我国推行全民健身计划、增强人民群众身心健康的重要大众体育项目之一。

2.项目起源与发展

舞龙的发端，一是与祈雨有关，每逢天旱，朝野都会采用舞龙的方式祈求上苍抛洒雨露，二是由“鱼龙漫衍”的舞蹈演变而来。

2.1 祈龙求雨

祈龙求雨最早可见于汉董仲舒撰《春秋繁露》卷十六的《春旱求雨》，也是最早有文字记载的舞龙。求雨的舞龙，是祭祀的一个环节，龙分五色，大小各有定数。尽管大龙可达九丈之长，每条龙的舞者仍仅为一人。后世的祈龙求雨仪式，显得更加庄重肃穆，舞龙在规模上比前代更繁盛。清代末期的祈龙求雨仪式，除了有龙舞外，还有狮虎鱼虾等舞蹈。

2.2 鱼龙漫衍

鱼龙之戏是一种由人装扮成巨鱼和巨龙进行表演的大型舞蹈。先由人装扮成一种怪兽在庭院里嬉戏，然后变化成鱼进入殿前的水中，戏水喷雾，最后变化成黄龙出水再到庭院里嬉戏。由于巨鱼和巨龙之间有一个“变”的环节，因此在表演时，可能还需要幻术、布景、烟雾等配合。鱼龙舞一直延续至清代。

3.项目规则

“龙灯扛阁”由舞龙和扛阁组成。龙灯、扛阁的舞龙者为青壮年，由两组轮番上场，每组 10 人或 14 人。其中 1 人擎珠，其他分执龙头、龙尾；8 副扛阁由 16 人表演，8 个成年人为“下扛”，8 个儿童为“上扛”，多扮作童男童女或神话故事中的人物形象，不时做出各种戏龙的惊险动作，场面精彩，引人入胜。

龙灯、扛阁的表演由擎珠者指挥，龙紧随珠舞动，基本套路有“站龙翻腾”“卧龙翻腾”“盘龙”“双窜龙”“泼龙”“滚龙”等，套路均以“速场”贯穿连接。动作要求“窜泼”一边倒，“翻腾”要抡圆，跑站记住“活”，时刻都不闲。扛阁则以“走场”为主，龙舞动作激烈时，扛阁在一侧交叉变换队形，舞龙舒缓时，扛阁即插入龙队中穿行回旋。

龙灯、扛阁用打击乐队伴奏，曲牌有“流水”“急急风”两种：前者节奏平稳，力度与速度视表演气氛而定；后者用在舞龙激昂如“窜龙”“泼龙”时，节奏快而热烈。表演进入高潮时，由专人在场外“打口哨”，以渲染气氛。

舞龙运动动作一

Dragon Dance action 1

4.项目器械

4.1　龙珠与龙体

龙珠：球体直径为 0.33～0.35 米，杆高（含珠）不低于 1.7 米。龙珠转动要流畅，杆与珠体的接口要牢固。

龙头：重量不得少于 3 千克，宽不少于 0.36 米，高不少于 0.6 米，长不少于 0.9 米，杆高不低于 1.25 米。龙头（含杆高）不低于 1.85 米。龙头嘴巴和眼珠活动要顺畅。龙须要柔顺，密度要适中，有飘逸的感觉。

龙身：以九节布龙参赛，龙身为封闭式圆筒形，直径为 0.33～0.35 米，全长不少于 18 米。龙身杆高（含龙身直径）不低于 1.6 米，两杆之间距离大致相等。龙体要饱满圆顺，色泽要亮丽。

龙尾：杆高（含龙身直径）不低于 1.6 米。

舞龙运动动作二

Dragon Dance action 2

4.2 鼓乐

舞龙的配乐普遍选用民间的打击乐器，根据地方特色选取相应的乐曲。乐曲可以是事先录制好的音乐也可以加其他电子琴之类的乐器合奏。

大鼓的鼓面直径约为 0.52 米，高度 0.52～0.56 米；小鼓的鼓面直径约为 0.25 米，高度约为 0.3 米。鼓面材料为牛皮，鼓身材料为木板制造。击打鼓面时声音要响亮，穿透力要强，声域范围要广。

大锣的直径为 0.3～0.35 米，小锣的直径为 0.20 米，用铜制造，以音质清脆为好。

大钹的直径为 0.3 米，小钹的直径为 0.15～0.20 米，用铜制造，以音质清脆为好。

5.动作解析

舞龙运动大部分是在行进动态中完成“龙”的游弋、起伏、翻滚、腾越、缠绞、穿插等动作，利用人体多种姿态将力度、幅度、速度、耐力等融入舞龙技巧之中，或动或静，组成优美形象的龙的雕塑，展现龙的精气神韵。按照《国际舞龙南狮北狮竞赛规则》(2011 年)的认定和划分，竞技舞龙包含“8”字、游龙、穿腾、翻滚、组图造型等五类动作。

5.1　“8”字舞龙动作

舞龙者将龙体在人左右两侧交替进行“8”字形环绕的舞龙动作，可快可慢，可原地，可行进，也可利用人体组成多种姿态，多种方法进行“8”字形舞动。

要求：龙体运动轨迹要圆顺，人体造型姿态要优美，快舞龙要突出速度、力量；每个动作左右舞龙各不少于 4 次，单侧舞龙每个动作上下各不少于 6 次。

5.2　游龙动作

舞龙者较大幅度奔跑游走，通过龙体快慢有致、高低、左右的起伏进行，展现婉转回旋，左右盘翻，屈伸绵延等龙的动态特征。

要求：龙体循着圆、曲、弧线的规律运动，运动员协调地随龙体的起伏行进。

5.3　穿腾动作

龙体运动路线呈纵横交叉形式，龙珠、龙头、龙节依次在龙身下穿过，称“穿越”；龙珠、龙头、龙节依次在龙身上越过称“腾越”。

要求：穿越和腾越时，龙形保持饱满，速度均匀，运动轨迹流畅，穿腾动作轻松利索，不碰踩龙体、不拖地、不停顿。

5.4　翻滚动作

龙体呈立圆或斜圆运动，展现龙的腾跃、缠绞的动势。龙体作立圆或斜圆状连续运动，当龙身运动到舞龙者脚下时，舞龙者迅速向上腾起依次跳过龙身，称“跳龙动作”；龙体同时或依次作 360°翻转，舞龙者利用滚翻、手翻等方法越过龙身，称“翻滚动作”。

要求：滚翻动作必须在不影响龙体运动速度、幅度、美感的前提下完成，难度较大，技术要求也高，龙体运动轨迹要流畅，龙形要圆顺，运用技巧动作要准确规范。

5.5　组图造型动作

龙体在运动中组成活动的图案和相对静止的造型。

要求：活动图案构图清晰；静止造型形象逼真，以形传神，以形传意，龙珠配合协调，组图造型连接、解脱要紧凑、利索。

6.项目继承

我国是一个有56个民族的大家庭，各民族都有各自传统的舞龙习俗。在不同的节日，不同民族的人们会用舞龙的形式进行庆祝，这些节日形成了各地区各民族既相似又各具特色的龙文化。

改革开放以后，由于受市场经济的影响，传统的舞龙习俗也在一定程度上受到冲击，艺术传承出现了断代。为了让华夏祖先遗存下来的宝贵文化资源得到延续，我国启动了对物质和非物质文化遗产的抢救、保护工作，各省、市、自治区等地方政府也相应成立工作组，挖掘、保护地方的文化资源，这对于弘扬民族文化传统、保护和发展民间艺术具有推动作用。

截至2011年，全国共公布了三批国家级非物质文化遗产保护名录，其中有36个舞龙项目在列。这也让世人有机会更真实地获得中国舞龙的文化信息，感受不同风格的龙舞。

7.项目的意义

舞龙这一传统文化是维系民族情感的纽带，在世界各地，只要有华人的地方就有中国龙。华人华侨将中国舞龙的习俗带到所在国，使中国传统文化在世界各地广泛传播并发挥深刻的影响。

在海外，舞龙习俗不断营造和渲染着一种浓郁的乡土文化氛围，潜移默化中，一种共同的精神和气质就会不知不觉地融入每一个龙的传人的血液和骨髓之中。当龙子龙孙看到巨龙飞舞，听到具有鲜明民族特色的喧天锣鼓时，就会自然而然地产生一种“我们是中国人”的民族认同感，这也是世界上凡有华人的地方就一定会有舞龙习俗传承的根本原因。

舞龙对于中国文化传承的意义既表现为它本身就是民间文化的重要载体，又表现为它可以为民间文化的传承提供一种有效的途径。世界上凡有华人生活的角落，就有舞龙活动。中华民族民间文化借此得以深入炎黄子孙生存繁衍的每一个地方，世代相传。巨龙飞舞，彰显中华民族的崛起，彰显国富民强，更是华侨华人爱国爱乡强大精神内核的体现。

Dragon Dance

1.Project culture

The dragon is the totem of the Chinese nation, and emblems a kind of spirit, sustenance and blessing. It's also a symbol of spirits of hardworking, bravery, striving and resolution in the Chinese nation. In Chinese culture, the dragon plays an important role, which has penetrated every aspect of Chinese society and become the cohesion and accumulation of culture. China is the birthplace of the dragon dance. For thousands of years, the dragon dance, a symbol of happy auspiciousness, has become the most representative folk activity to celebrate the festivals in rural and urban areas in China. In the meantime, it is also one of the most important popular sports in China's national fitness program to enhance the physical and mental health of people.

2.Project origin and development

First, the origin of dragon dance is related to praying for rain. Every time of drought, governments in the past usually prayed for rain through drag dance. Second, it is said to be a variant of mixed dancing performances with giant fish and dragon, which is called "yulongmanyan".

2.1 Praying for rain by the dragon

Praying for rain can be seen in *Luxuriant Gems of the Spring and Autumn Annals*, Volume 16, *Praying for Rain in Spring Drought* written by Dong Zhongshu. It is also the earliest record of the dragon dance. The dragon praying for the rain is a part of fete. There are five colors of dragons that have their own fixed sizes. Although dragons can be up to nine feet long, each dragon has only one dancer. In later ages, the ceremony of praying for rain was more solemn, and the dragon dance was more prosperous in scale. The ceremony of the dragon praying for rain included not only the dance of the dragon, but also the dance of the lion, tiger, fish and shrimp in late Qing Dynasty.

2.2 Mixed dancing performances with giant fish and dragon

The play of the fish and dragon is a large dance performed by people dressed up as giant fish and dragon. First, people dress up as a monster and play in the courtyard. Then they change into fish into the water before the temple to paddle. Finally, they change into the yellow dragon came out of the water and play in the courtyard. Since there is a problem of how to change between the giant fish and the dragon, the performance may also require illusion, scenery, smoke and other cooperation. This kind of dance has continued through the Qing Dynasty.

3.Sports rules

Dragon Lantern Carrying Pavilion ("longdengkangge") consists of dragon dancing and carrying pavilion. The dragon dancers who carry the dragon lantern and the pavilion are young adults. Two groups of 10 or 14 players take turns to perform. One of them holds the bead, while the others hold the head and tail. The performance is performed by 16 people, with 8 adults carrying the bottom of the dragon, and 8 children carrying the upper part of the dragon. Most of them play the roles of boys and girls or fairy tales, such as the characters in the Eight Immortals Crossing the Sea. They make a variety of breathtaking actions to play the dragon from time to time, which is fascinating. The performance of the dragon lantern and carrying the pavilion is conducted by the performer that holds the bead. The dragon follows the bead. The basic routines include "standing dragon tumbling", "lying dragon tumbling", "coiling dragon", "double dragons playing", "pouring dragon" and "rolling dragon", etc. The routines are at the fast speed. They must play the dragon on the same side. The action of somersault is round. They also must remember the time that they should run or stand. The performers carrying pavilion run around the field. When the dragon dance is intense, they will run on one side to change the formation. When the dragon dance is slow, they will go through the team of the dragons.

This performance with perk band has different styles. There are two kinds of tunes "liushui" and "jijifeng". The first tune has a nice steady beat and the dynamics, and the speed depends on the atmosphere of this performance. The latter tune uses in the stirring dragon dance when the performers play "chuanlong" or "polong". The rhythm is fast and warm. When the performance comes to a climax, someone will whistle outside to heighten the atmosphere.

4.Project apparatus

4.1 Dragon ball and the body of the dragon

Dragon ball: The diameter of sphere is 0.33 to 0.35 meters, and the height of pole (including the Dragon Ball) is not less than 1.7 meters. The rotation of the dragon ball should be smooth, and the interface between the pole and the dragon ball should be firm.

Head of the dragon: The weight of the dragon's head should not be less than 3kg, the overall size of which is not less than 0.36 meters in width, 0.6 meters in height and 0.9 meters in length. The height of the pole should not be less than 1.25 meters. The head (including the height of the pole) should not be less than 1.85 meters. The mouth and eyes of the dragon head should move smoothly. The dragon beard should be smooth and the density of them should be moderate to have an elegant feeling.

Body of the dragon: The dragon that is made of the cloth in the field is nine-section. The body of the dragon is a closed cylinder with the diameter of 0.33 to 0.35 meters and the length of no less than 18 meters. The height of the pole (including the diameter of the body) of the dragon body is no less than 1.6 meters and the distance between the two poles is roughly equal. The body of the dragon should be full and round, and the color should be bright.

Tail of the body: The height of the pole of the tail (including the diameter of the body) should not be less than 1.6 meters.

4.2 Drum corps

Folk percussion apparatuses are generally selected for the music of dragon dance. In addition, the performers usually select appropriate music according to local characteristics. The music can be prerecorded, or it can be played in an ensemble with other apparatuses such as a keyboard.

The diameter of the bass drum is about 0.52 meters, and the height is from 0.52 to 0.56 meters. The snare drum is about 0.25 meters in diameter and 0.3 meters in height. The surface of the drum is made of cowhide and the body of the drum is made of wood. When you hit the drum, the sound must be loud and powerful and it should also travel far.

Big gongs are from 0.3 to 0.35 meters in diameter, while small gongs are 0.20 meters in diameter. They are made of the copper with a clear sound.

The large cymbals are 0.3 meters in diameter and the small cymbals are from 0.15 to 0.20 meters in diameter. They are made of the copper with a clear sound.

5.Action parsing

Most of the dragon dancers complete the movements such as swimming, fluctuation, roll, leap, entangling and interspersing in the dynamic movement. The strength, amplitude, speed and endurance are integrated into the dragon dance skills by using various human postures. The dances are sometimes moving or static which is forming a graceful dragon sculpture and showing the essence and charm of the dragon. According to the identification and division of *International Dragon Dance Competition Rules for Southern Lion and Northern Lion* (2011), competitive dragon dance includes five types of movements, such as "Figure 8", dragon flying, crossing, roll and shape.

5.1 Figure 8 dragon dance

The athletes will alternate the dragon body on the left and right sides of the people as the figure 8 around the dragon dance action. The action can be fast or slow. The athletes may be in a place, and they may feasible forward.

They can also use the body to form a variety of gestures using different methods to make the figure 8 shape dance.

Requirements: the movement trajectory of the dragon body should be round and smooth, the posture of the human body should be graceful, and the fast dragon dance should highlight the speed and strength. The movement of the left and right dragon dance has not less than 4 times. The movement of one side dragon dance has not less than 6 times.

5.2 The action of flying dragon

The athletes run on a large scale to show the dynamic characteristics of the dragon, such as roundabout, turning around, bending and stretching, through the ups and downs of the dragon body.

Requirements: The dragon body follows the regular movement of circle, curve and arc. The athletes march in coordination with the ups and downs of the dragon body.

5.3 The action of crossing

The movement route of the dragon body is in the form of crossing. The dragon ball, the dragon head and the dragon section pass under the dragon body in turn, which is called "crossing". The dragon ball, the dragon head, and the dragon section over the body of the dragon turn, which is called "leap".

Requirements: When crossing and leaping, the shape of the dragon should be full, and the speed should be uniform. The movement trajectory should be smooth. In addition, the movement should be easy and quick, and the body of the dragon should not be touched by the performers. It should not touch the ground. The movement can't stop.

5.4 The action of rolling

The movement of the body of the dragon is in vertical circle or oblique circle, showing the posture of the dragon's prancing and entangling. When the dragon body moves to the foot of the dragon dancer, the dragon dancer will jump over the dragon body quickly, which is called "dragon jumping action".

The body of the dragon turns 360° at the same time or in turn, and the athlete passes the body of the dragon by means of rolling and handspring, which is called "rolling".

Requirements: The action must be completed without affecting the speed, amplitude and aesthetic feeling of the dragon. It is difficult and it requires high technical requirements. The trajectory of the dragon should be smooth, and the dragon shape should be round and smooth. The athlete uses some skills to make the action accurate and standard.

5.5 The action of shaping

The body of the dragon forms a moving pattern and a relatively static shape in motion

Requirements: The pattern is clear. The static modeling image is lifelike. The dragon ball and the dragon coordinate in phase. The action of the shape must form quickly and disperse neatly.

6.Project inheritance

China is a big family of 56 ethnic groups, each of which has its own traditional dragon dance customs. In different festivals, people of different ethnic groups will celebrate with the dragon dance. These festivals have formed the dragon culture of different ethnic groups in different regions with some similarities and differences.

After the reform and opening-up, due to the influence of market economy, the traditional custom of dragon dance was also impacted to a certain extent, and the artistic inheritance disappeared in some generations. In order to inherit the precious cultural resources that have carried down from our ancestors, our country has started to rescue and protect the tangible cultural heritage and the intangible cultural heritage. Local governments such as provincial government, municipal government and autonomous regional government also set up corresponding working group to excavate and protect the local cultural resources, which plays an important role in carrying forward the national cultural tradition and protecting the folk art.

By 2011, China had published three batches of national intangible cultural heritage protection lists, among which 36 dragon dances were included in the list. It also presents the world with cultural information of Chinese dragon dance and shows different styles of dragon dance.

7.Significance of project

The traditional culture of dragon dance is the bond that maintains the national emotion. Wherever there are Chinese people, there are Chinese dragons all over the world. The overseas Chinese brought the custom of Chinese dragon dance to the countries where they live, which made the traditional Chinese culture spread widely and exerted a profound influence all over the world.

The custom of dragon dance constantly creates a rich local cultural atmosphere overseas. In this cultural atmosphere, a common spirit and temperament will be imperceptibly integrated into the blood and heart of each dragon's descendants. When "descendants of the dragon" see the dragon flying and hear the loud music with distinctive national characteristics, they will naturally develop a sense of national identity of "We are Chinese". This is also the reason why there will be the tradition of dragon dance wherever there are Chinese in the world.

The significance of dragon dance for the inheritance of Chinese culture is that it is not only an important carrier of folk culture, but also an effective way for the inheritance of folk culture. Wherever Chinese live in the world, there are dragon dances. The folk culture of the Chinese nation has been passed down from generation to generation in every place where the descendants of the Chinese and Yellow dynasties live and thrive. The dragon dance shows the rise of the Chinese nation, the prosperity of the country and the strength of the people. And it is also the embodiment of the strong spirit of the overseas Chinese to love their country and their hometown.

第9节 山东秧歌

1.项目文化

秧歌是中国(主要在北方地区)广泛流传的一种极具群众性和代表性的民间舞蹈类别,不同地区有不同的称谓和风格样式。在民间,秧歌的称谓分为两种,踩跷表演的称为"高跷秧歌",不踩跷表演的称为"地秧歌"。近代所称的"秧歌"大多指"地秧歌"。秧歌历史悠久,南宋周密在《武林旧事》中介绍的民间舞队中就有"村田乐"的记载,清代吴锡麟的《新年杂咏抄》中明文记载了现存秧歌与宋代"村田乐"的源流关系。现各地的秧歌一般以秧歌舞队为主要形态,舞队人数少则十数人,多时达上百人,既有集体舞,也有双人舞、三人舞等多种表演形式。根据角色的需要,演员手持相应的手绢、伞、棒、鼓、钱鞭等道具,在锣鼓、唢呐等吹打乐器的伴奏下尽情舞蹈。各地秧歌的舞法、动作和风格各不相同,有的威武雄浑,有的柔美俏丽,千姿百态,美不胜收。

山东秧歌动作一

Shandong Yangko action 1

秧歌是中国北方最具代表性的民间舞种之一，既有表演性的，也有自娱性的，自娱娱人，深受老百姓的喜爱。各地均出现过一些有代表性的民间秧歌艺人，很多民间艺人对新中国舞蹈事业的建设发挥过重要作用。在农村经济快速发展、文化环境随之发生变化的今天，能够掌握传统秧歌技艺和纯正舞蹈风格的民间艺人已寥若晨星，保护和传承工作亟待进行。

一说起秧歌，人们的脑海中就会映现出红绸翻飞、脚步跳跃的舞蹈场面。在隆重的庆典时刻，在平常的百姓生活中，我们都很容易见到这种以十字步为主要特点的秧歌。而在中国众多的秧歌形式中，这种十字步秧歌仅仅是其中的一种。20世纪40年代，毛泽东发表了《在延安文艺座谈会上的讲话》，其核心思想就是要让革命文艺工作者到广大的农村中去汲取营养，创造出具有时代意义的文艺作品。由此，陕甘宁边区掀起了一场群众性的"新秧歌运动"。在陕北秧歌的基础上，文艺工作者创造出了新的秧歌样式，也就是十字步秧歌。在日后的岁月里，从农村到城市，它成为人们最喜闻乐见的舞蹈形式之一，并且，它的流传并没有使其他的秧歌衰落。逢年过节的时候，在中国北方地区的广大农村，还存在许多形态各异、内容丰富的秧歌。

秧歌作为北方汉族地区极为普遍的民间歌舞形式，通常是百姓欢度传统农历正月十五元宵节的重要内容。南方地区的民间歌舞形式也非常丰富，但大都不同于秧歌，而是在各地小戏、民间舞蹈基础上产生的舞蹈形式，如安徽的"花鼓灯"、云南的"花灯"等。

宋代文人笔记小说中就已经有秧歌的踪迹，主要是说百姓在农事中唱秧歌。后来，清代的记载对各种装扮人物都有详细的描述，如"耍和尚""耍公子""打花鼓""田公""渔妇""货郎"等。这充分说明，在清代，秧歌已经定型为我们今天所看到的样式。

在千余年的历史中，秧歌的发展演变大体经历了四个阶段：先有伴随劳动生活的小曲，之后发展成独立的民间歌舞演唱，后来由歌舞演唱逐渐向小戏过渡，最后秧歌发展到今天，逐渐向纯粹的舞蹈艺术过渡。秧歌演唱的内容多为神话传说、民间故事，且在表现男女爱情时非常大胆和直率，所以在历史上曾被很多时代的王朝所不容，屡遭查禁。从艺术的角度去看秧歌，它集合了诗歌、音乐、舞蹈、戏剧表演等各种成分。但从秧歌本身的生存状态来看，它有着非常多的文化意义，如祭祀祖先、民俗礼仪等功能。

在民间，老百姓对秧歌有个生动的概括，那就是"锣鼓鞭炮，红火热闹，旗罗伞扇,花里胡哨”,说的就是秧歌表演时的场面。一般秧歌表演都会有一支角色分工明确的队伍,舞者扮成生活中和神话传说里的各种人物,手执扇子、手帕、伞、鼓、棒等道具。这支队伍里的各种人物不仅仅有身体上的舞动,还有丰富的假形,如“旱船”“竹马”“狮子”“龙灯”“高跷”“大头娃娃”等,它们都是秧歌队的重要组成部分,有的地方还有民间小演唱和传统戏曲的片段,再有就是现代歌舞和自编自唱的活报剧。

若有人认为秧歌是一种非常简单易学的“玩意儿”,那可就大错特错了。因为秧歌的形式除了在地面上舞蹈,还有踩高跷的形式,把丈余高的木跷缚在秧歌人的腿上,不仅要完成行走,还要进行跳跃、翻筋斗、跨越障碍等高难动作,这可不是人人都能胜任得了的。同时,秧歌也不是从头到尾就一个规模,它在表演的进程中分为大场和小场。大场包括舞蹈开头和结尾,中间穿插各种小场,小场为几个人的舞蹈和歌舞小戏表演。大场一般由十余人到数十人组成,由一两个领舞者率领秧歌队边舞边走各种队形图案,所以领舞者的工作并不轻松,一定要心中有数并且记忆超强,否则阵脚一乱,那可就得闹大笑话了。

有人曾说汉族是不爱歌舞的民族,可当我们真正走入民间去感受形式各样的秧歌时,就会被它们的多彩而感动,而秧歌人身体里所传达的对于历史、文化和生命的演绎又如何说明汉族人不爱歌舞呢?只是我们对秧歌的了解太少。由此,我们应重新发现和认识这具有深厚历史积淀和群众基础的汉族歌舞典范。

山东省的秧歌以鲁西、鲁北新胶东半岛流传最盛,而以曲阜为中心的鲁中南地区,在方圆几百里内却很少有秧歌流传,这可能与儒家“重雅轻俗”的思想影响有关。流传在鲁南、鲁北和鲁西边缘地区的各种秧歌,如“渔灯秧歌”“花鼓伞”“柳林秧歌”“凤秧歌”等,均与邻省的某些秧歌在某些方面(如苏北的“花鼓洛子”、河南的“花鼓秧歌”、河北的“地秧歌”等)有相似之处。而最负盛名的山东三大秧歌——鼓子秧歌、胶州秧歌、海阳秧歌则以各自鲜明的风格成为汉族秧歌中的舞蹈典范。总体看来,山东秧歌不仅形式多样,而且风格各异,从不同角度展示了齐鲁人民粗犷豪爽的性格特点,浓缩了千百年来齐鲁大地的风尚习俗,同时也体现出山东人民所特有的审美情趣和精神风貌。

2.项目起源

南宋陆游有诗:时雨及芒种,田野皆插秧,家家麦饭羹,处处秧歌长。明代洪熙年间,海阳《赵氏家谱》记载,欣逢五世同堂,舞生闻诏率其创练之秧歌舞唱于庭，这时秧歌有歌有舞。明代嘉靖年间《夏津县志》记载，窃喜时和民同乐，秧歌方起又弦歌，这时秧歌歌舞分开。清代《晃州厅志》记载，岁，农人连袂步入田中，以趾带锄，且行且拨，塍间击鼓为节，疾徐前却，这时秧歌有舞无歌。清代《武林新年杂咏抄》记载，秧歌，南宋舞队之村田乐也，所扮有花和尚、花公子、打花鼓、拉花姊、田公渔婆、装态货郎、杂沓灯街，以得观者之笑，这时秧歌也是有舞无歌。明清《商河县志》均无"秧歌"一词记载，但载有在元宵节期间里人行户扮渔读耕樵诸戏，酒宴悦收竞为欢会。综上所述，至少可以说明以下两点：

首先，秧歌是古时农人在插秧时节，田间击鼓鸣歌跳舞而得名，它可以有舞有歌，也可以有舞无歌，但以舞为主体。之后它逐步发展成综合性的群众文艺活动，多在元宵节期间演出。从概念上和实地情况分析，秧歌不单指民间舞蹈，而是民间歌舞杂要的泛称。秧歌一词始见南宋，上溯北宋称"舞队"，唐称"乐舞"，汉称"百戏"，春秋称"夷狄之乐"。商河的民间歌舞虽然冠名为"鼓子秧歌"，但当地群众仍叫"跑十五""闹玩艺儿"。"跑"是舞，"闹"则是鼓子，既有曲有舞，也有杂要了，可见它仅是不同时期不同地域不同阶层的不同叫法而已。

其次，由于鼓子秋收扎根于民众之中，因而有着强大的生命力和创造力，是艺术精品的源泉。

古时歌舞没有专业和业余之分，但自从有了阶级以后，乐舞艺术被统治者所利用，才逐渐有了专业和业余的说法。早在汉代，国家就有了训练乐舞人才的专业机构，从历史唯物主义角度讲，这两部分文化不能被分开，它的根在民间是无疑的。现在有些西方国家的许多民间艺术已走向败落，并被歪曲、篡改和商品化了。而我们国家则强调建设有中国特色的社会主义，在"特色"中又突出中国特色的社会主义文化，所以必须立足于"源泉"，立足于中国五千年的文明史，古为今用、洋为中用、他为我用，除去糟粕、取其精华、锤炼提高。舞台艺术是这样，广场艺术也是这样。

2.1　胶州秧歌

有着"地秧歌""跑秧歌""三道弯""扭断腰"等别名的胶州秧歌活跃在胶州市郊广大农村。此外，在即墨、黄岛、胶南和高密等县(市)的部分地区也有流传。

胶州秧歌是山东三大秧歌之一，起源于清咸丰年间，据清代宋观炜所作《秧歌词》的描述推测，当时的胶州秧歌舞蹈动作、行当名称、服装道具等与现在基本相同。

胶州秧歌有膏药客、翠花、扇女、小、棒槌、鼓子等角色，基本动作主要有“翠花扭三步”“撇扇”“小扭”“棒花”“丑鼓八态”等，表演程序有“开场白”“跑场”“小戏”三部分，跑场队形有“十字梅”“四门斗”“两扇门”“正反挖心”“大摆队”“绳子头”等，还有《送闺女》《三贤》《小姑贤》《双推磨》等小戏。胶州秧歌里五种角色的性格动态各有不同：“翠花”开朗大方、“扇女”温柔淑静、“小妞”活泼俏丽、“鼓子”潇洒诙谐、“棒槌”英武矫健。其中女角最具特色的是姿态造型上的“三道弯”。“三道弯”是指全身各部位分别向不同方向连续做“oo”形或弧线运动，任何部位不能出现棱角，使膝部、腰部、肩胸部始终在“三道弯”的造型中变换舞姿，以充分展示女性特征的魅力。其音乐由打击乐、唢呐牌子、民间小调三大部分组成。小戏秧歌原有 72 个剧目，现存 135 个。胶州全市现有秧歌队 100 多支。中华人民共和国成立后，有关人员曾先后七次对胶州秧歌进行挖掘整理，现已将其编列为汉民族舞蹈的教材之一。1996 年，小屯村被文化部授予“中国民间艺术之乡”的称号。

胶州秧歌萌生于乡土，活跃于民间，在发展中自行流变，是群众自发参与、自由宣泄、自娱自乐的广场民间艺术，展现了胶东农村女性特有的健美体态和情性魅力，具有较高的审美价值和艺术研究价值。

在教育提倡传承发展和创新的今天，胶州秧歌从民间素材上升到课堂教材，尽量做到规范，对原生态舞蹈素材精挑细选，力求既保持民间的生活气息及动作特色，又能加以提炼升华。

胶州秧歌的动律特征概括起来有以下三个方面：

（1）下肢在脚的带动下，腰胯随之向左向右平旋拧动，脚沿脚跟随之。双膝并靠，脚的拾、踩、扰、踞、压始终保持身躯在流动中的三道弯及前俯后仰的姿态中。

（2）上肢则由手带动、肘随肩追，形成推、闪、盘、划八字姿态，变化中轮番缓发快收，融入抻劲。

（3）上下身向反方向运转，带出自上而下的持续三道弯、连动八字扭。整体动作手与脚合、肘与膝合、肩与胯合、眼随头转、头随腰走、有刚有柔、刚柔并济。

2.1.1 乞讨的传说和秧歌小调

传说在明末清初时，有姓马和姓赵的两家人从外地逃荒到此落户，但又因兵荒马乱此地无法维持生计，这两家人就弃家合伙闯了关东。他们长期流浪在外以卖艺为生，家中老头手执货郎鼓，儿子舞着“横天棍”，原来就是乞讨时打狗用的工具，儿媳和孙女则各执团扇、彩巾，歌舞说唱。老婆背起兜售妇女用品的翠花包，沿途叫卖，艰难度日。在秧歌《关东五更》里有这样的唱词："五更里，在关东两泪满腮，闯关东十二年未曾发财，我有心待要回家转，等一年盼一年实实难挨。"秧歌词真实地反映了当时闯关东的百姓十几年的血泪生涯。十二年后，两家重返故地定居，并将流浪途中学到的民歌小调与当地艺术相互融汇而形成了胶州秧教的雏形。以后又经过约七八十年的光景，到清乾隆年间基本上形成了小调秧歌，直到乾隆末年才基本定型。

2.1.2　秧歌团体的建立和师承方式

清同治年间，第一个具有科班性质的秧歌团体——安锅，在胶州马店镇楼子埠村诞生。它标志着秧歌的传承方式从家传到村传的改变。这个由当时著名秧歌艺人组成的安锅的组织者被称为"班主""老板"，秧歌团体开始时招收学员 40 人左右，经过训练逐渐筛选至 20 人左右。学生多为 14 至 18 岁的穷家男孩，由于经济条件和时间的限制，训练期限为从农历的十月初一至腊月二十三的三个月，期间训练紧张而严格。安锅的教授方式十分奇特，师傅在前面用两根秫秸做牵引，学生在身后双手握一端，另一端由师傅牵动，使学生与师傅的动作统一，一招一式不能马虎，直至达到要求方罢。据说当年武功演员在沙地上练"上纹"（乌龙绞柱），不仅磨破了皮革帽子，连头皮都磨出血来，所以中途打退堂鼓者大有人在。这也说明安锅的师承方式，基本上具备了专业化的性质。

2.2　海阳秧歌

2.2.1　"悦庙"和"拜大户"的年节风俗

海阳秧歌在民间有"耍正月，闹二月，哩哩啦啦到三月"的说法。秧歌队组织好后要在头年腊月排练，次年正月初开始扮装，称"包头"，然后要悦家庙、拜祖宗（俗称"悦庙"就是敬请祖宗鬼神同乐），接着要"拜大户"，即给本村有钱有势及德高望重之人上门拜年。从正月初三开始，各村秧歌队就开始互相串演，共贺新春，互道吉利，到正月十一秧歌演出才算达到高潮。在民间这样说道："十一庄稼会吃了干饭拉大陪。""大陪"就是指这一天百姓们相约在一起去看秧歌。此外，正月二十五日囤神生日及二月二也都有秧歌活动，这样哩哩啦啦地闹下来就到三月了，可见过年期间闹秧歌是当地一个多么重要的内容。

2.2.2　"抓胎"与"外援"

海阳秧歌的艺人没有严格的师徒关系，先由有名望的艺人商量后，从部分少年后生中挑选出优秀者随同学艺，名曰"抓胎"，即在排练秧歌中学，其中聪明伶俐者掌握技艺好的，当年就可以替代年老体弱者上场演出，学得不好者，可先充当打旗的、跑腿的，等到来年还可再学。

海阳秧歌的完善与成熟，离不开各种外来艺术精华的渗透，在乾隆三十五年(1770 年)海阳柳树庄人陈英弼编写的秧歌剧《陈老喜劝子跑四川》序中就有记载。可见早在二百多年前，海阳秧歌的音乐唱腔就已经借鉴蜀歌了。另外有关花鼓的传说也证明了这一点，相传当地老辈的花鼓个头小，舞动鼓槌的双手只在脸前划拉，被群众戏称为"猫洗脸"，关键是击鼓的声音不响亮，缺乏气势。后来，当地艺人向在本村做长工的外地人学演大花鼓，很受群众喜爱。"猫洗脸"终于被淘汰，而大花鼓则流传至今。武术也是促使海阳秧歌发展变革不可忽视的一个重要因素。据当地老人讲，早在清代，少林高徒就将少林武术架势教给本村后生，用于花鼓舞蹈。而海阳曾有习武健身之风，渐渐地拳术成为秧歌中单独表演的内容，之后逐渐融进秧歌角色的动作中，淘汰了纯武术表演而形成新的舞蹈形式。

2.2.3　男扮女和"扭断腰"

海阳秧歌中的男性动作因受武术影响较大，强调"铺身刹架""脚底生根"的沉重、稳健风格，而女性动作则讲究飘逸舒展。旧时，因为秧歌中的女角全部由男性扮演，所以艺人们在模仿的基础上夸大了动作姿态，特别是为了表现古代女性小脚走路的体态，创作出了秧歌中女角的出脚规律(落脚跟、碾脚边、压脚掌，两膝靠紧微屈又自然地带动了出胯、扭腰、压肩腮)，从而形成"拧曲"的基本舞姿。

人体的腰部最能体现女性特征，而海阳秧歌恰恰最为强调女性动作腰部的灵活性。观众评价舞者技艺水平的高低要以院部的柔软度而论。"拧腰"则是构成女性动作体态"拧曲"的主要因素，而"大扑腰""大闪腰"等动作也是通过腰部的拧、转、旋、提来带动双臂在身体上下左右做大幅度的回旋。民间艺人王发因此技出众而获得"扭断腰"的艺名，深受百姓喜爱。

2.3　鼓子秧歌

鼓子秧歌广泛流传在鲁西北的商河、惠民、乐陵、陵县、阳信、济阳、临邑等地区。春节期间，到处都有震耳欲聋的锣鼓和追随围观秧歌表演的人海。秧歌场上祖孙三代共舞屡见不鲜。在商河县 978 个村就有 724 个村有秧歌队这个统计数字足以证明当地民众对鼓子秧歌的参与性。

2.3.1　水灾的传说

听老人讲，北宋年间商河县一带连年水灾不断，包公便奉命从河南到此赈济灾民。包公和下官们送来粮食的同时，也把秧歌传授给了当地人。从此，人们每逢元宵佳节时便跑起秧歌，以表达对包公的感激之情。

还有一个传说也和水灾有关，是说北宋年间河南黄河水患不断，大批灾民背井离乡沿着黄河东下，寻找可安家落脚之地。到达此地时，还是一片蛮荒之地。当移民们开荒种地获得第一次丰收时，喜悦的心情无以言表，于是，人们用筛面用的箩圈蒙纸作鼓，蒸馒头时架篦子用的锅梁置柄为伞，跳起了家乡的秧歌。从此，该秧歌便在当地流传开来。

2.3.2　祭祀仪式和秧歌

旧时，各村的秧歌队在出外演出的前一天晚上，必须到本村寺庙或祠堂举行祭祖敬神的仪式。祭祀队伍由族长或德高望重的长者担任散“路灯”者，又叫“祭香包”，他们用棉纸包松枝，用油浸后点燃散在路两旁，走在队伍的前端，然后是开道锣，撒小米者、烧纸钱者、供桌(上有猪、牛、羊三牲供品)、锣鼓队、秧歌队等。这支浩浩荡荡的祭祀队伍，伴随着缓慢深沉的锣鼓声到达寺庙或祠堂后，开始献供品、烧香纸、三拜九叩，祭奠神灵和先祖，祈祷神灵和先祖保佑来年风调雨顺、五谷丰登，同时保佑秧歌队出村演出事事如意、人人平安。祭祖敬神之后的第二天就可安心地出村演出了。

2.3.3　“博士”和传承方式

秧歌的传承方式有三种：

第一种是家传，即父传子，子传孙，一般不串角色，伞传伞、鼓传鼓、棒传棒。他们打小开始就每年看长辈跑秧歌，受其熏陶，到了十三四岁即可下场。

第二种方式是拜师学艺，如某村没有人会跑秧歌，就把其他村的“博士”请来教授，从动作、跑场以及服装道具全部教会，不过“博士”是收授课费的。

第三种是“偷”学，每年的农历正月初十以后，总有几十支秧歌队云集县城，竞相献技，各亮“绝招”。各村的秧歌艺人都认为这是切磋技艺、提高水平的一次机会。有不少艺人在此期间背着干粮遍游乡镇，不辞辛苦地将人家的长处“偷偷地”吸收到自己的秧歌中来。

2.3.4　丰富的场图

鼓子秧歌的场图设计得十分有趣，它的取材之广泛令当代人钦佩，其形态来自劳动工具、生活用具、花卉、建筑、服装头饰、历史故事、神话传说、战争阵式等各个方面。例如，散发着浓郁乡土气息的构图“黄瓜架”“牛鼻钳”“勾心梅”“石榴花”“鸳鸯图”等，还有包含着历史故事或神话传说的构图“炮打临清”“十二连城”“八仙过海”“八门阵”“力杀四门”“紧闭四门”等。在跑法上也有一定的规律和要求,如“左进门、右出门”,进门前出门后必须绕“驳花”“跑场交叉,对脸就打”“前等后、后找前、前后对茬”等。

2.3.5　尚礼的民俗和串秧歌的规矩

出村串门送秧歌是鼓子秧歌过年期间重要的内容,但村与村之间的关系亲疏有别,这就决定了串秧歌时需要采用不同的方式。关系很好的村子,只要提前打个招呼,便可直接带秧歌队进村演出。如要建立新关系的村子,需先派探马去联络,经同意后方可前往演出。如果想通过串秧歌改善原本有矛盾的村子之间关系,其过程就要复杂一些,需经探马三探:一探对方是否同意;二探对方村中是否有秧歌队;三探对方是否准备好。经过三探,待一切确定安排停当后方可前去演出。秧歌队在族长率领下抵达另一个村庄时,先鸣炮示意串村的秧歌队已到,该村也需由族长带领村人到村口迎接,并鸣放鞭炮表示欢迎。在隆重的欢迎仪式后,秧歌队才开始演出。串秧歌可以使两村的矛盾得以解决并握手言好,事后还要商量回访事宜。

有时在行进途中两支秧歌队相遇,双方必须偃旗息鼓,相互让路,以示对对方的尊重。如有一方敲击锣鼓,对方则认为是有意挑衅,必会引起纠纷。另外,秧歌队在串村时大概需经过许多村庄,探马要提前探明所经过的村子是否有秧歌队演出,如有则不能进村,一直要等到该秧歌队演完才能进村。某村如果要请过路的秧歌队在此停下演出,可在路中央放一条长凳子,并燃放鞭炮以示欢迎,秧歌队有意表演就停下来。演完后村里要送给秧歌队一些烟、糖、点心之类的礼物表示谢意。这种良好的礼俗对改善民风及秧歌自身的发展起到了积极作用。

山东商河县地处济南市北郊,位于济南、德州、滨州三市交会处,交通便利、通信发达,能源充足,气候宜人,总面积 1162 平方公里,人口 58 万。在这块肥田沃土上,河渠路林交错纵横,农林牧副渔阡陌流金,工业立县初具规模,是济南市在鲁西北的经济辐射中心。这里民风淳朴,人民勤劳善良,热情豪爽,能歌善舞,是闻名遐迩的鼓子秧歌之乡。全县 978 个自然村村村都能跑秧歌、能上妆下场参加演出鼓子秧歌的人数众多。鼓子秧歌被誉为“民族民间文化的奇葩,齐鲁文化的骄傲”,于 1955 年、1980 年、1989 年、1992 年、1996 年、2002 年六次代表山东省和济南市参加全国民舞大赛,五次获大奖。1996 年被文化部命名为“中国民间艺术之乡”。

商河鼓子秧歌被时代认可,秧歌队员的足迹踏进了全国 20 多个省市的广场和舞台，如全国城运会（济南）、全国民运会（昆明）、中国旅游节（济南）、国际风筝节（潍坊）、国际灯会（淄博）、国际旅游文化节（北京）、蓉城之秋（成都）、三峡之夏（重庆）、龙山文化艺术节（济南）、国际秧歌节（沈阳）、国际舞蹈节（北京）、纪念反法西斯战争胜利五十周年（泰安）、七省一市元旦晚会（石家庄）、龙潭花会（北京）、中国新秧歌大赛（威海），以及有 260 名秧歌队员参加过中华人民共和国成立五十周年大庆，他们在北京天安门广场上的演出活动，饮誉海内外。专业文艺团体深入生活，根据鼓子秧歌舞蹈语汇创作的节目参加了世界青年联欢节，其中的《花鞭鼓舞》获金奖（莫斯科），在卡乌斯蒂宁民间艺术节（芬兰）、阿蒂纳河谷艺术节（意大利）及东南亚、北美等国家的演出引起强烈反响。鼓子秧歌以其独特魅力进入中国和世界人民文化生活范围，可以预料在不远的将来，它将以独特舞蹈形式风靡全世界。注入了时代活力的鼓子秧歌将青春永驻，继往开来，与时俱进，再谱新篇章！

2.4　起源与发展

2.4.1　商河鼓子秧歌起源于抗洪斗争

黄河养育了我们古老而伟大的民族，是中华民族的摇篮，但黄河自古善淤善决、善涉，决口和改道极为频繁，在四千多年中，较大的迁涉改道达 26 次之多，其中大改道就有 7 次。

在黄河腰穿县境的岁月里，县内屡受黄水危害，毁房舍，败田禾，饿殍遍地，民不聊生，民间财产付之于漂流者，更不知几千万计矣，经过洪水多次冲刷淤积，境内高凹地海拔高度竟有 10 米之差，72 个盐研涝洼分布全县各地，城南的清水洼最大时达 4 万多亩，季节性滞留水，还出现过海市蜃楼幻象。人生在世，一要活着，二要温饱，三要发展生产提高生活水平，就必须参与适应和变革现实的社会实践。黄河岸边的商河百姓为了生存，群起奋勇抗洪抢险，导水排涝，灾后散墒抢种，辛勤劳作，喜有收成，情不自禁拿起锅碗瓢盆、棍棒、簸箕、雨伞等随手用具，聚集在一起唱起来跳起来，抒发灾后余生抗灾夺丰收的欢悦心情，这就是鼓子秧歌的雏形。从现在流传的秧歌样式里，可以看到对古时人们劳动过程的模仿和重现，或是劳动过程中的各个环节，或是劳动的复习与预演，这些与当时的生产方式、生活方式有密切关联，留至今日与此有关的秧款阵图就有 20 多个，如“扁担勾”“值餐子”等。

2.4.2　鼓子秧歌以武舞成型，舞魂锤炼于军事战争

史上齐、秦、汉、唐在开国初期到中期，都有过经济繁荣的鼎盛时期，诗、歌、

舞也与历史的发展相一致，表现出封建制青春期特有的乐观情绪和朝气蓬勃精神，即便是艰苦的战争也义无反顾、一往无前，如唐睿宗年间王翰的“葡萄美酒夜光杯，欲饮琵琶马上催。醉卧沙场君莫笑，古来征战几人回”。唐僖宗年间农民起义领袖黄巢的著名反诗“待到秋来九月八，我花开后百花杀。冲天香阵透长安，满城尽带黄金甲”。这些体现了那个时代诗人豪迈的气概和宽广的胸怀。作为唐宋年间以武舞成型的商河鼓子秧歌，很具有那个时代的精神特点，被打上了时代的烙印。商河鼓子秧歌经过千百次的演出，锤炼出军事化的组织形式，变化莫测的舞蹈阵式，具有粗犷豪放的将士风格，无往不胜的英雄气势，这就是山东大汉的气质和性格，也就是舞蹈之观。作为将生命情调和冲动形诸人体动作的鼓子秧歌表演者，能尽情地抒发自己的情感，展示自己的力量，在美与力里自我陶醉：它忽如蛟龙摆尾，忽如短搏杀，忽如群虎下山，忽如行云流水，但却又什么都不像，看到听到感觉到的是一些虚的实体，是抽象的艺术，是灵与肉的结合，是力的起落和节奏变化，是力的集聚和所向披靡，是生命力的呐喊，是人对生命系统的自我认识、觉醒、肯定、追求和表现，是在时间延续着、变动着的空间样式里洋溢着的炎黄子孙的感情色彩，跳动着的中华儿女顽强的生命脉搏。这种情感的传递能使表演者与观众产生共鸣，因而具有强烈的震撼力。

2.4.3　鼓子秧歌从实用功利艺术逐渐向自娱性转化

随着社会进展、生产发展、文化发达，鼓子秧歌从减轻劳动重负、鼓舞战斗热情、祭礼驱禳的实用功利艺术逐渐向祝福游艺、自我娱乐的精神功利艺术转化，主调由重神秘演化为喜庆欢乐，在明清时期发达昌盛。

元末明初从河南、河北、山西、云南等省，明末清初从枣强、武邑等县迁来大批灾民，这几次移民不仅促进了当地的经济发展，还由于各地的乐舞文化在商河大汇合，使民间歌舞更加丰富多彩，绚丽多姿。

鼓子秧歌当地俗称“跑十五”“闹玩艺儿”，突出一个“跑”字和“闹”字，一个完整的鼓子秧歌演出包括“伞鼓舞”、秧歌调和杂要三部分，载歌载舞，由于舞者不歌，歌者不舞，所以秧歌队人数众多，多者可达六七百人，表演顺序是：前场（武场）—伞鼓舞—杂要秧歌调—伞鼓舞，这种综合性的表现形式可上溯到汉代的“百戏”。

“百戏”就是集歌、舞、杂要于一场，汉代称“百戏”为“角抵戏”，南北朝称“百戏”为“散乐”。宋代“百戏”复盛，南宋孟元老《东京梦华录》载：“每逢元宵节，歌舞百戏，鳞鳞相切，乐声嘈杂十余里。”商河的“百戏”保留至今，除伞鼓舞外，尚有花鞭鼓、凤阳花鼓、花棍、采茶、小车、大头、高跷、龙灯、狮包、灯官、虎牛斗、荷花灯、独竿轿、二人转、旱船、跑驴、赶脚、行车、马叉、武场、撮播子，背媳妇、二人摔、摇葫芦、打杈、哈哈等三十余种。

山东秧歌动作二

Shandong Yangko action 2

3.角色、服饰、道具

“伞”:有“头伞”“花伞”之分。“头伞”亦称“丑伞”，由中老年男性扮演，多以4～8 人配置，是秧歌队的群体指挥。头伞中的一二把伞称领伞，为正副指挥，服饰为白发、白髯、白袍、黄头带、红裤、浅鞋，左手持伞，右手持“驳棰”。花伞是“花”头领，由青年男性扮演，人数一般与头伞相等，服饰为青衣、青头带、黑髯、黑靴，持伞和铜铃(有的用江湖医生使用的虎曾)。

“伞”道具运用有其古文化因素，伞为平顶皇伞，有庇护四方风调雨顺的含义。“伞”黄色头带，黄是亮色、吉祥色，炎黄子孙，黄皮肤，饮黄河水，尊黄帝神，皇帝用色，故也为权威之色。“插伞”的伞头直径为 80～100 厘米，“打伞”的伞头直径为 70～80 厘米，杆长都是 100～120 厘米，“举伞”的伞头直径为 50～70 厘米，杆长 70 厘米。伞罩颜色，头伞为黄、白、红色吉祥图案，花伞为蓝、灰色吉祥图案。女性“花伞”的伞罩用绸花系成，花团锦簇、典雅华贵。“插伞”“扛伞”用的驳棰是牛胯骨，是远古打击乐器的一种。也有的驳棰用桑柘木制成，长 1 尺(按四时中的春)，上宽3寸6(按360日)，下宽1寸2(按12个月)。“插伞”腰间的小孩鞋寓意子孙在身边平平安安，鞋中酒盅寓意不仅有饭吃，而且有酒喝。

“鼓”：亦称“鼓子”，是秧歌队的主力军，由青年男性扮演，多以24、32、48、64人配置，左手持双面圆鼓，右手持棍击打起舞，鼓面直径26厘米，厚12厘米，鼓腔用红布封好，布上缀几条红绸，底端用皮条环跨在手腕上可自由翻转(鼓子秧歌的手鼓与山东汉画像石中的“踏鼓”鼓形相似，不同的是，一个手持，一个脚踏。服饰为黄衣、黄裤、黄头巾上慧英雄胆，身上十字披红英雄带，浅鞋。现在北乡有些村女性扮“鼓”，服饰全身红，英姿飒爽，不让须眉。

“棒”：亦称“棒棰”，由青年男性扮演。人数少于“鼓”，多以8、16人配置演员。持双棒，棒长60厘米，棒端缀彩缨、服饰全身黑，十字披绿英雄带，黑头巾上悬铁箭头(红蝴蝶、小圆镜)。

“花”：女角，分地花、跷花两种。地花就是双翼在地上跑的，跷花就是踩着高跷跑的。跷高50厘米，解放前后一般是男性扮演，现在是少女少妇扮演，服饰为花袄、花褶裙、斗篷，头饰红绸花，左手花篮(花束、花灯、花环)，右手拂尘(绸巾)，也有左手巾。现在的服饰则什么好看穿什么，主要是炫耀自身美丽。

“丑”：亦称“外角”，由男性扮演，多扮成“二癫子、王先生、傻老婆”等，“丑”熟悉秧歌场阵，跑场时在暗中指挥。在两场“伞鼓舞”中间穿插补空，亦说亦唱，插科打挥，不俗不丑，风趣活泼，逗人捧腹。

“伞”“鼓”“棒”“花”的服饰均受角色影响，以稳健、潇洒、英武、俊美为主调。如“伞”像《打渔杀家》中的萧恩，“鼓”像武侠，“棒”像燕青，“花”像《租柯寨》中的女兵。“丑”的服饰及化妆则以丑为美。

歌手：2～10人不等，着便服，主要演唱秧歌调。

民乐队：包括唢呐、笙、笛、管、二胡、三弦、京胡、堂鼓、板胡、小锣、小镲等，主要为秧歌调伴奏或器乐合奏。

杂耍：包括武术、旱船、狮子、高跷等，表演人数根据各村条件而定。

鼓乐队：由大鼓1、铙2、镲2、锣2组成，大鼓鼓面直径80～120厘米，鼓响如雷鸣。大鼓为指挥、与“领伞”配合默契。

编制：“伞”“鼓”“棒”“花伞”“花”的配置比例一般为1∶4∶2∶1∶4。某秧歌队如“头伞”为4，“鼓”则为16(亦可24、32、48)，“棒”为8(亦可16、24)，“花伞”为4、花为16(亦可24、36)，“丑”为双数，一般2～4人角色配备，总人数都是以2为基数。只有如此，才能保持秧歌场子对称、平衡，完整与丰满。

Shandong Yangko

1.Project culture

Yangko is a popular and representative folk dance in China (mainly in the North). Different regions have different titles and styles. In folk, there are two names for Yangko: those performed on stilts are called "Gaoqiao Yangko", and those performed without stilts are called "Di Yangko". In modern times, "Yangko" mostly refers to "Di Yangko". Yangko has a long history. There is a record of "village field music" in the folk-dance team introduced by Zhou Mi in *The Old Stories of Wulin* in the Southern Song Dynasty. The source relationship between the existing Yangko and the "village field music" in the Song Dynasty is clearly recorded in Wu Xilin's *Copy of New Year's Miscellaneous Chants* in the Qing Dynasty. At present, Yangko dance teams are generally in the form of Yangko dance teams. The number of people in dance teams varies from ten to more than 100. There is not only group dance, but also many performance forms such as double dance and triple dance. According to the needs of the role, they hold corresponding handkerchiefs, umbrellas, sticks, drums, whips and other props and dance heartily with the accompaniment of percussion apparatuses such as gongs and drums, suona and so on. The dance methods, movements and styles of Yangko vary from place to place. Some are powerful, and some are soft and beautiful.

Yangko is one of the most representative folk dances in northern China. It is both performative and self-entertaining. It also entertains people and is deeply loved by the people. There have been some representative folk Yangko artists all over the country, and many folk artists have played an important role in the construction of dance in the PRC founded in 1949. With the rapid development of rural economy and the change of cultural environment, there are few folk artists who can master the traditional Yangko skills and pure dance style. The protection and inheritance need to be carried out urgently.

When mentioning Yangko, people often remind of the dancing scenes of red silk flying and footsteps jumping. At the grand celebration moment, it is easy to see this kind of Yangko characterized by cross step in ordinary people's life. Among many forms of Yangko in China, this cross step Yangko is only one of them. In the 1940s, Mao Zedong published *The Speech at the Yana's Literature and Art Symposium*. Its core idea was to let revolutionary writers and artists go to the vast rural areas to absorb nutrition and create literary and artistic works of contemporary significance. Therefore, a mass "new Yangko movement" was launched in the Shaanxi, Gansu, and Ningxia Border Region. Based on Northern Shaanxi Yangko, writers and artists have created a new Yangko style, that is, cross step Yangko. In the years to come, it has become one of the most popular forms of dance from rural areas to cities. Moreover, its spread did not make other Yangko forms decline. During the Spring Festival, there are many Yangko songs with different forms and rich contents in the vast rural areas of northern China.

Yangko, as a very common form of folk song and dance in northern Han areas, is usually an important content for people to celebrate the Lantern Festival on the 15th day of the first lunar month. The forms of folk songs and dances in southern China are also very rich, but most of them are different from Yangko. They are dance forms based on local operas and folk dances, such as "flower drum lantern" in Anhui and "flower lantern" in Yunnan.

The trace of Yangko has been recorded in the notes and novels of literati in the Song Dynasty, mainly saying that people sing Yangko in farming. Later, the records of the Qing Dynasty had detailed descriptions of various dressed up characters, such as "monk", "childe", "flower drum payer", "farmer", "fisherwoman", "merchant" and so on. This fully shows that Yangko in the Qing Dynasty has been shaped into the style we see today.

In the history of more than a thousand years, the development and evolution of Yangko has generally experienced four stages: First, there are small songs accompanied by working life, then developed into independent folk song and dance singing, and then gradually transition from song and dance singing to small drama. Finally, Yangko has transited to pure dance art today. The content of Yangko singing is mostly myths, legends, and folk stories, and it is very bold and straightforward in expressing the love between men and women. Therefore, it has been forbidden by many dynasties in history. From the perspective of art, Yangko combines poetry, music, dance, drama performance and other components. However, from the survival state of Yangko itself, it has a lot of cultural significance, such as sacrificing ancestors, folk etiquette, and other functions.

Folk people have a vivid summary of Yangko, that is, "gongs, drums and firecrackers sound noisy; and flags, umbrellas and fans fly colorfully", which is the scene of Yangko performance. Generally, Yangko performances have a team with a clear division of roles. Dancers dress up as various characters in life and myths and legends, holding props such as fans, handkerchiefs, umbrellas, drums, and sticks. The characters in this team not only dance physically, but also have rich false shapes, such as "dry boat", "bamboo horse", "lion", "dragon lantern", "stilt", "big head doll", etc. They are all important parts of the Yangko team. In some places, there are fragments of small folk songs and traditional operas, as well as modern songs and dances and self-made and self-singing newspaper dramas.

If people think that Yangko is a very simple and easy to learn "thing", it is a big mistake. Because the form of Yangko is not only dancing on the ground, but also walking on stilts. It requires not only walking, but also difficult movements such as jumping, somersaulting, and crossing obstacles. Not everyone can be competent. At the same time, Yangko is not one style from beginning to end. It is divided into large-scale performance and small-scale performance in the process of performance. The large-scale performance starts and ends with dance, with various small-scale performances interspersed in the middle. The small-scale performance is about the dance and song and dance performances of several people. The large-scale performance is generally composed of more than ten to dozens of people. One or two leading dancers lead the Yangko team to dance and walk in various formation patterns. Therefore, the work of the leading dancers is not easy. They must know well and have a strong memory. Otherwise, if they are in a mess, they will have to make a big joke.

Some people once said that the Han people do not love singing and dancing, but when we really go among the people to feel various forms of Yangko, we will be moved by their colorful forms. With the interpretation of history, culture and life conveyed in their bodies, how can we say that Han people do not love singing and dancing? That's because we know too little about them. Therefore, let's rediscover and understand this model of Han song and dance with profound historical accumulation and mass foundation.

Yangko in Shandong Province is the most popular in the new Jiaodong peninsula in western Shandong and Northern Shandong. In central and southern Shandong, centered on Qufu, there are few Yangko spread within a few hundred miles, which may be related to the influence of the Confucian thought of "emphasizing elegance and neglecting vulgarity". Various Yangko dances, such as "Yudeng Yangko", "Huagusan", "Liu Lin Yangko" and "Feng Yangko", which are popular in the southern, northern and western regions of Shandong Province, are similar to some of the Yangko dances of neighboring provinces in some respects (such as "Huagu Luozi" in northern Jiangsu Province, "Huagu Yangko" in Henan Province and "Di Yangko" in Hebei Province). The three most famous Shandong Yangko dances, Guzi Yangko, Jiaozhou Yangko and Haiyang Yangko, have become the models of Yangko dances of the Han nationality with their own distinct styles. Overall, Shandong Yangko not only has various forms, but also has different styles. It shows the rough and forthright character characteristics of Qilu people from different angles, condenses the customs of Qilu for thousands of years, but also reflects the unique aesthetic interest and spiritual style of people in Shandong.

2.Project origin

In Lu You's poem in the Southern Song Dynasty "During the Mangzhong season, rice seedlings are planted in the fields, wheat rice soup is found in every family, and Yangko is played everywhere". During the reign of the emperor Hongxi of the Ming Dynasty, the *Family Tree of Zhao* in Haiyang recorded that "When five generations gather together in the hall, the dancers perform Yangko. In this situation, Yangko is accompanied by dancing and signing". In the *Annals of Xiajin County* during the Jiajing period of the Ming Dynasty, it was recorded that "I enjoyed with the people when I was happy, and Yangko was performed." In this situation, Yangko is in separation from dances and songs. According to the *Records of Huangzhou Hall* in the Qing Dynasty: "Farmers walk together in the fields, and move the hoe with their toes. They walk while playing drums. The Yangko is accompanied by dance but without songs. According to *Wulixinian Zayongchao* in the Qing Dynasty, Yangko is the music in the field in the Southern Song Dynasty, and performers dress like monks, boys, girls, fishermen and salesmen to entertain the audience by ridiculous movements. In this case, the Yangko is also accompanied by dance but without songs. There is no record of "Yangko" in *Shanghe County Annals* in the Ming and Qing dynasties, but it contained the record that "During the Lantern Festival, people dress up as fishermen for entertainment in a banquet". To sum up, at least the following two points can be drawn:

First, "Yangko" is named after the ancient farmers beating drums and dancing in the field during the rice transplanting season. It can be accompanied by dance and song, or dance without song. However, taking dance as the main body, it has gradually developed into a comprehensive mass literary and artistic activity, which is mostly performed during the Lantern Festival. From the conceptual and field situation analysis, "Yangko" does not only refer to folk dance, but a general term for folk song, dance and vaudeville. The word "Yangko" was firstly found in the Southern Dynasty. Yangko was called "dance" in the Northern Song Dynasty, "music" in Tang Dynasty, "baixi" in the Han Dynasty, "music of yidi" in the Spring and Autumn dynasties. The folk music and dance in Shanghe is called "Guzi Yangko", and local people also call it "Paoshiwu", and "Naowanyier". "Pao" means dancing, and "Nao" means Guzi. There are music, dance, and vaudeville. So, it can be seen that Yangko has different names among different levels of people in different periods and regions.

Second, because Guzi takes root among the people, it has a noble vitality and creative vitality, and is the source of fine art.

In ancient times, there was no distinction between professional and amateur singing and dancing, but since there was a class society, the art of music and dance was used by rulers, and then there was a saying of professional and amateur gradually. As early as the Han Dynasty, the state had professional institutions for training music and dance talents. From the perspective of historical materialism, it is no doubt that the two parts of culture cannot be separated, and their roots are rooted in the folk. At present, many folk arts in some western countries have fallen, distorted, tampered with and commercialized. Different from western countries, China emphasizes the construction of socialism with Chinese characteristics and highlights the "socialist culture with Chinese characteristics" in the "characteristics". Therefore, we must absorb the quintessence from the ancient times and the western world, and throw away defects to improve our skills both for the stage art and plaza art based on the "source" and China's 5000-year history of civilization.

2.1 Jiaozhou Yangko

Jiaozhou Yangko with the nicknames of "Di Yangko", "Pao Yangko", "sandaowan" and "Waist twisting" is active in the vast rural areas in the suburbs of Jiaozhou and Jimo, Huangdao, Jiaonan and Gaomi counties (cities). It has also spread in some areas.

Jiaozhou Yangko is one of the three major Yangko in Shandong. Jiaozhou Yangko originated in the reign of Xianfeng in the Qing Dynasty. According to the description of Yangko Lyrics written by Song Guanwei in the Qing Dynasty, the dance movements, trade names and clothing props of Jiaozhou Yangko at that time were basically the same as those now.

Jiaozhou Yangko has the roles of gaoyaoke, cuihua, shannv, xiaoniu, bangchui, and guzi. The basic actions mainly include "cuihua niusanbu", "pieshan", "xiaoniu", "banghua" and "guchoubatai". The performance procedures include "opening speech", "running field" and "small play". The running field formation includes "shizimei", "simendou", "liangshanmen" and "zhengfanwaxin" "dabaidui", "shengzitou", as well as small plays such as *Songguinv*, *Sanxian*, *Xiaoguxian*, *Shuangtuimo*. In Jiaozhou Yangko, the characters of five roles are different: "cuihua" is generous; "xiaoniu" is lively; "guzi" is handsome, and witty; "bangchui" is vigorous. The most characteristic movement in female roles is the "sandaowan", meaning that all parts of the body make actions in different directions successively in the "oo" shape or arc shape smoothly, and the knees, waist, shoulders and waist of the players should always change in the shape of "three bends" to fully represent female charms. Its music consists of percussion, suona brand and folk minor. There are 135 minor Yangko operas out of the original 72. Jiaozhou has more than 100 Yangko teams. After the founding of the People's Republic of China, relevant personnel have excavated and sorted out Jiaozhou Yangko seven times, and now it has been listed as one of the teaching materials of Han nationality dance. In 1996, Xiaotun Village was awarded the title of "Hometown of Chinese folk art" by the Ministry of culture.

Jiaozhou Yangko was born in the countryside, active in the folk, and has changed itself in the development. It is a square folk art with the spontaneous participation of the masses for self-entertainment. It shows the unique body-building posture and emotional charm of rural women in Jiaodong and has high aesthetic value and artistic research value.

Today, when education advocates inheritance, development, and innovation, Jiaozhou Yangko has been taught in classroom as a folk art, which should be standardized with careful selection of original dances. The aim is to maintain the original folk life atmosphere and action characteristics while refining and promoting them.

The dynamic characteristics of Jiaozhou Yangko can be summarized in the following three aspects:

(1) Driven by the feet, the waist and crotch rotate horizontally to the left and right, and the feet follow them. Lean on your knees and keep your body in the three bends in the flow and the posture of pitching forward and backward when picking up, stepping, disturbing, squatting and pressing your feet.

(2) The upper limb is driven by the hand and followed by the elbow with the shoulder, forming the posture of pushing, flashing, turning and drawing eight characters. In the change, it takes turns to slow down and quickly close, integrating people's stretching strength.

(3) Turn the upper and lower body in the opposite direction to bring out the continuous three turns and continuous eight-character twist from top to bottom. The whole movement is hand and foot, elbow and knee, shoulder and crotch, eyes turn with the head, and the head walks with the waist, with hardness and softness combined.

2.1.1 The Legend of begging and Xiaodiao Yangko

It is said that in the late Ming Dynasty and early Qing Dynasty, people from two families surnamed Ma and Zhao fled from other places and settled here. However, they were unable to make a living here because of the chaos of war. They abandoned their homes and went to Guandong together. They were wandering outside during their growing up by performing arts. The old man in the family held a peddler drum and his son danced a "horizontal stick". It turns out that it is a tool for beating dogs when begging. The daughter-in-law and granddaughter each held group fans and colored scarves for singing and dancing. The wife took up the Cuihua bag and sold women's products along the way. In the Yangko *Five Watch in Guandong*, there is such a lyric: "In the five watches of the night in Guandong, two tears are full on my cheeks. I haven't made a fortune in Guandong for 12 years. I want to go home. It's hard to go through each year while waiting for returning." Yangko's lyrics truly reflect more than ten years of tough times of those who have attempted to make a living in Guandong at that time. Twelve years later, the two families returned to their hometown to settle down, and merged the folk tunes learned in the wandering way with the local art to form the prototype of "Jiaozhou Yangjiao". After about 70-80 years, Xiaodiao Yangko was basically formed in the reign of Qianlong of the Qing Dynasty, and it was not basically finalized until the end of Qianlong.

2.1.2 The establishment of Yangko group and its teaching methods

During the Tongzhi period of the Qing Dynasty, the first Yangko group with the nature of a scientific class, Anguo, was born in Louzibu Village, Madian Town, Jiaozhou. It marks the establishment of the inheritance mode of Yangko from family to village. The organizer of Yangko Anguo consisting of famous Yangko artists at that time, was known as the "leader" and "boss". At the beginning, about 40 students were recruited, and gradually screened to about 20 after training. Most of the students are poor boys aged 14 to 18. Due to economic conditions and time constraints, the training period was three months, from the first day of October to the 23rd day of the twelfth lunar month. The training was intense and strict, and the teaching method of pot installation was very strange. The master used two sorghum stalks as traction in front, while the students held one end with both hands behind them, and the other end was influenced by the master to ensure uniform actions of the students and the master. One can't be careless until the action meets the requirements. It is said that when martial arts actors practiced "Shangwen" (oolong twisted column) on the sand, they broke the leather hat, and even rubbed the scalp to bleed, so many people withdrew halfway. The way of teacher inheritance of Anguo basically has the nature of specialization.

2.2 Haiyang Yangko

2.2.1 New Year customs of "Yuemiao" and "worshiping big families"

"Haiyang Yangko" has the saying of "playing in the first month, making trouble in February, and cheering until March". After the Yangko team is organized, rehearsal starts in the twelfth month of the first year, and dressing up (known as "Baotou") begins at the beginning of the first month of the next year. Then, ancestors are worshiped in the family temple, commonly known as "Yuemiao". Then, New Year's greetings are expressed to the rich, powerful and respected people in the village. From the third day of the first lunar month, the Yangko teams of each village begin to perform with each other to celebrate the New Year and say good luck to each other. The Yangko performance reaches its climax on the eleventh day of the first month. It is said in the folk that "On the eleventh day, Dapei performance is viewed after dining". "Dapei" means that people meet together to see Yangko on this day. In addition, on the 25th of the first month, there are Yangko activities on Tunshen's birthday and February 2 in lunar calendar. After these activities, March comes. It can be seen how important role the Di Yangko plays during the new year.

2.2.2 "Grasping the excellent disciple" and "foreign aid"

The artists of "Haiyang Yangko" do not have a strict apprenticeship relationship. After consultation with famous artists, they select the excellent ones from some young students to follow their classmates, which is called "Grasping the excellent disciple" ("Zhuatai"), that is, in the rehearsing of Yangko, those who are smart and have good skills can perform in replace of the old and weak in that year. Those who do not learn well can first act as flag bearers and errands runners, and improve their skills in the next year.

The development of "Haiyang Yangko" is based on the infiltration of all kinds of exotic art essence. In the 35th year of Qianlong, this was recorded in the foreword of *Chen Advised His Son to Go to Sichuan*, a Yangko opera written by Chen Yingbi from Liushu Zhuang. As early as more than 200 years ago, the musical singing of "Haiyang Yangko" had learned from Shu songs. In addition, the legend about the flower drum also proves this. It is said that the previous flower drum was small, and the performers had to move their hands at the front of their faces when moving the drumstick. It was jokingly called "maoxilian" by the masses. The sound of beating the drum was not loud and lacks momentum. Later, local artists learned to play big flower drums from outsiders who worked long in the village, which was very popular with the masses. The action "maoxilian" was finally eliminated, and the big flower drum has been handed down to this day. Martial art is also an important factor that cannot be ignored in promoting the development and reform of "Haiyang Yangko". According to local elders, as early as the Qing Dynasty, Shaolin masters taught Shaolin martial arts posture to the younger generation of the village for flower drum dance. Haiyang once had the atmosphere of practicing martial arts and fitness. Gradually, boxing became a separate performance in Yangko. Later, it gradually integrated into the actions of Yangko characters, eliminated pure martial arts performance and formed a new dance form.

2.2.3 Disguised as a woman and "Waist twisting"

The male's movements in "Haiyang Yangko" are greatly influenced by martial arts, emphasizing the heavy and steady style of "spreading the body" and "taking root in the soles of the feet". Actions for women require elegant and comfortable movements. In the old days, because the female characters in Yangko were all played by men, artists exaggerated the movement posture based on imitation, especially the posture of ancient women walking with small feet and created the stepping rule of female characters in Yangko defeat: Heel landing grinding the side of the foot pressing the soles of the feet. The knees are close and slightly bent, and are naturally moved out of the crotch. Twist the waist and press the shoulders and cheeks to form the basic dance posture of "twisting".

The waist of the human body can best reflect women's characteristics, and "Haiyang Yangko" emphasizes the flexibility of women's waist. The audience's evaluation of the dancer's skill level is based on the softness. "Twisting the waist" is the main factor that constitutes the "twisting" of women's posture, and the actions such as "throwing at the waist" and "flashing the waist" also drive the arms to make a large swing up, down, left and right through the twisting, rotation, and lifting of the waist. Folk artist Wang Fa won the stage name of "Niuduanyao" because of his outstanding skills, who is deeply loved by the people.

2.3 Guzi Yangko

"Guzi Yangko" is widely spread in Shanghe, Huimin, Leling, Lingxian, Yangxin, Jiyang, Linyi and other areas in northwest Shandong. During the Spring Festival, there are deafening gongs and drums and a number of people watching Yangko performances. It is common for three generations to dance together on the Yangko field. Statistics are sufficient to prove the participation of the local people in "Guzi Yangko". There are 724 Yangko teams in 978 villages in Shanghe County.

2.3.1 Legend of flood

According to the old man, during the Northern Song Dynasty, there were continuous floods in Shanghe County, and Bao Gong was ordered to provide relief to the victims from Henan. While Bao Gong and the lower officials sent grain, the lower officials also taught Yangko to the local people. Since then, people have performed Yangko every Lantern Festival to show their gratitude to Bao Gong.

Another legend is also related to floods. It is said that during the Northern Song Dynasty, the Yellow River in Henan was flooded continuously, and many victims left their homes and went down the Yellow River to find a place to settle down. When they arrived here, it was still a wilderness. When the immigrants cultivated land for the first harvest, their joy was unspeakable. Therefore, people made drums with baskets and paper covered with screen noodles. When steaming steamed bread, the pot beam with grate was set as an umbrella and jumped up the Yangko of their hometown. Since then, the Yangko has spread locally.

2.3.2 Sacrificial ceremony and Yangko

In the old days, the Yangko teams of each village had to go to the temple or ancestral hall of the village to hold a ceremony of ancestor worship the night before they went out to perform. The sacrificial team was composed of clan leaders or highly respected elders, also known as "sacrificial sachets". They wrapped pine nuts in cotton paper, lighted them on both sides of the road after being soaked in oil, and walked in the front of the team. Others played gongs, sprinkled millet, burned paper money, offered tables (There are three animal offerings of pigs, cattle and sheep), and performed Yangko, etc. After arriving at the temple or ancestral hall with thc slow and deep sound of gongs and drums, this vast sacrificial team began to offer offerings and burn incense paper, praying for the gods and ancestors to bless the good weather and bumper harvests in the coming year, bless the Yangko team to perform smoothly out of the village; and that everything is going well and safe. The next day after offering sacrifices to ancestors and gods, people can go out of the village to perform Yongko at ease.

2.3.3　"Bo shi" and inheritance mode

There are three ways of Yangko inheriting:

The first is family inheritance, that is, the father passes on the son and the son passes on the grandson. Generally, the same roles (those playing umbrella, drum, and stick) are passed on to next generations. Since childhood, the young watch their elders perform Yangko every year, and they can perform at the age of 13-14.

The second is to learn skills from teachers. If no one in a village can perform Yangko, the "Bo shi" (the person skilled at Yanko) from other villages will be invited to teach it, including movements, running fields and clothing props. Of course, the "Bo shi" collects teaching fees.

The third is learning skills "secretly". After the tenth day of the first lunar month every year, dozens of Yangko teams gather in the county to show their skills and especially their "unique skills". Yangko artists in all villages believe that this is an opportunity to learn skills and improve their levels. During this period, many artists traveled around the villages and towns with dry food on their backs, taking pains to secretly absorb the strengths of others into their own Yangko.

2.3.4　Rich drawings

The drawings of Guzi Yangko are interesting, which are drawn from a wide variety of materials and admired by modern people. The forms come from working tools, living utensils, flowers, buildings, clothing and headdress, historical stories, myths, and legends, as well as war styles. For example, the drawings with rich local flavors include "cucumber rack", "plum", "pomegranate", and "mandarin duck". Drawings from historical stories or legends include "Attack Linqing with cannons", "12 cities", "Eight fairies", "Eight arrays", "Attach four doors" and "Close four doors". There are certain rules and requirements on performing, for example, "entering doors from left" and "exiting doors from right". After entering and exiting doors, one must run the court, and hit the opponent's face, as well as "the front person should wait for the follower, and the follower should follow up the front person and they should align with each other", etc.

2.3.5 The folk custom of advocating etiquette and the rules of performing Yangko in other villages

Performing Yangko out of the village is an important content of "Guzi Yangko" during the Chinese New Year. The relationship between villages determines that different ways should be adopted when performing Yangko. The Yangko team can directly go to the village with a good relationship for performance after advance notification. If one village wants to establish a new relationship with another, it needs to send a contact person (called "tanma") to contact first, and can go to another village for performance only after consent. To improve the originally contradictory relationship between villages by performing Yangko, the process will be more complicated. The village needs to learn three things through tanma: First, check whether the other village agrees their performance; second, find out whether there is already a Yangko team in the other village; third, check whether the other village has been prepared for welcoming it. The performance is only allowed when everything is determined. When the Yangko team arrives at another village under the leadership of the clan leader, it should first fire firecrackers to signal the arrival of the Yangko team. The clan leader of the receiving village should lead the villagers to the entrance of the village and fire firecrackers as a welcome. After the grand welcome ceremony, the Yangko team can perform Yango. Performing Yangko can solve the contradiction between two villages and establish good relationship. Afterwards, they need to discuss the return visit.

Sometimes, when two Yangko teams meet on the way, both sides must stop and give way to each other to show their respect for each other. If one party strikes gongs and drums, the other party will see it as provoking, which will lead to disputes. In addition, the Yangko team may have to pass through many villages when visiting the village. The tanma must find out in advance whether there is a Yangko team performance in the passing village. If so, it cannot enter the village until the Yangko team has finished its performance. If a village wants to invite a passing Yangko team to stop performing here, it can put a bench in the middle of the road and firecrackers to show welcome. The Yangko team stops if it wants to perform. After the performance, the village will give the Yangko team some gifts such as cigarettes, sugar and snacks to express their gratitude. This good etiquette and custom have played a positive role in improving folk customs and the development of Yangko itself.

Shanghe County is in the northern suburb of Jinan City and the intersection of Jinan, Dezhou and Binzhou. It has convenient transportation, developed communication, sufficient energy, and pleasant climate, with a total area of 1,162 square kilometers and a population of 580,000. On this fertile land, rivers, canals, roads and forests are crisscross; agriculture, forestry, animal husbandry, sidelines, fish and fields are rich, and the industrial county is beginning to take shape. It is the economic radiation center of Jinan in northwest Shandong. With simple folk customs, hardworking and kind people are warm and forthright and good at singing and dancing. It is the famous hometown of Guzi Yangko. All the 978 natural villages in the county can perform Yangko and take part in the performance. Guzi Yangko is known as "the extraordinary model of national folk culture and the pride of Qilu culture". In 1955, 1980, 1989, 1992, 1996 and 2002, the Shanghe Yangko team participated in the national folk-dance competition on behalf of Shandong Province and Jinan City six times and won the grand prize five times. In 1996, it was named "hometown of Chinese folk art" by the Ministry of culture.

Shanghe Guzi Yangko is recognized by the times, and the footprints of Yangko players have stepped into the squares and stages in more than 20 provinces and cities in China, such as the National Urban Games (Jinan), the National Democratic Games (Kunming), the China Tourism Festival (Jinan), the International Kite Festival (Weifang), the International Lantern Festival (Zibo), the International Tourism and Culture Festival (Beijing), the Autumn of Chengdu (Chengdu), the Summer of the Three Gorges (Chongqing), the Longshan Culture and Art Festival (Jinan) and the international Yangko Festival (Shenyang), International Dance Festival (Beijing), 50th Anniversary of Commemorating the Victory of the Anti-fascist War (Tai'an), New Year's Party of Seven Provinces and One City (Shijiazhuang), Longtan Flower Fair (Beijing), China New Yangko Competition (Weihai). In addition, 260 Yangko players once participated in the performance on Beijing's Tiananmen Square for the celebration of the 50th Anniversary of the Founding of the People's Republic of China. Professional literary and artistic groups are rooted in people's life. They participated in the World Youth Festival according to the programs created by Guzi Yangko dance vocabulary. Among them, *Flower Whip* won the Gold Award (Moscow), which had strong repercussions in Kaustinin Folk Art Festival (Finland) and Atina Valley Art Festival (Italy), Southeast Asia, North America and other countries. Guzi Yangko has been immersed in the cultural life of people in China and the world with its unique charm. It can be expected that soon, Guzi Yangko will be popular all over the world in the form of worldwide dance. Infused with the vitality of the times, Guzi Yangko will carry forge ahead, keep pace with the times and write a new chapter!

2.4 Origin and development

2.4.1 Shanghe Guzi Yangko originated from the struggle against floods

The Yellow River has nurtured our ancient and great nation and is the cradle of the Chinese nation. Since ancient times, the Yellow River often silted, burst dikes, and rerouted frequently. The large transference involving rerouting is as much as 26 times, including 7 times of major rerouting in more than four thousand years.

In the years the Yellow River ran through the county, the floods destroyed houses and broke homes and fields of people there, causing starvation and death. Being scoured by the flood, the altitude intercept in the county reached 10 meters. Seventy-two saline depressions distributed throughout the county, clear water pools in the south of the city has a maximum area of more than 40,000 mu, with seasonal stagnant water and mirage illusion. To live in the world, first, we must live; second, we must eat and wear; third, we must develop production and improve living standards. Therefore, we must participate in social practice to adapt to and change reality. During the flood season of the Yellow River, the people of Shanghe River on the Bank of the Yellow River strive to fight against the flood by leading the water, draining the water logging, and dispersing the soil moisture. They rush to plant seeds after the disaster, work hard and enjoy the harvest. People can't help picking up pots and pans, sticks, dustpans, umbrellas, and other handy utensils, gathering to sing and dance to express their joy in fighting the disaster and winning a bumper harvest for the rest of their lives after the disaster, which is the prototype of Guzi Yangko. This combination of folk movements and dances is credible, although there is no written record about it. From the popular Yangko style, we can see the imitation and reproduction of people's labor process in ancient times, or a link in the labor process, or the review and rehearsal of labor. These are closely related to the mode of production and lifestyle at that time. For example, there are more than 20 seedling patterns related to them, such as "shoulder pole hook" and "tableware".

2.4.2 Guzi Yangko is shaped by martial dance and tempered in military war

In history, the Qi, Qin, Han and Tang dynasties had their heyday of economic prosperity from the early to the mid-term of the founding of the country. Poetry, songs, and dance were also consistent with the development of history, showing the unique optimism and vigorous spirit of the feudal system in adolescence. Even if it was a hardware, they were bound to move forward. For example, during the reign of emperor Ruizong of the Tang Dynasty, Wang Han wrote "Exquisite wine in cups that glitter at night; The pipa playing on horseback urges us to drink. Laugh not if we lie drunk on the battlefield". The famous poem of Huang Chao, the leader of the peasant uprising during the reign of emperor Xiaozong of the Tang Dynasty, wrote "When autumn comes, I will invade Chang'an wearing golden armor". How heroic and broad-minded the poet is. Shanghe Guzi Yangko, which was formed by martial dance during the Tang and Song dynasties, has the spiritual characteristics of this era and is branded with the brand of the times. After thousands of performances, militarized organizational form, unpredictable dance formation, straightforward and bold style of soldiers and men, and invincible heroic momentum are formed in this form of art, which also show the temperament and character of the men in Shandong, and the concept of dance. The Yangko performers express their emotions, show their strength, and present their beauty and strength. It is sometimes like a dragon waving its tail, a short Bo killing, a group of tigers descending the mountain, a moving cloud and flowing water. Sometimes, it is like nothing. It feels like some virtual entities and abstract art. It is the combination of soul and flesh, the rise and fall and rhythm change of force, the outline to which the force is gathered, the battle song of wrestling, and people's self-awareness and awakening of the life system. Affirmation, pursuit and performance are filled with the emotional color of the children of Huang in the space style that continues and changes over time, beating the tenacious life pulse of the Chinese people, and the actors resonate with the audience with strong shock.

2.4.3 Guzi Yangko has gradually transformed from practical and utilitarian art to self-entertainment

With the social progress, production development and cultural development, Guzi Yangko gradually transformed from the practical utilitarian art of reducing the burden of labor, encouraging fighting enthusiasm and sacrificial ceremony to the spiritual utilitarian art of blessing entertainment and self-entertainment.

The main tone evolved from mystery to joy, which developed and prospered in the Ming and Qing dynasties.

Many victims moved from Henan, Hebei, Shanxi, Yunnan and other provinces in the late Yuan and early Ming dynasties and from Zaoqiang, Wuyi and other counties in the late Ming and early Qing dynasties. These immigrants not only promoted the local economic development, but also made the folk songs and dances more colorful due to the confluence of music and dance cultures in Shanghe. Guzi Yangko is commonly known as "paoshiwu" and "naowanyier", highlighting the words "running" and "playing". A complete Guzi Yangko performance includes three parts, namely "umbrella drum", Yangko song and vaudeville, with singing and dancing. Because dancers don't sing and singers don't dance, there are many Yangko teams, most of which can reach 600 or 700 people. The order of performance is as follows: In the front stage (martial arts field), umbrella and drum dance performance, acrobatic Yangko, and umbrella and drum dance performance. This comprehensive form of expression can be traced back to the "Baixi" (hundred operas) of the Han Dynasty.

"Baixi" is a collection of songs, dances, and vaudeville. In the Han Dynasty, "Baixi" was called "jiaodixi", in the Northern and Southern dynasties, "Baixi" was called "Sanyue", and flourished. Meng Yuanlao of the Southern Song Dynasty recorded in the dream of China in Tokyo: "Every Lantern Festival, there are hundreds of songs and dances, the scales are tangent, and the music is noisy for more than ten miles."

The "hundred operas" in Shanghe County have been preserved up to now. In addition to umbrella and drum dance performance, there are more than 30 kinds of operas, such as those named huabiangu, fengyanghuagu, huagun, caicha, xiaoche, datou, gaoqiao, longdeng, shibao, dengguan, huniudou, hehuadeng, duganjiao, er ren zhuan, hanchuan, paolv, ganjiao, xingche, macha, wuchang, cuobozi, beixifu, errenshuai, yaohulu, daquan, and haha, and so on.

3.Roles, costumes, props

"San": The role of "san" can be divided into "tousan" and "huasan". "tousan", also known as "chousan", is played by middle-aged and elderly men, mostly configured with 4-8 people. It is the Group Commander of the Yangko team, which is banned by the party. One or two of the tousans are called leading umbrellas, which are the principal and deputy commanders. The dress includes white hair, white beard, white robe, yellow headband, red trousers and light shoes. The left hand holds the umbrella, and the right hand holds the "barge hammer". Huasan is the leader of the "flower", which is played by young men in general equal to "tousan", the costumes are green clothes, green headband, black beard, black boots, umbrella holding and bronze bell (some use Huzeng used by Jianghu doctors).

The use of "san" props has its ancient cultural factors. "san" is a flat top imperial umbrella, which has the meaning of sheltering the four directions and good weather. "san" has a yellow headband. Yellow is a bright and auspicious color, representing Chinese people with yellow skin who drink Yellow River water; and respect of the Yellow Emperor God. In addition, the emperor uses the yellow color, so it is the color of authority. The head of "inserting san" has a diameter of 80-100 cm". The diameter of the head of "san" is 70-80 cm, the rod length is 100-120 cm. The head diameter of "dasan" is 50-70 cm, and the rod length is 70 cm. The color of "san" cover is yellow, white and red, and "huasan" is blue and gray. The cover of female "huasan" is made of silk and flowers, and the flower brocade are elegant and luxurious. "Jucan", the barge hammer used for "carrying san" is cattle crotch bone, which is a kind of ancient percussion apparatus. Some barge hammers are made of Sangzhe wood, which is 1 foot long (according to the spring in the fourth season) and 3 feet wide 6 inches (based on 360 days), and 1 inch 2 inches (based on 12 months). Children's shoes tied to the waist represent the praying for their children and grandchildren to be safe. The wine cup in the shoes means that there is not only food to eat, but also wine to drink.

"Gu": Also known as "guzi", it is the main force of Yangko team played by young men. It is mostly configured with 24, 32 and 48, and 64 people. The left hand holds a double-sided round drum, and the right hand holds a stick to beat and dance. The drum surface is 26 cm in diameter and 12 cm thick, the drum cavity is sealed with red cloth and decorated with several strips of red silk, and the bottom end is covered with a leather strap ring on the hand cell, which can be turned freely (the hand drum of guzi Yangko is similar to the drum shape of "stepping on the drum" in the portrait stone of Han Dynasty in Shandong, except that one hand and one foot). The costumes are yellow clothes, yellow trousers, yellow head, bright hero courage on the scarf, red hero belt and shallow shoes. Now some women in Beixiang village dress up as "gu", and their clothes are red and heroic.

"Bang": Also known as "bangchui", it is played by young men. The number of people is less than that of "Gu", which is often 8 and 16. The actors are equipped with double sticks, with a length of 60 cm, a slow colored tassel at the sample end, black clothes, green hero belt on the cross, iron arrows hanging on the black head (red butterfly, small round mirror).

"Hua": There are two kinds of this role "dihua" and "xiaohua", played by female actors. "Dihua" is the person with two wings running on the ground, and "xiaohua" is the one running on stilts. The stilt is 50 cm high. Before and after liberation, it is generally played by men. Now it is played by girls and young women. The costumes are flower jackets, flower pleated skirts, cloaks, red silk flowers, left-hand flower baskets (bouquets, lanterns, wreaths), right-hand dusts (in silk), and left-hand scarves. Now, most of the costumes are to show off their own beauty "appearance" and high "bright boxes". They are mainly painted with paint and powder. They wear beautiful clothes.

"Chou": Male actors, also known as "waichou", "erdianzi", "Mr. Wang", "silly wife", etc. "Chou is skilled in the Yangko field array and commands secretly for performing Yangko. They filled in the space between the two "umbrella dances".

They also sing and speak, with funny words to amuse people.

The costumes of "Gu", "Bang", "Hua" and "Chou" are influenced by dance, with steady, natural and unrestrained, heroic and handsome as the main tone. For example, "San" is like Xiao En in *A Fisherman's Struggle*, "Gu" is like Wu Xia, "Bang" is like Yan Qing, and "Hua" is like the female soldiers in *Zuke Stronghold*. Chou's clothing and makeup take ugliness as beauty.

Singer: Ranging from 2 to 10 people, wearing casual clothes, mainly singing Yangko tune.

Folk band: It includes suona, sheng, flute, pipe, erhu, sanxian, jinghu, tanggu, banhu, small gong, small sickle, etc., mainly accompanied by Yangko tune or instrument.

Juggling includes martial arts, dry boats, lions, stilts, etc. The number of people performing in the form of juggling depends on the conditions of each village.

Drum band: It is composed of one big drum, 2 cymbals, 2 cymbals and 2 Gongs. The diameter of big drum surface is 80-120 cm. The drum sounds like thunder. The big drum is the conductor and cooperates with the "leading umbrella".

Preparation: The allocation ratio of "San", "Gu", "Bang", "Huasan" and "Hua" is generally 1:4:2:1: 4. For a Yangko team, if "Tousan" 4 and "Gu" 16 (24, 32, 48), "Bang" 8 (16,24), "Huasan" (4), and "Hua" (16, or 24, 36), "Chou" is an even number, generally 2. The role allocation and total number of 4 people are based on 2. Only in this way can it maintain the symmetry, balance, integrity and fullness of Yangko field.

第 10 节　商羊舞

1.项目文化

商羊舞属汉族民间舞蹈，流传于山东省菏泽市鄄城县李进士堂乡杏花岗村（又叫"陈刘村"）一带，为杏花岗村一带所独有。杏花岗上有座三官庙，庙内塑有尧、舜、禹三大圣贤像，历代香火盛行，热闹非凡，古老的商羊舞就起源于这里。商羊舞过去是祈雨祭祀专用舞蹈，相传商羊舞最早可追溯到商周时期，距今已有数千年的历史，后渐演变为该村在三官庙前祈雨专用舞蹈。新中国成立以后，又逐渐演变成为一种民间娱乐艺术形式的舞蹈，由此完成了从“娱神到娱人”的转变。

商羊舞历史悠久，既带有浓浓的神话色彩，又带有浓厚的古老历史文明与文化气息，在历代的风俗中都占据着极其重要的地位。

2.项目起源

商羊舞是具有地方风格和民俗特色的民间舞蹈之一，是菏泽鄄城人民传统文化的一种表现形式。它植根于鄄城人民群体的文化传统和文化历史之中，也是被广泛认同的中华民族具有美好象征意义的舞蹈之一。

相传商羊是一种吉祥的水鸟。每当快要下雨时，它们便从高山、树林中飞出来，落在杏花岗上，边戏耍边啄食，或蹦跳追逐，或仰天低鸣，或曲颈浅水，直到天降大雨方散。人们见商羊出现，就知道雨要降临。每当天旱久不下雨时，人们就盼望商羊的出现。后来，不知是因为强烈的地震还是涛涛的水患，或是人类的繁衍使杏花岗一带不再适应商羊鸟的生存，不管天气如何干旱，商羊鸟都不再出现。人们求雨心切，为了感动上天，就自扮商羊鸟，戴面具、拿响板、结彩铃，模仿商羊鸟的动作，舞蹈蹦跳。这种模仿商羊鸟求雨的动作与传统的祭祀仪式逐渐结合在了一起，经过鄄城先民们的不断升华、完善，逐渐成为一种民间舞蹈——商羊舞，并且这种活动除了在天旱求雨时进行外，还形成了固定的举行日期——每年三月三，自商周起，世代相传至今。

3.项目规则

过去商羊舞是祈雨的专用舞蹈，由 12 个赤背光脚少年组成。而现在它已经演变为一种群众性自娱集体舞蹈，舞队也变成由 12～16 人组成(男女各半)。队员上穿彩衣，下着彩裤，腰系彩带，手拿响板，上系铜铃一对和红缨结成的花一朵，脚脖上各系铜铃一对，在乐队的伴奏下，手持响板跳舞，模仿商羊鸟的动作，同时双手执板边舞边打节奏，响板撞击发出脆响。队员表演时，动作有时蹦跳热烈，有时嬉戏玩闹，把商羊鸟的神态表现得活灵活现。

商羊舞动作一

Shangyang Dance action 1

4.动作解析

商羊舞的主要动作有:①行走动作:双手托响板于胸前竖立撞击,一脚抬起跳动向上。②泰山压顶:女队员蹲下手持响板撞击,男队员站立手持响板,响板头向下击节,表现商羊鸟的欢快起舞。③抵头:男女队员各持响板分两队,响板头互相抵着,并且击节表演(传说商羊鸟抵头,天空就会下雨)。另外,此舞还有"商羊腿""前仰后合步""前跳步""后弓步""咯噔步""踌躇步"等动作。其中"咯噔步"是商羊舞基本步法之一,它模仿的是商羊一足蹦跳行走的样子。"踌躇步"的要领是前脚掌向前点地迅速收回,就像行走在河边或沼泽地似的,大有一不小心就会陷进泥潭的感觉,这可能是商羊鸟因为此地古代遍布河流沼泽所形成的一种行为习惯。

商羊舞的队形变化较为丰富,主要队形有:①上山:集体上场。②下山:集体下场。③卷箔:向内转圈,交叉队形。④二龙吐须:男女两队由中心向外翻转。⑤交麻花。⑥商羊戏水等。商羊舞是一种舞者将舞蹈与伴奏相结合的艺术形式,表演动作独特、节奏明快,颇有上古舞蹈之遗风,原始古朴、别具韵味,具有浓郁的鲁西南文化气息及风格特点。

商羊舞动作二

Shangyang Dance action 2

5.项目器械

商羊舞的伴奏最初就是以鼓为主，兼以锣、钹、镲、梆等打击乐器，所以商羊舞也叫“商羊鼓舞”。后来，人们又根据气氛和场合的需要增加了笛、笙、二胡、坠琴等乐器。商羊舞的音乐最初主要以祭祀乐为主，后来受民间音乐及地方文化的影响，逐渐形成极具特色的商羊舞专用伴奏。领奏乐器为鲁西南地方特色乐器坠琴，其音色高亢、浑厚，极具表现力。音乐节拍为板眼相间的 2/4 拍，节奏快、富有动感。

表演道具响板也叫“阴阳板”，是商羊舞的主要道具，材质为枣木，分红、黄两种颜色(黄色代表丰收，红色代表财运)，分别刻印龙凤图案。响板由主板和侧板组成，主板长 65 厘米，侧板长 55 厘米。表演时男舞者持黄色响板，演奏时左手执响板之主板，右手套在侧板线圈内，女舞者则持红色响板，右手执主板。

6.项目传承人

商羊舞自商周起历经三千多年流传至今，主要是通过“族内袭承”的模式进行传承。所谓“族内袭承”，就是以血缘关系为纽带代代相传，即同宗族家庭成员间的世代传承，主要以“口传心授”的方式进行。由于缺少文字性史料记载，关于商羊舞和其传承的问题，很多已不可考证。

从商羊舞的传承谱系来看，其与中国大多数戏曲和民间艺术形式一样，采用的都是较为传统、保守的家族式传承，虽然有一定的局限性，但这种口传心授的方式却能使所传技艺保持原汁原味并更加精益求精。富有地方特色和民俗特色的商羊舞是鄄城传统文化的代表，它涉及鄄城节日习俗的方方面面，具有重要的人类学、民俗学研究价值。现在因时代变迁，商羊舞后继乏人，生存困难，亟待保护。

7.项目新发展

商羊舞经过数千年的传承发展，在鄄城县杏花岗一带落地扎根，在这片古老的土地上延续着自己独特的艺术形式。新中国成立后，随着社会生产力的不断提高，科学技术的迅速发展，农业经济发展得到较好的保障，人民生活水平不断提高，祭神求雨的活动越来越少。商羊舞祈雨祭神的性质逐渐消失，而在舞蹈中逐渐融入了娱乐的性质，商羊舞也随之逐渐演变为自娱自乐的广场舞蹈艺术形式。在商羊舞从祈神求雨到娱人自娱转变的同时，也说明了智慧的鄄城人在中国共产党的带领下，从愚昧走向了科学，从贫穷走向了富裕。商羊舞作为鄄城县杏花岗村一带所独有的舞蹈形式，并没有形成众多的流派、门类，而是在当地一脉相传。

商羊舞在自身发展的过程中也影响到了当地的其他民间艺术形式。20 世纪 50 年代初，为了庆祝解放，菏泽城内民权街游艺班个个献艺，有个叫卞寿起的青年，把商羊舞和高跷揉为一体，创造了“独脚高跷”，这项新的民间艺术形式，备受观众喜爱。他还曾到济南表演，也给省城观众留下了深刻的印象。近年来，随着民族文化的弘扬，独脚高跷也在菏泽民间广泛流传。

Shangyang Dance

1.Project culture

Shangyang Dance is the folk dance of Han nationality, which is popular in the area of Xinghuagang Village (Chenliu Village), Lijinshitang Town,

Juancheng County, Heze City, Shandong Province. In the village, there is a Sanguan Temple, where there are three statues of sages—Yao, Shun, and Yu. The temple was prosperous in the past and is still so nowadays. The Shangyang Dance originated right here. The dance was especially for praying for rain, which conveyed people's yearning for rain after too long drought in order to have a good harvest. That is also people's wish for a better life. According to the legend, the Shangyang Dance has a history of thousands of years, which can be traced back to the Shang Dynasty, and then gradually evolved into the special dance in front of the Sanguan Temple. After the founding of the People's Republic of China, it gradually became a folk entertainment dance, completing the transition from "entertaining the gods" to "entertaining people".

Shangyang Dance has a long history with a strong mythological color, a rich ancient civilization and a dense cultural atmosphere. It occupies an extremely important position in the customs of the past dynasties.

2.Project origin

Shangyang Dance is one of the folk dances with local folklore characteristics, which is a manifestation of the traditional Juancheng culture. Hence, it is rooted in the tradition and history and is one of the widely recognized beautiful and symbolic dances of the Chinese nation.

According to the legend, Shangyang was a kind of auspicious water bird. When it was about to rain, they flew out of the mountains and woods and landed on the Xinghuagang area, playing, pecking, jumping, chasing, or rising to the sky and bending their necks in shallow water, until a heavy rain fell. When people saw the Shangyang bird, they knew that the rain was coming. Therefore, whenever the drought weather lasted too long, people looked forward to seeing the Shangyang bird. Later, perhaps because of strong earthquake, flash flood, human reproduction or other unknown reasons, the Xinghuagang area became an unsuitable place for Shangyang birds to live. Therefore, they did not appear anymore, no matter how dry the weather was.

So, in order to move God to rain, people imitated Shangyang bird's movements to jump and dance with masks on face, castanets and ring bells in hand, pretending Shangyang birds came back. This imitation for rain is gradually combined with the traditional sacrificial rituals. After the continuous improvement of the ancestors in Juancheng County, it has gradually become a kind of folk dance—the Shangyang Dance. And it is not only performed for rain during the drought, but also danced on a fixed date—March 3 of each year—since the Shang and Zhou dynasties. It has been passed down for generations.

3.Project rules

In the past, Shangyang Dance was a special dance for praying for rain, which was composed of twelve male teenagers who were bare-foot and bare-upper body. Nowadays it has evolved into a collective dance for self-entertainment, and the dance team has turned to 12-16 people (men and women by half). The players wear colorful clothes and colored ribbons on the waist, with castanets in hands and a pair of copper bells on the ankles. On the castanets, there is also a pair of copper bells and a flower of red tassel. Accompanied by the band, they imitate the movements of Shangyang birds and beat the rhythm with castanets in hands to make a crisp sound. The movements are sometimes bouncing, sometimes frolicking to show Shangyang birds' demeanor vividly.

4.Action parsing

The main movements of Shangyang Dance are as follows: (1) Walking movement: Performers hold the castanets to hit upright before the chest. At the same time, one foot lifts up to jump upwards. (2) Taishanyading (hitting castanets): Female performers squat down and hold the castanets to hit, while male ones stand upright and hold the castanets to hit them (the castanets' heads down), which show Shangyang birds' dance with joy. (3) Against heads: Male and female performers are divided into two teams, and each of them holds castanets of which heads are against each other. And they hit the beat to dance. (Legend has it that when the Shangyang birds' heads are against each other, it will rain.). In addition, there are some other dance steps, such as Shangyang leg, forward and backward steps, forward jump, backward lunge step, jump step, hesitation step and so on. Jump step is one of the basic footwork of Shangyang Dance, which imitates Shangyang bird's jump on one foot. Hesitation step is to put the front of the sole forward and then retract quickly, just like walking on a river or a swamp carefully to avoid sinking, which may be a living habit left under the geographical environment of rivers and swamps in ancient times.

The formation of Shangyang Dance is quite varied, and the main ones are as follows: (1) Going up the mountain. Performers show up on the stage collectively. (2) Going down the mountain. Performers go off the stage collectively. (3) Rolling foil. The performers line up to turn inward and make crosses. (4) Two dragons spitting the whiskers. The men's and women's teams turn outwards from the center separately. (5) Crossing twists. (6) Shangyang bird playing in the water, etc. Shangyang Dance is an art form that contains dance and music accompaniment. The performance is unique, and the rhythm is bright and lively, which is quite reminiscent of ancient dance. It is primitive and simple with unique charm, and it has a strong flavor and style of the culture in southwestern area, Shandong Province.

5.Project apparatus

Originally, drums were the main accompaniment apparatus of Shangyang Dance, combined with percussions such as gongs, cymbals, cymbals, and bang-zi (a kind of Chinese traditional wooden percussion), therefore Shangyang Dance was also called "Shangyang Drum Dance". Later, to heighten the atmosphere and conform to the scene, other apparatuses were also added, such as flute, sheng, erhu, and zhuiqin (a kind of Chinese traditional string apparatus). At first, accompaniment music was mainly sacrificial and then formed a special one influenced by folk music and local culture for Shangyang Dance. Today the leading accompaniment apparatus is zhuiqin, a local characteristic one in southwestern area of Shandong Province, which has a high-pitched, vigorous and expressive tone. The beat of accompaniment music is 2/4, which has alternate strong and weak ones. The rhythm is fast and dynamic.

The castanets, also called "yin and yang boards", are the main props of Shangyang Dance. The material is jujube wood and has two colors: red and yellow (yellow represents a good harvest and red represents wealth). The dragon and phoenix patterns are engraved respectively on them. The castanets are composed of a main board, 65 cm long, and a sideboard, 55 cm long. Male dancers hold the yellow castanets during the performance, with the main board in the left hand, and the right hand in the sideboard coil. While female dancers hold the red ones with the main board in the right hand. When they hold the castanets with both hands and swing their arms left and right, up and down to tap the castanets, the main board hits the side one, making a clear and loud sound, which is quite imposing.

6.Project inheritor

Shangyang Dance has been passed down for more than 3,000 years since the Shang and Zhou dynasties, mainly with the mode of "inheriting within the patriarchal clan" from generation to generation by blood relationship. In other words, the passing down of Shangyang Dance is only among members in the same patriarchal clan by the way of "oral instruction". Due to the lack of written historical records, many things about Shangyang Dance and its inheritance are unverifiable. Now, it has been passed down to the 16th and 17th generations, represented by Chen Zechuan and Chen Fenge in Xinghuagang Village.

From the perspective of the inheriting, Shangyang Dance adopts a relatively traditional and conservative way, just as Chinese operas and many folk arts. Although it has certain limitations, this oral teaching way can keep the traditional skill original and keep Shangyang Dance improving.

The Shangyang Dance has many local and folk characteristics, which is the representative of the Juancheng county traditional culture. It involves many aspects of Juancheng's festival customs and has an important value in anthropology and folklore research. Due to the changes of the times, at present the Shangyang Dance is short of successors and difficult to survive, therefore it needs immediate protection.

7.New development

After thousands of years of passing down and developing, Shangyang Dance has taken root in Xinghuagang area, Juancheng County, and has also kept its features in the ancient land. After the founding of the People's Republic of China, the agricultural economic development has been guaranteed and the people's living standard has been improving with the continuous improvement of social productivity and the rapid development of science and technology. There are fewer and fewer activities of praying to the gods for rain, so the original meaning of Shangyang Dance gradually disappeared, and the entertainment was gradually integrated into it. Later it evolved into a square dance for self-entertainment. The changing process from praying for rain to entertaining themselves, also shows that Juancheng people have changed from ignorance to science, from poverty to wealth under the leadership of Communist Party of China. As a unique dance in Xinghuagang area, Juancheng County, Shangyang Dance does not have many genres and categories, but is only passed down in one local patriarchal clan.

Shangyang Dance also influenced other local folk arts during its development. In the early 1950s, in order to celebrate the liberation, the entertainment group at Minquan Street, Heze City made a performance. A young man named Bian Shouqi created a new "one-legged stilt", combining Shangyang Dance and stilts together, which were very popular with the audience. He also performed in Jinan and gave a deep impression on the audience in the provincial capital. In recent years, with the promotion of national culture, the one-legged stilt is still widely spread among the people of Heze.

第11节　鼓舞

1.项目文化

中华鼓舞多以鼓谱丰富、情绪热烈、底蕴深厚为特点，流行于全国各地，影响遍及全世界。《易·系辞》中有“鼓之舞之以尽神”之语，既反映了中华鼓舞历史的悠久，又提纲挈领地道出了其主要功能。从原始的“击石拊石，百兽率舞”到后世的流行遍及大江南北，华夏鼓舞始终一脉相承，绵延不绝。中华鼓舞形制多样，分布广泛，舞蹈姿态各异，种类千差万别，其中较为典型的形态有腰鼓舞、鼗鼓舞、花鼓(灯)舞、木鼓舞、长鼓舞、扁鼓舞、铜鼓舞、龙鼓舞、扇鼓舞、黄泥鼓舞、象脚鼓舞、猴儿鼓舞、花鞭鼓舞、竹鼓舞、铃鼓舞、羊皮鼓舞等多种。

鼓是人类最早发明的乐器之一，也是人类最早用于舞蹈表演的道具之一。在蛮荒年代，鼓就陪伴在人类身边。在中华民族大家庭中，汉族和各个少数民族很早就都拥有了带有自己本民族特色的鼓和鼓舞。在漫长的发展历史中，各民族的鼓和鼓舞都成为民族文化不可分割的重要部分。

在汉族数千年的社会发展历史中，鼓的应用非常广泛，上起古代帝王的祭祀大典、宫廷宴乐，下至普通百姓祈雨庆丰、年节自娱，几乎所有需要乐舞的集体活动都离不开鼓的参与。

在汉族聚居的地方表演鼓舞已经成为一种生活习惯。由于区域文化的不同，鼓舞的表演形式又分化为具有地方特色的多样化形式，如开封盘鼓、凤阳花鼓、山西威风锣鼓、陕北腰鼓等。由于鼓舞的广泛普及和鼓舞表演时振奋人心的情绪特质，以至于“鼓舞”这个词语本身在汉语中具有了特定的含义，即振作、奋发，取振奋人们的信心，增强人们的勇气之意。汉代扬雄在《法言·先知》中提道：“鼓舞万物者，雷风乎？鼓舞万从者，号令乎？”

汉族的日常生活，正在使用着为数众多跟鼓和鼓舞相关的词语和成语，如“鼓动”“鼓吹”“鼓舞”“鼓掌”“鼓励”“鼓足干劲”“鼓舞人心”“鼓舞士气”“一鼓作气”“鼓角齐鸣”“鼓舞欢欣”“鼓唇弄舌”“鼓乐齐鸣”“鼓乐喧天”等。从这些词语和成语的使用频率和适用范围来看，鼓和鼓舞早已深入到汉族人民的生活之中。

虽然现在西方音乐和乐器在中国已经司空见惯，但在大多数需要乐舞的场合，唱主角的仍然是以鼓为主的中国传统乐器。

2.项目起源

鼓和鼓舞紧密相连，有鼓才有鼓舞。作为一种对中国各民族具有重要意义的乐器和舞蹈表演形式，有必要对鼓舞的产生状况进行仔细研究。考察汉族和少数民族地区鼓的起源就能得知鼓舞的起源。

2.1　汉族鼓舞的起源

鼓作为汉族音乐舞蹈艺术最主要的乐器之一，起源非常早，具体的形成时间不详。但是根据史料记载，关于蒙皮鼓的创制起源主要是圣人制鼓说，如《山海经·大荒东经》认为鼓是由黄帝发明的，《礼记·明堂位》认为鼓是由伊耆氏发明的，而明代罗欣在其著作《物原·乐原》中认为鼓是由神农氏发明的，种种传说不一而足。从考古发掘的成果来看，现存最早的蒙皮鼓——陶鼓，其历史可以上溯到新石器时代，《图说中国舞蹈史》中记载了一件新石器时代“永登乐山坪陶鼓”，这是一件原始社会晚期的打击乐器，用红陶土制成，原为喇叭口处蒙兽皮而作鼓声。其实鼓的起源历史应该更早，据《尚书正义·益稷第五》记载：“於！予击石拊石，百兽率舞，庶尹允谐。”另外《列子全译·黄帝第二》也有记载：“尧使夔典乐，击石拊石，百兽率舞，《箫韶》九成，凤凰来仪，此以声致禽兽者也。”从这两条史料来看，远古时期就有敲击石头作为舞蹈伴奏乐器的做法，虽然有石头做的专门乐器——石磬，但是客观上还是起到了鼓的作用。鼓被创造出来之后即受到广泛的应用，所以汉族鼓的起源即鼓舞的起源。

2.2　少数民族鼓舞的起源

少数民族地区的鼓舞起源也相当早，从现在能查到的资料来看，少数民族鼓舞起源跟汉族鼓舞的起源时间相差无几。这一点也显示出人类文化发展的共通性，由于鼓的形制相对简单，制作难度较小，所以鼓是各族人民最先发明和使用的主要乐器之一。相比汉族鼓的起源在各种史籍中被详细记载，少数民族鼓的起源大都流传于神话传说之中。尤其在中国西南的少数民族地区，有的民族对鼓具有十分特殊的喜好，甚至于把鼓当作跟自己祖先一样神圣的圣物。这种情况在佤族尤为典型，根据刘金吾《中国西南少数民族的鼓文化》中的研究，佤族中流传的木鼓起源是跟佤族祖先同时出现的。他们认为，佤族祖先是从一个被称为“司岗里”的地方出来的，与这些人一起出来的有一些动物，另外还有一个木鼓。其他少数民族也有类似的民族祖先和鼓起源的传说，虽然这种传说是建立在想象虚构的基础之上，但我们从中可以看出鼓在这些少数民族人民心中的重要地位。《中国西南少数民族的鼓文化》还列举了更为可信的鼓起源的传说，分别是佤族和哈尼族的木鼓。传说在古代，佤族有一对男女在山上，碰见一只老虎正在走来，这位佤族男子灵机一动，马上敲击一棵空心的树干，发出像鼓一样的响声，老虎听到后被吓走了，后来佤族人民便模仿空心树干创造出了木鼓。一直到现在，佤族的村寨中还有专门存放木鼓的木鼓房，里面供奉着一公一母两个木鼓。而哈尼族当中也流传着类似的传说，在古代，哈尼族主要以狩猎为生，猎人们在山火烧过的树林中打猎，无意中击打到空心树，空心树干发出很大的响声，哈尼族人受到启发创造出了木鼓。根据考古发掘的结果来看，现存历史最为久远的少数民族鼓的种类是铜鼓，主要分布于云南、贵州和广西等地区。考古学者通过考查出土的众多铜鼓发现，这些地区的铜鼓历史久远，从春秋战国一直到清代，都有各种类型的铜鼓，并且在众多少数民族地区中都有发现，包括苗族、壮族、彝族、傣族、瑶族、佤族、布依族、水族等。戴宁在《中国打击乐研究——古代鼓的起源与分类》中认为，铜鼓是从工具铜釜蜕变而来，楚雄万家坝和牟定小香贝苴出土的鼓是现知最原始的铜鼓，年代约相当于2600年前的春秋早期。钱茀在《土鼓访真》一文中也认为，在东周时期，南方少数民族就造出了神圣而又精美的铜鼓。由此可见，少数民族鼓的起源应该略晚于汉族鼓。

3.项目器械

鼓的形制分为两个方面：一为形，即形状；二为制，即大小。在汉族和少数民族使用的鼓中，存在着形状和大小各异的众多类型。

汉族鼓从最开始“击石拊石”，敲击石头发出声响形成节奏作为舞蹈的伴奏，这些石头起到了鼓的作用，可以说这是汉族最早的鼓——石鼓。由于远古时期技术手段极为落后，要把大块石头钻孔做成空心鼓是极为困难的，可以想见作为初级伴奏乐器的原始实心石鼓使用起来十分不便，音响效果也极差。随着社会生产力的发展，先民们学会了烧制陶器，并且将这一项技术用在了鼓的制作当中，发明了“土鼓”，即用陶土塑造为鼓身，再将兽皮蒙于鼓身之上，成为严格意义上的“鼓”。古代文献《周礼注疏》中有关于土鼓制作的记载，“土鼓，以瓦为框，以革为两面，可击也。”郑注《礼运》云：“土鼓，筑土为鼓也。蒯桴，桴谓击鼓之物，以土块为桴。”由此两条资料可以看出，最初的土鼓，其形应该是圆的，其制应该不太大，因为较大的陶质鼓身容易破裂，如果为了结实而将鼓身造得很厚的话，鼓的重量就要大大增加，使用时会更为不便。钱茀在《土鼓访真》一文中也认为，远古人多用瓦桶为鼓，鼓面可能是在兽皮的边沿直接钻孔，再以藤蔓或动物筋连接捆扎在鼓桶上的。戴宁在《中国打击乐研究——古代鼓的起源与分类》一文中也提到，鼓最初的形制是以土为鼓腔，用草扎的鼓棒敲击，后发展成烧土为陶以作鼓腔，最后形成了木制鼓腔、铜制鼓和石制鼓。从鼓的形制分析，根据戴宁的研究，中国古代汉族鼓大概有以下几种类型：①从鸣响的类别上可以分为两种——膜鸣类和体鸣类，汉族鼓都属于膜鸣类，体鸣类鼓主要见于少数民族地区的铜鼓和石鼓。②根据不同形制可分为大鼓类、建鼓类、鼗鼓类、悬鼓类、手鼓类五大类型，大鼓类主要包括大鼓、赤鼓、花腔鼓、教坊鼓和大将鼓，这类鼓的特征为体积大，蒙皮、凸腹，放置于鼓架之上，双槌击打；建鼓类主要包括建鼓、应鼓、晋鼓、树鼓、楹鼓，这类鼓的特征是体积中等，蒙皮、凸腹，以木柱树贯之，双槌击打。鼗鼓类包括鼗鼓、拨浪鼓、雷鼗、头鼓、路鼗、灵鼗、两耳鼓等，这类鼓的特征为体积小，蒙皮、凸腹，拿在手中摇动，使鼓两边的耳槌自行击打鼓面；悬鼓类包括悬鼓、灵鼓、鼖鼓、雷鼓和路鼓等，这类鼓的特点是体积中等，蒙皮、凸腹，用钩将鼓悬挂在鼓架之下，双槌击打；手鼓类包括手鼓、提鼓、扁鼓、太平鼓、小鼓子和八角鼓等，这类鼓的特征为体积小、鼓身扁，蒙皮、凸腹，既可以握在手中，也可以放置在鼓架上或挂在胸前，用手或者鼓槌击打。[①]

4.项目分类

4.1　陈官短穗花鼓

陈官短穗花鼓是一种独特的民间舞蹈，流传于山东省东营市广饶县陈官乡一带及商河县等地，它原是流浪艺人借以乞讨谋生的手段。清朝时，广饶县陈官乡陈官村的张洪祥、张洪果跟随父亲张延水逃荒要饭，在此过程中逐渐学会了打花鼓。另据商河县的张凤云、李喜平等老艺人传述，清光绪二十九年以卖唱为生的王立礼、王立义兄弟与广饶艺人流浪到北京时学习并掌握了打花鼓技艺，随后便将这种表演形式传到广饶、商河一带的黄河下游地区。

陈官短穗花鼓由一人打镲说唱，一人击鼓表演，动作舒展、奔放，讲究“打场

① 参见戴宁：《中国打击乐研究——古代鼓的起源与分类》，《交响（西安音乐学院学报）》1997 年第 4 期。

脚微颠，八字腿弓箭；击打头略晃，跑鼓轻如仙”。击鼓有三四十种套路，如张飞骗马、苏秦背剑等。现突破为一人唱或两人对唱，多人以锣、镲等伴奏，代表曲目有《串九州》《枕头记》等。

新中国成立后，党和政府对陈官短穗花鼓非常重视，将其加工提炼后搬上舞台，使这一民间舞蹈由过去的要饭手段变成了艺术。1956 年，广饶张延水的徒弟李宏元和商河县张凤云、李喜平的短穗花鼓舞参加山东省民间艺术会演获奖。民间艺人张毅特地到陈官乡学习短穗花鼓，她表演的《花鼓舞》在 1957 年世界第六届青年联欢节上荣获金奖。

陈官短穗花鼓用鼓声歌声来表现对幸福生活的追求，独具当地的乡土风情，是当地传统文化的代表，具有人类学、民俗学研究价值。

陈官短穗花鼓动作难度大，因而流传不多。近年来，由于文化生态环境的改变，陈官短穗花鼓面临着严重的生存危机，如人才匮乏、传承不力，急需保护扶持。

4.2 柳林花鼓

山东省冠县的柳林花鼓是“鼓子秧歌”的一种，其最初表演形式为“地秧歌”，后逐渐发展演变成“走街秧歌”。柳林花鼓约起源于清朝初年，所演绎的故事起源于《水浒》，百姓将宋江、吴用等化装成花鼓艺人劫法场救卢俊义的故事与本地流传的鼓子秧歌结合，变成固定表演形式延续下来，最终发展成“柳林花鼓”这种独特的民间舞蹈。目前，它仅存于山东省冠县柳林镇，演出范围及于周边临清、聊城的数十个乡镇和河北馆陶等地。

柳林花鼓原来包括两部分内容：第一部分表现梁山好汉一路载歌载舞、化装进城的情形；第二部分表现他们劫法场营救卢俊义的战斗场面。现在保留下来的仅是第一部分。

柳林花鼓由舞蹈和武术融合而成，文武兼备、粗犷豪放、泼辣火爆。从艺术角度看，柳林花鼓特色鲜明、风格独特，在形形色色的“鼓子秧歌”中独树一帜，而且具有浓烈的地方特色，是土生土长的民间艺术，唱词中充满了当地的俗词俚语，对于研究当地民间文化发展具有重要意义。柳林花鼓在冠县当地享有很高声誉，历史上一直是临清庙会的重点节目。新中国成立初期，柳林花鼓曾在华东民间艺术会演中获得一等奖，并赴抗美援朝前线慰问演出。近年来，柳林花鼓的艺人队伍日益老龄化，传承面临危机，前景堪忧，亟待抢救保护。

4.3　花鞭鼓舞

山东省商河县地处山东省鲁北平原，南距黄河 35 千米，东邻惠民县，北达乐陵市，西与临邑县接壤，花鞭鼓舞即流传于这一地区。清光绪年间商河的王立礼、王立义兄弟到北京卖艺，拜流落在京的艺人李桂珍、李明雄兄弟为师，学会花鞭鼓舞，回家后勤苦练习，技艺日进后王立礼兄弟将花鞭鼓舞技艺传授给乡人，一直流传至今。目前花鞭鼓舞在商河县张坊乡一带大为盛行，张坊乡苟家村的张氏家族几代都会跳花鞭鼓舞，逢年过节即进行演出，热闹非常。

花鞭鼓舞表演使用的是一般的腰鼓，同时以小锣、小镲伴奏。舞者头系白毛巾，身着短衣，左肋下斜挎腰鼓，双手各持一鞭，鞭杆长 22 厘米，鞭条长 50 厘米，鞭梢系成疙瘩。表演时两条鞭上下翻飞，甩至背后，在胸前和胯下准确地击打鼓面，鞭飞鼓鸣，独具一格，引人入胜。花鞭鼓舞有前八步、后八步、鹞子翻身、鲤鱼跳龙门、古树盘根、张飞骗马、苏秦背剑、二龙吐须、金丝葫芦、菊花盖顶、黑狗钻裆、就地十八滚等三十余种动作。表演时花鞭翻腾似金蛇狂舞，令人眼花缭乱，目不暇接；鼓音咚咚若战马奔腾，使人精神振奋，情绪高涨。

花鞭鼓舞充满鲁北地方色彩，具有历史文化、民俗学、舞蹈学等方面的研究价值。近年来，这一民间舞蹈的传承陷入窘境，发展前景令人忧虑，急需保护。

4.4　八卦鼓舞

八卦鼓舞是山东省唯一归属于道教文化的广场舞蹈，主要流传于山东省栖霞与福山交界的庙后镇一带，现只有庙后镇上林家村有传人。据史料记载，元代以来栖霞的道教活动十分频繁，重阳宫鼎盛之时，道士有百人之多，声势浩大。传统的道教斋醮仪式需以鼓乐配合，八卦鼓舞由是而产生。栖霞独特的地理位置和文化根基造就了与道教文化联系密切的八卦鼓舞，这种民间舞蹈与传统武术相融合，以祭祖、祈福、避邪等为目的，反映了当地人民祈求风调雨顺的理想和愿望。

八卦鼓舞以男女对舞形式演出，表演中步法、手势、队形都要求走八字，显示出轻、飘、蹲、转的特点。舞队一般由八男八女组成，男队员腰前挎八卦鼓，左手扶鼓，右手持鼓槌，女队员双手握圆形平顶古铜色伞舞蹈。整个表演以鼓为主，以伞为辅，鼓伞配合，相得益彰。八卦鼓舞队形变化较为简单，常出现“八条街”“双龙吐须”“单串花”“圆”中见“转”等样式。

鼓舞

Drum Dance

八卦鼓舞是山东民间舞蹈的瑰宝，也是中国道教艺术的一朵奇葩。近年来，大环境的变迁使它逐渐陷于濒临失传的境地，急需抢救保护。

Drum Dance

1.Project culture

Chinese drum dance is famous for its rich drum music, warm emotions and profound connotations. It has spread throughout the country and influenced the whole world. There is a saying in *Yi* · *Xi-Ci* that "the dance of drum is perfect", which not only vividly reflects the long history of Chinese drum dance, but also outlines its main functions. From the original "clapping stone, animals rate dance" to the later popularity throughout the country, the Chinese drum dance has always been a lineage of continuity. Chinese drum dance is widely distributed in various forms and styles. Typical forms include waist drum dance, la drum dance, flower drum (lamp) dance, wooden drum dance, long drum dance, flat drum dance, bronze drum dance, dragon drum dance, fan drum dance, yellow mud drum dance, elephant foot drum dance, monkey drum dance, flower whip drum dance, bamboo drum dance, bell drum dance, sheepskin drum dance and so on.

Drum is one of the earliest musical instruments invented by human beings, and also one of the earliest props used in dance performances. In the wild times, drums had accompanied human-beings. In 56 Chinese nations, the Han nationality and various ethnic minorities have long had their own ethnic characteristics of drum and drum dance. In the long history of development, drum and drum dance of all ethnic groups have become an integral part of national culture.

In thousands of years of social development of the Han Nationality, drum has been widely used from ancient emperors' sacrificial ceremonies and court feasts to ordinary people. It has been used for praying for rain and celebrating harvest, and annual festival entertainment. Almost all group activities requiring music and dance cannot be separated from the participation of drum.

It has become a living habit to perform drum dance in places inhabited by Han people. Because of the differences in regional culture, the performance forms of drum have been divided into diversified forms with local characteristics, such as Kaifeng Pangu, Fengyang flower-drum, Shanxi Weifeng logo and waist drum in North Shanxi. Due to the widespread popularity of drum dance and the exciting emotional characteristics, the word "encouragement" itself has a specific meaning in Chinese, that is, to cheer up and make progress; boost people's confidence; strengthen people's courage. Yang Xiong of the Han Dynasty mentioned in the *Fa Yan* • *Prophet*: "Who inspires all things, thunder and wind? Encourage all followers, the order? "

In the daily life of Han people, there are numerous words and idioms associated with drums and dancing, such as "encouraging" and "advocating", "inspiration", "applauding", "mustering", "inspiring", "morale", "pursuing", "beating the drums and blaring the trumpets", "inspiring delight", "drum lip tongue", "the music is everywhere", "happy music fills the air" and so on. From the frequency and scope of application of these words and idioms, drum and drum dance have already penetrated the life of the Han people.

Even today, western music and musical instruments are common in China, but in most occasions where music and dance are needed, traditional Chinese musical instruments, mainly drums, still play the leading role.

2.Project origin

Drum is closely related to drum and drum dance. Drum is the precondition of drum dance. As a musical apparatus and dance performance form of great significance to all ethnic groups in China, it is necessary to conduct a careful study on the emergence of drum. If we study the origin of drum in Han and minority regions, we can know the origin history of drum dance.

2.1 Origin of drum dance in Han nationality

As one of the most important musical instruments in the music and dance art of the Han nationality, the origin of drum is very early, and the specific formation time is unknown. But according to historical records, the origin of the creation of the skin drum is mainly that the saints make drums. For example, the *Book of Mountains and Seas · Great Wilderness East Classic* holds that drum was invented by the Yellow Emperor, the *Book of Rites · Mingtangwei* holds that drum was invented by Yi Qi family, and Luo Xin of the Ming Dynasty, in his book *Wuyuan · Yueyuan*, believes that drum was invented by Shennong family, as well as many other legends. From the results of archaeological excavations, the earliest extant skin drum-pottery drum can be traced back to the Neolithic age. A Neolithic "Yongdeng leshanping pottery drum" is recorded in the *History of Chinese Dances with Drawings*, which is a percussion apparatus in the late primitive society. It is made of red clay. It was originally made of animal skin at the bell mouth. In fact, the origin history of drum should be earlier. According to the *Shangshu Zhengyi · Yiji V*, it is recorded that "when you hit the stone, all animals lead the dance". In addition, it is also recorded in the *Complete Translation of Liezi · Yellow Emperor II*: Yao envoys Kui classical music, hit stones and stones, led by hundreds of animals, 90% of Xiao Shao, and the phoenix came to the apparatus, which caused birds and animals with sound. From these two historical materials, it can be seen that in ancient times, there was the practice of knocking stones as dance accompaniment apparatuses. Although there was a special apparatus made of stones (stone chime), it objectively played the role of drum. Drum was widely used after it was created, so the origin of Han drum is the origin of drum.

2.2 Origin of drum dance in ethnic minority

The origin of ethnic drum dance in ethnic minority is also quite early in ethnic minority areas. According to the available data, the origin of drum dance in ethnic minority is almost the same as that of drum dance in Han nationality, which also shows the commonality of human cultural development. Because the shape of drum is relatively simple and the production is less difficult, drum is one of the main musical instruments first invented and used by people of all ethnic groups. Compared with the origin of Han drum recorded in various historical records, the origin of minority drum is mostly spread in myths and legends. Especially in the minority areas in Southwest China, some ethnic groups have a very special preference for drums, and even regard drums as sacred objects like their ancestors. This situation is very typical among the Wa nationality. According to Liu Jinwu's *Research for Drum Culture of Ethnic Minorities in Southwest China*, the origin of wooden drum spread among Wa people appeared at the same time as Wa ancestors. They believe that Wa ancestors came out from a place called "Sigangli". With these people, there were some animals and another wooden drum. Other ethnic minorities also have similar legends about the origin of national ancestors and drums. Although this legend is based on imagination and fiction, we can see the important status of drums in the hearts of these ethnic minorities. *Drum Culture of Ethnic Minorities in Southwest China* also lists more credible legends about the origin of drums, namely the Wa and

Hani wooden drums. It is said in ancient times, there was a young couple who were playing on the mountain, seeing a tiger coming, the man had a brainwave, immediately hit a hollow tree trunk, like a drum, then, the tiger was scared away. Later, the Wa people created wooden drums imitating hollow tree trunks. Up to now, there are special wooden drum rooms in the village of Wa nationality, in which there are two wooden drums, one male and one female. And there is also a similar legend among the Hani people. In ancient times, the Hani people lived mainly by hunting. When hunters hit hollow trees in the burning woods, the hollow trunks made a loud noise, which inspired the Hani people to create wooden drums. According to the results of archaeological excavation, the type of ethnic drum with the oldest history is tongue, which is mainly distributed in Yunnan, Huizhou, Guangxi and other regions in the south. Through the examination of many unearthed drums, archeologists have found these regions have a long history, from the Spring and Autumn and Warring States to the Qing Dynasty, there are various types of drums, and are found in many ethnic areas, including Miao, Zhuang, Yi, Dai, Yao, Wa, Buyi, Shui and so on. In *Research on Chinese Percussion—Origin and Classification of Ancient Drums*, Dai Ning believes that "the bronze drum is derived from the bronze kettle, and the drums unearthed from Wanjia Bay in Chuxiong and Muding are the most primitive known drums, dating from about 2,600 years ago in the early Spring and Autumn Period." Qian Fu also argued in his article *Investigation of Drums* that, "In the Eastern Zhou Dynasty, the minority nationalities in the south created sacred and exquisite drums." Therefore, it can be seen that the origin of drum of minority nationality is a little later than that of Drum of Han nationality.

3.Project apparatus

The shape of the drum is divided into two aspects, one is shape, and the other is size. Among the drums used by Han and ethnic minorities, there are many types of drums in various shapes and sizes.

The Han Chinese drums have been used as a rhythm for dancing since the very beginning of the drumming process, when stones were struck to make a sound. This kind of stone can be said to be the earliest drum of the Han nationality—stone drum. In ancient times, it was extremely difficult to drill holes into large stones to make hollow drums because of extremely poor technology, thus it can be imagined that the original solid stone drum as a primary accompaniment apparatus was very inconvenient to use, and the sound effect was very poor. With the development of social productivity, ancient people learned to fire pottery, and this technology was used in the production of drums that is "earth drum" —the clay is molded into the drum body, and then the animal skin is covered on the drum body to become a "drum" in the strict sense. In the ancient document *Shouli Zhushu*, there is a record about the making of earth drums: "Earth drum uses tiles as a frame and leather as two sides, then it can be hit". "Zheng notes in *Li Yun* that: Earth drums are drums made of earth. Quine, beam is drumming thing, with clods of earth as beam. From these two data, it can be concluded that the original earth drum should have been round in shape and not too big, because the large clay drum body is easy to crack, because if the drum body is made very thick in order to be strong, the weight of the drum will be greatly increased, and it will be more difficult to use. In his article *Investigation of Drums*, Qian Fu also believes that "Most of what we see now are wooden drums. But, at that time, people had not learned to hoop barrels, and it was too laborious to hollow out logs, but skilled in pottery technology. Therefore, ancient people used earthen barrels as drums, the drum was probably drilled directly into the edge of the hide and tied to the drum with vines or animal sinews." Dai Ning also mentioned in his article *Research on Chinese Percussion — The origin and Classification of Ancient Drum* that the drum was originally made of earth and hit with straw sticks. Later, it developed into earth burn pottery as the drum, and finally formed wooden drum, copper drum and stone drum." Analysis from the shape of drum, and Dai Ming's *Research on Chinese Percussion — The origin and Classification of Ancient Drum*, there are probably the following types of drums in ancient China:

Firstly, it can be divided into two types from the categories of ringing — membrane-ringing and tone-ringing. All drums of the Han nationality belong to membrane ringing. Tone-ringing drums are mainly found in bronze drums and stone drums in minority areas. Secondly, it can be divided into five types as big drum, jian drum, tao drum, hang drum and tambourine, big drum category mainly includes big drum, red drum, flower cavity drum, jiao fang drum and big general drum. This kind of drum is characterized by large volume, skin, convex abdomen, placed on the drum frame, and beat with double hammers. The table category includes table, drum, flat drum, taping drum, small drum and octagonal drum and so on. This type of drum is characterized by its small size, flat body, skin and protruding belly. It can be held in the hand, placed on the drum stand or hung on the chest, and beaten with the hand or drumstick.

4.Sports classification

4.1 Chenguan short spike flower drum

Chenguan short spike flower drum is a unique folk dance, which is popular in Chenguan Township, Guangrao County, Dongying City, Shandong Province, and Shanghe County. It was originally a means for wandering artists to make a living by begging. In the Qing Dynasty, Zhang Hongxiang and Zhang Hongguo of Chenguan Village, Chenguan Township, Guangrao County, followed their father Zhang Yanshui to beg for food and gradually learned to play flower drum in the process. According to Zhang Fengyun, Li Xiping and other old artists in Shanghe County, in the twenty-ninth year of the Reign of Emperor Guangxu of the Qing Dynasty (1903), Wang Lili and Wang Liyi brothers, who made a living by singing, learned and mastered the art of flower drum while wandering to Beijing with artists from Guangrao, and then spread this form of performance to Guangrao and the lower Reaches of the Yellow River along the Shanghe River.

Chenguan short spike flower drum is played by one hit cymbals, one drum performance, action stretch, bold and unrestrained, pay attention to the "field foot slight bump, eight-legged bow. Hit the head slightly shake, run drum light as fairy". There are 30 or 40 kinds of drum sets, such as Zhang Fei's horse deception, Su Qin's holding sword and so on, now it has developed into one or two sing in pairs, many people with gongs, cymbals, and other accompaniment. Representative songs are *Chuanjiuzhou*, *Pillow* and so on.

After the PRC founded in 1949, the Party and the government attached great importance to Chenguan short spike flower drum. After being refining, the folk dance was put on the stage, turning it into an art form from a beggaring means in the past. In 1956, short spike flower drum performed by Zhang Yanshui's apprentice Li Hongyuan from Guangrao and Zhang Fengyun from Shanghe County, and Li Xiping was presented in Shandong province folk art performance awards. Zhang Yi, a folk artist, went to Chenguan Town to learn short spike flower drum. Her flower-drum performance won the gold medal at the sixth World Youth Festival in 1957.

Chenguan short spike flower drum expresses people's pursuit of happy life with drum sound and song. It is a representative of local traditional culture with unique local customs and has the value of anthropology and folklore research.

Chenguan short spike flower drum movement is difficult, so it is not popular. In recent years, due to the change of cultural and ecological environment, Chenguan short spike flower-drum is facing a serious survival crisis, lack of talent, poor inheritance, and needs urgent protection and support.

4.2 Liulin Flower Drum

Liulin flower drum in Guan County, Shandong Province is a kind of "Drum Yangko". It was originally performed in the form of "ground Yangko" and gradually developed into "Di Yangko". Liulin flower drum dates from the early Qing Dynasty, and the story it tells originated in water Margin. The story of Song Jiang and Wu Yong, disguised as Huagu artists, rescuing Lu Junyi, was combined with the local popular Guzi Yangko, which became a fixed form of performance and continued, and eventually developed into

"Liulin Huagu", a unique folk dance. At present, it only exists in Liulin Town, Guan County, Shandong Province, and has been performed in dozens of towns and villages in neighboring Linqing and Liaocheng as well as Guantao in Hebei Province. The Liulin Huagu originally consists of two parts. The first part shows the heroes of Liangshan singing and dancing all the way to the city in disguise. The second part shows the battle scene of their rescue of Lu Junyi. Only the first part remains nowadays.

Liulin Huagu is a combination of dance and martial arts. It is bold, vigorous and hot. From the artistic point of view, Liulin Huagu has distinct characteristics and unique style. It is unique among all kinds of "Guzi Yangko" and has strong local characteristics. It is a homegrown folk art, the lyrics are full of local slang words, which is of great significance to the study of the development of local folk culture. Liulin Huagu enjoys a high reputation in Guan County and has been the focus of Linqing Temple fair in history. In the early days of the founding of the People's Republic of China, Liulin Huagu won the first prize in the East China Folk art performance and went to the front line to show condolences to the United States and Korea. In recent years, the artists of Liulin Huagu are aging day by day, and their inheritance is facing a crisis, with a bleak future and urgent need for rescue and protection.

4.3 Huabian drum dance

Shanghe County, Shandong Province is located in the Lubei Plain of Shandong Province, which is 35 km from the Yellow River. It is adjacent to Humin County in the east, Leling City to the north, and Linyi County in the west. The Huabian drum dance is popular among this region. Brothers Wang Lili and Wang Liyi in Shanghe County in Guangxu Period of the Qing Dynasty went to Beijing for making a living as performer, and took Li Guizhen and Li Mingxiong who wandered in Beijing as their teachers, and learned Huabian drum dance. After they returned home, they practiced hard and improved their skills. Then, they taught Huabian drum dance to their fellow villagers, which has been passed down today. Currently, Huabian drum dance is popular in Zhangfang Town, Shanghe City. Generations of Zhang Family in Goujia

Village, Zhangfang Town can perform this. They perform Huabian drum dance every holiday and festival, which is lively.

The drums used in the performance are common waist drums, accompanied by small gongs and small cymbals. The dancers wear white towels, and short cloths, with the drums hanging on their left rib. In addition, both hands hold a whip with the rod length of 22 cm, and the whip of 50 cm. The end of the whip is tightened. When performing, the performers make two whips fly up and down, and hit the drum surface at the front of their chest and under their rib. The whip flies and the drum sounds, which is distinctive and attractive. It has over thirty kinds of actions such as front steps, rear steps, flipping like a crane, jumping over the dragon gate by carp, coiling of roots of old trees, cheating horses by Zhang Fei, taking swords by Su Qin, spitting out whiskers by two dragons, gold wire gourd, covering with chrysanthemum, drilling crotch like a black dog, and rollings 18 times in place. During performing, the whip is tossing like a golden snake, making people dazzle; the drum is inspiring like galloping horse.

The Huabian drum dance is full of local characteristics in the north of Shandong Province, and has the study values in history, culture, folklore, and dance. In recent years, the inheritance of this folk dance falls into difficulty, with worrying development prospects, and needs urgent protection.

4.4 The Eight Diagrams drum dance

The Eight Diagrams drum dance is the only square dance belonging to Taoist culture in Shandong Province. It is mainly spread in Miaohou town at the junction of Qixia and Fushan in Shandong Province. At present, only the Linjia Village in Miaohou Town has descendants. According to historical records, Taoist activities in Qixia have been very frequent since the Yuan Dynasty. When the Chongyang palace was in its heyday, there were as many as 100 Taoists. The traditional Taoist fasting ceremony needs to be accompanied by drum music, and the eight trigrams' drum dance comes from it. Qixia's unique geographical form and cultural foundation created the eight diagrams drum dance, which is closely related to Taoist culture. This folk dance is integrated with traditional martial arts to worship ancestors, pray for good fortune and ward off evil spirits, reflecting the ideal and desire of local people praying for good weather and rain.

The Eight Diagrams drum dance is performed in the form of male and female dance. In the performance, footwork, gestures and formation are required to walk eight character, showing the characteristics of light, floating, squatting and turning. The dance team is generally composed of eight men and eight women. The male team members carry Eight Diagrams drums at the waist, hold drums in the left hand, hold drumsticks in the right hand, and the female team members dance with round flat topped bronze umbrellas in both hands. The whole performance is dominated by drums, supplemented by umbrellas. Drums and umbrellas complement each other. The formation change of Eight Diagrams drum dance is relatively simple, and there are often patterns such as "eight streets", "double dragons spit whiskers", "single string flowers" and "turn" in "circle".

The Eight Diagrams drum dance is not only the treasure of Shandong folk dance, but also a miracle of Chinese Taoist art. In recent years, with the changes of the environment, it is gradually on the verge of being lost and in urgent need of rescue and protection.

第 12 节　青州花毽

1.项目文化

花毽亦称"踢花毽"或"踢毽子"。青州花毽主要分布于青州市,而今扩展到潍坊市。青州花毽历史悠久,源远流长。春秋战国时期,青州已盛行蹴鞠(踢球)之类的游艺活动。蹴鞠逐渐演化为蹴毛丸,进而演化为踢毽子,至今已有两千多年的历史。青州花毽在制作技艺与踢弄技艺两个方面都有丰厚积累。

2.项目起源

青州花毽历史悠久,至今仍为青州人所喜爱。青州花毽由毛丸发展而来,相传齐国有一孩童，不小心将毛丸踢破，羽毛露了出来，他急中生智，用一细线将破球从中间缠了一下，形成月牙葫芦状，上为羽毛，下有皮革为托，不想由于阻力增加，踢起来更加稳健，这就是毽子的原型。后经过改进，以公鸡花翎为主体的鸡毛毽产生。清雍正八年(1730 年)，青州建立“满洲驻防旗城”，旗城一位王爷擅长踢花毽，并为雍正表演，受到重赏，花毽也因此在京津地区广为流传。青州民间踢毽开展广泛，老艺人杨庆来等四人围井踢毽，时间长、花样多而毽不坠地，成为青州一绝。

3.项目规则

平时踢毽健身，比赛时以花样多少、难度高低、时间长短、动作优美程度为考核标准。青州花毽分单人踢和多人踢，多人踢是单人踢的组合，难度更高，但艺术感染力和观赏性更强。青州花毽花样繁多，有 108 种。其中较为精彩的有连升三级、鸳鸯拐、大踹马、童子拜佛、转印、凤凰摆尾、垂首龙等。现在，青州花毽爱好者们还在不断创新，编排练习一些新的花毽花样，如“云驼三山秀”“毽穿云门洞”“洋溪晚钓”等。

多人踢

Multi-player kick photographed by book writing group

(资料来源:本书编写组拍摄)

单人踢

Single-player kick photographed by book writing group

（资料来源：本书编写组拍摄）

4.项目器械

青州花毽以花毽制作、踢毽运动和花样比赛为基本内容。花毽分一般毽、比赛毽和艺术毽。一般毽的制作过程首先是选毛，以白色乌鸡绒毛为最佳，其优点是柔软不易断，容易上色；其次是染色，把绒毛染成红、黄等五颜六色，使其绚丽多彩，具有观赏性。花毽的毽身以一根不易折断的尼龙杆为主，最多分5层捆扎，1层1～2根，2层3根，3层4根，4层5～7根，须长度一致，前左后右对称，使其不偏不歪、弹力好、落地稳，其高度不超过15厘米；最后是制作毽托，用一元硬币大小的皮革做垫，中间穿孔，用皮革作毽绳穿起，配有垫钱两个，其分量不超过15克，然后将毽身、毽托用细线捆牢，即成完整的花毽。比赛专用毽的制作程序与普通毽一样，主要选用上等优质羽毛如火鸡毛、雕翎毛等，每支毽最少两根，造价较高。观赏毽属于工艺品，其制作随心所欲，花样百出，如高20厘米、30厘米、1～2米等，各种绒球需6、8、20、40个不等，一般不实踢，只供欣赏把玩。

5.动作解析

花毽以高超的毽技、灵活的步伐和优美的动作著称，如想踢好花毽，必须掌握花毽技巧。经过辛勤的努力和科学的训练，抓好提高控制毽的能力和提高身体素质才能取得成功。要提高控制毽的能力，能够支配毽子，让它随人的意志去运动；要熟悉并掌握毽的性能，包括毽的弹性、重量、运动中的阻力等因素；还要熟练掌握各种踢法的技术要点，如用力大小、用力角度以及怎样赋予毽子在空中正确的运行轨迹等；最后总结经验，找出适合自己的方法并不断创新，在速度、耐力、弹跳力、灵敏性、协调性和柔韧性等方面加强练习。

青州花毽品种丰富，无论是游艺毽、健身毽、观赏毽还是比赛毽，无不配料科学、制作精美。踢弄花毽讲究身形架步优美、心意相随、眼到脚到、反应灵活、人随毽舞、毽随人转；低踢毽如彩蝶飞舞，高踢毽如凌空飞燕。青州踢毽花样繁多，有 108 式，即天罡 36 式和地煞 72 式。天罡 36 式是将踢花毽技艺形象与青州风土民情、山川景物紧密结合来命名，富有鲜明的青州地方特色；地煞 72 式是指历代积累的踢花毽各种技巧动作的名称。青州花毽与天地人文融会贯通，富有浓郁的传统文化内涵。

6.项目传承人

青州花毽技术动作是经过几代人的研发和传承而形成的。现有技术动作 66 种，分为一般基础性动作和高难度竞技性动作。基础性动作简单易学，人们在很短的时间内就可以掌握，但竞技性动作就非常复杂和难练。一些具有地域文化特色的技术面临失传的危险，如“一柱擎天”“童子拜佛”“垂首龙”三种花样只有花毽协会王志刚一人会踢，而“转印”“双蹁马”“孔雀开屏”只有方新柱会踢，“连升三级”“鸳鸯拐”“蜻蜓点水”等花样也只有马振乾会踢。随着这些人年龄的增长，这些技术也就慢慢成了真正的遗产。

目前，青州花毽入选第三批国家级非物质文化遗产名录，第四代传承人李贤臣为将青州花毽传承下去，在学校、社区举办了多个免费培训班，同时组建了青州花毽协会。

青州花毽动作

Qingzhou Huajian action photographed by book writing group

（资料来源：本书编写组拍摄）

7.项目新发展

近年来，青州市成立花毽协会，设立培训、辅导、联络站及分会，有系统、有计划地培训协会成员。同时，市政府共投入50多万元，通过“政府买服务”的形式请花毽传承人在青州古街现场表演，授徒传承。现在，青州花毽已列入国家级非物质文化遗产保护名录。

Qingzhou Huajian

1.Project culture

Huajian（shuttlecock）is also called“kicking Huajian” or “kicking shuttlecock”. Qingzhou Huajian is mainly popular in Qingzhou City, and extends to Weifang City now. Qingzhou Huajian has a long history. During the Warring States Period, games like Cuju (football) were popular in Qingzhou, which was gradually evolved into Cumaowan (a kind of ball for kicking in ancient times), and turned into the Huajian eventually with more than 2,000 years of history. Qingzhou Huajian has rich accumulation in terms of manufacturing skills and kicking skills.

2.Project origin

Qingzhou Huajian has a long history and has been liked by Qingzhou people. It developed from Maowan (a kind of ball in ancient times). It is said that a child in the State of Qi broke Maowan carelessly when playing, and the feather came out. Then, he used his quick wits and twined a string surrounding the center of broken ball which formed the shape of crescent-cucurbit, with feather above and leather at the bottom. Then, the ball became more steadily to be kicked due to increased resistance, which was the prototype of the Huajian. After improvement, chicken feather Huajian came out, mainly made of beautiful plumes of roosters. During the 8th year of Yongzheng Period in the Qing Dynasty (1730), Qingzhou built up "Manzhou Banner City". In the city, one lord was good at kicking Huajian, and performed it for Yongzheng Emperor and won his appreciation. After that, Huajian was popular in Beijing and Tianjin Area, and wide spread in Qingzhou folk. Yang Qing and other four senior artists surrounded a well to kick Huajian with various skills, without letting Huajian fall for a long time, which became a unique skill in Qingzhou.

3.Project rules

In daily life, kicking Huajian is a kind of fitness activity. During the competition, the examination is based on the variety of tricks, the level of difficulty, the length of playing time, and the beauty of the movements. Qingzhou Huajian is divided into single-player kick and multi-player kick. As the combination of single-player kicks, multi-player kick is more difficult, but has more artistic appeal and appreciation. Qingzhou Huajian has 108 kinds of styles, among them, the exciting ones include "Lianshengsanji", "Yuanyangguai", "Dapianma",

"Tongzibaifo", "Zhuanyin", "Fenghuangbaiwei", "Chuishoulong" and so on. Now, Qingzhou Huajian enthusiasts are still innovating, arranging and practicing new Huajian skills, such as " Yuntuosanshanxiu ", " Jianchuanyunmendong ", "Yangxiwandiao", etc.

4.Project apparatus

The basic contents for Qingzhou Huajian include Huajian making, Huajian kicking and trick competition. Huajian can be divided into ordinary Huajian, competition Huajian and art Huajian. The production process of ordinary Huajian starts from feather selection, with white feather from black-bone chicken as the best choice. This kind of feather is soft, easy to dye and not prone to break; the next step is dyeing: feathers are dyed into different colors, like red, yellow, etc. to make the Huajian colorful and ornamental. The body is mainly made of one nylon rod that is not easy to break, which is tied up by at most 5 layers of feathers. For example, 1 to 2 pieces of feathers are tied on the first layer, 3 pieces of feathers on the second layer, 4 pieces of feathers on the third layer, 5 to 7 pieces of feathers on the fourth layer with the height not more than 15 cm. What's more, these feathers should be in symmetry at the front, back, left and right, so that Huajian is not skewed with good elasticity, and can be fell on the ground steadily. The last step is to make the base of Huajian. A piece of leather, which has the same size of a one-yuan coin, is used as the base and perforated in the middle, with a leather string stringing them together. It is also equipped with two coins with the weight not more than 15 grams. Then, the Huajian body and Huajian are tied with thin wires to form a complete Huajian. The production process of the special competition Huajian is the same as the ordinary Huajian. And they are all made of high-quality leathers, such as turkey leather, eagle plume, etc. There're at least 2 of these leathers in each Huajian, whose cost is relatively high. Appreciation Huajian belongs to artwork. They can be made at will and in a variety of patterns, ranging from 20 cm, 30 cm, 1 to 2 meters. The number of pompoms is 6, 8, 20, 40, and so on. Appreciation Huajian is not for practical kicking, but for appreciation.

5. Action parsing

Huajian is famous for its superior skills, flexible paces and elegant postures. To kick Huajian well, you must grasp the skills. Diligent efforts, scientific training, good control of Huajian, and physical fitness are the key to success. You should improve your ability of controlling Huajian with your will, be familiar with its characteristics, such as its elasticity, weight, resistance in movement, etc., and proficiently grasp the technical points of various kicking methods, such as the amount and angle of force, and how to move the Huajian in the correct trajectory in the air. Finally, you look for suitable ways to continuously make innovations, and practice more in terms of speed, endurance, bounce, agility, coordination and flexibility, etc.

There're many kinds of shuttlelocks in Qingzhou, including entertainment Huajian, fitness Huajian, appreciation Huajian and competition Huajian, which are all produced delicately. Huajian kicking emphasizes the beautiful posture, following the spirit, kicking with sight, and quick response. Players dance with the Huajian and the Huajian flies with the players. High-flying Huajian is like colorful butterflies flying, and low-flying Huajian is like swallows flying. There're 108 styles of kicking Qingzhou Shuttlelock, including 36 Tiangang styles (Tiangang is the name of star in ancient times, it also means immortals in the heaven) and 72 Disha styles (Disha means evil star in ancient times, and it also means devil). 36 Tiangang styles are named by the combination of the image of kicking Huajian with local customs and landscapes in Qingzhou that has obvious local features. 72 Disha styles are named after skills of kicking Huajian in history. Qingzhou Huajian integrates with the culture of heaven and earth and is rich in traditional cultural connotations.

6. Project inheritor

The skills and actions of Qingzhou Huajian have been formed by several generations' research and inheritance. Now, there're 66 kinds of skillful actions, including general basic actions and highly competitive actions respectively. It's easy to learn and grasp basic skills in short time. However, it's difficult to grasp highly competitive skills. Some skills with regional cultural features are at the risk of being lost. For example, "Yizhuqingtian", "Tongzibaifo", "Chuishoulong" can only be performed by Wang Zhigang, a member of Huajian Association; " Zhuanyin ", " Shuangpianma ", "Kongquekaiping" can only be performed by Fang Xinzhu; "Lianshengsanji", "Yuanyangguai", "Qingtingdianshui" can only be performed by Ma Zhenqian. As these performing artists grow older, these skills will slowly become a heritage.

Currently, Qingzhou Huajian has been selected in the third batch of National Intangible Cultural Heritage List. In order to inherit Qingzhou Huajian, Li Xianchen, the fourth generation inheritor, has set up many free training courses in schools and communities, and organized Qingzhou Huajian Association.

7.New development

In recent years, Huajian Association has been established in Qingzhou for training, coaching, coordination, and branches to systematically train the members of association. At the same time, the municipal government has totally invested more than 500,000 RMB in inviting inheritors of Huajian to perform on site in Qingzhou ancient streets to receive and teach students by the form of "government buying service". Today, this project has been listed on the third National Intangible Cultural Heritage List.

第 13 节　高跷

1.项目文化

高跷，是民间流传已久的乡土体育娱乐活动，是我国劳动人民在长期生产、生活中积累起来的集养生、健身、娱乐为一体的活动形式，有着悠久的历史和丰富文化蕴涵，它的发展与民间戏剧、杂技、舞蹈、灯展相融合，不仅仅是一项体育活动，也是一项艺术活动。近年来，在大力弘扬民族文化的氛围里，人们对这项运动不断创新，高跷又展现出新的活力。

2.项目起源

关于高跷的起源存在多种观点：

第一种观点认为高跷起源于原始氏族的图腾崇拜。尧舜时代的丹朱氏族以鹤为信仰，在祭礼中要踩着高跷绿鹤一样跳舞，以此作为宗教祭祀仪式。其依据是《山海经·海外西经》载："长股之国在雄常北，被发，一曰长脚。"另外，甲骨文中有一字可以解释为"像一个人双脚蹈矩棍而舞"，以及出土的北魏石棺上有高跷、杂技的图画也可为佐证。非洲扎伊尔巧克威（tchokwe）部落宗教仪式中，也有踩跷的表演，一名巫师腿上绑着长跷，徐徐走动，两手缓缓起舞。

第二种观点认为高跷起源于杂技表演。《列子·说符篇》中记述了一个叫兰子的人，他为宋元公表演跷技时，小腿上绑着比身体长一倍的两根木棍，快速地跑跳，并向空中循环抛弃七把短剑，五把常在空中，元公看后非常吃惊。这个故事说明高跷是一种杂技表演形式。今出土的北魏时期墓碑上的"百戏图"也有当时"乔人"形象。

第三种观点认为高跷起源于人们的生产劳动。依靠采摘野果为生的原始人群在采摘山实野果时，常常需要借助木叉枝芽的登踩，从而受到启发，产生了类似高跷的"踏跷"。同时，生活在海边的"长脚人常负臂人入海中捕鱼也"，即沿海的渔民脚上绑扎着长木跷，手持长木制成的原始捕鱼工具在浅海中捕鱼。

3.项目规则

表演者双脚着跷，奔跑跳跃，灵活自如，加以折腿腕、水蛇腰、抖肩膀、甩担子、摆头甩髯等身上功夫，跷功腿力，身段眼神，糅合在一起，形成高跷独特的艺术风格与表演形式。演出程序分为行进、小场、大场。行进是高跷队进村、进街，双行前进队形，有时以"扒皮""别篱笆"的形式进行变换。小场即一般撂场，用于主要街头、路口、较大单位门前与观众稠密处，紧点、圆场略施技巧，一晃即过。大场为正式演出场，首先演员集体跑场，即打场子，随即分场表演，称为过对。集体跑场，队行花样有"单行进行""二龙吐须""剪子股""转'8'字""走方社”“龙摆尾”和“四门斗”等，跑场间隙加唱。分场表演由一对表演者分别登场表演，表演中竞相发挥技巧，即兴抓眼逗趣，送上祝福。高跷表演场面活跃，气氛热烈，广大观众沉浸在祥和欢乐之中。

4.项目器械

高跷由 4×6 厘米的方木制做，高 80、100、120 厘米不等，上扁下圆，底径 3～4 厘米。

5.动作解析

表演有双跷、单跷之分。双跷多绑扎在小腿上，以便展示技艺；单跷则以双手持木跷的顶端，便于上下，动态风趣。表演又有“文跷”“武跷”之分。文跷重扮相与扭逗，重于扭和踩；武跷则强调个人技巧与绝招，以演特技为主。在表演中，有“跳桌子”“越头跳”“后滚翻”“单腿跳”等技巧动作。高跷讲究队形变换，其基本变换形式有“踏街”“一条龙”“剪子股”“转‘8’字”“麒麟送子”。还有的在高跷表演过程中，表演者头戴公子帽，上穿黄褂，下穿红色高脚裤，双脚缚木制跷棍，跷棍高 1～4.6 米不等。表演队形有单排、双排、“Z”字形等，表演队伍为男女混合、老中青少混合。为了增强活动的趣味性，表演还设计一定的情节，生动有趣。

武跷

Wu Stilt

6.项目传承人

齐玉杰，山东德州人，被评为高跷传承人。他 18 岁开始跟随老师曲长恩学习高跷艺术，在多年的高跷表演过程中掌握了全部高跷艺术表演绝活，现已有同辈徒弟、晚辈徒弟 30 余人。齐玉杰曾带队荣获 1979 年、1984 年德州市民间文艺演出优秀奖、1999 年德城区民间文艺展演优秀参演奖、2007 年德城区首届民间文化艺术节民间文艺大赛特别奖。在齐玉杰等老一辈高跷艺人的带领下，小锅市的高跷不仅在当地非常出名，还被传授到了外地，为传承德州高跷这一艺术形式做出了贡献。

7.项目新发展

高跷这种表演活动机动性大，行动比较自如，可以在大场面中表演，也可走街串巷表演。过去表演时间固定，但如今踩高跷已经不再是只有节庆才能进行的娱乐内容，在乡镇、社区人们一有空闲就能玩。而且踩在高跷上的人不仅仅限于男人，越来越多女子也参与进来。在我国江西省赣县，有一支专门以青少年女子组成的高跷表演队，是江西省唯一的青少年高跷表演队伍。民间艺人王昭富老师在民间高跷表演艺术上大胆创新，创下了高跷与杂技表演融合、高跷上变魔术的新记录。这些变化不仅是高跷技术和表演的创新，也是人们男女平等观念的变革。

高跷

Stilt

高跷不仅是节庆时候的表演活动，还是我国民族传统体育的优秀项目，其竞技方法有竞速、竞艺等形式。目前，高脚竞速已被列为全国少数民族传统体育运动会的竞赛项目。随着该项运动的广泛开展和竞技水平的提高，人们对竞技高跷要求也不断严格。在器材方面，高跷从造型到制作工艺都进行过多次大胆的改进与创新，这也为高跷运动的发展起到了巨大促进作用。

现代高跷运动不仅在民间广泛开展，而且还进入了学校，并成为具有民族特色的体育教材内容，在北京密云地区许多学校，还开展了高跷教学的研究。

Stilt

1.Project culture

The stilt is a kind of folk sport and entertainment activity that has been popularized among the people for a long time. It is created by the working people of our country in the long-term production and life and is a combination of health maintenance, fitness and entertainment. Having a long history and rich cultural connotation, stilt has been developed by integrating with folk drama, acrobatics, dance, and lantern show, which is not only a sports activity, but also an artistic activity. The stilt has shown new vitality through vigorous promotion of the national culture and people's continuous innovation of the sport in recent years.

2.Project origin

There are multiple views about the origin of stilts:

The first viewpoint holds that stilts originated from the totem worship of the primitive clan. In the Yao and Shun eras, the Danzhu clan believed in cranes. They stepped on stilts and danced like cranes during rituals. This was a religious ritual, which is based on *The Classic of Mountains and Seas · Overseas Western Classic*, "Long-thigh country is located in the north of Xiongchang, and their people has long hair, which is called Long-feet country." In addition, this opinion can be confirmed by a word in the oracle bone inscriptions interpreted as "a person dancing with a stick on his feet" and the excavated sarcophagus with stilts and acrobatics pictures of the Northern Wei Dynasty. In the religious ceremonies of the tchokwe tribe in Zaire, Africa, there are also stilt-walking performances. A wizard with stilts tied to his legs walks slowly and dances with both hands.

The second view is that stilts originated in acrobatics. *Lie Zi · Shuo Fu* described a man called Lan Zi. He performed for Emperor Song Yuan having two sticks with twice the length of his body tied on his calves, running and jumping quickly, and dropped seven swords in turn in the air, five of which were remained in the air. The Emperor was very surprised after watching this performance. This story illustrates the stilt is a form of acrobatics. The "Hundred Operas" on the excavated tombstone of the Northern Wei Dynasty also has the image of "Qiao Ren" at that time.

The third view believes that it originated productive labor. The primitive people who depended on picking wild fruits for a living often needed to step on the branches and buds of wooden forks when picking wild fruits in the mountains. Inspired by this, they produced "stepping stilts" like stilts. Meanwhile, people living by the sea often go fishing in the sea with stilts to catch fish in shallow seas.

3.Project rules

Actors run and jump on stilts flexibly. They often fold their legs, twist their waists shake their shoulders, burdens, heads and whiskers. They show their leg strength with the help of the expressions and the body. It forms the unique artistic style and performance form of stilts. Performance procedure has three steps—marching, small field and big field. Marching means that the team enters the village and the street with two lines. Sometimes, they advance in other formations such as "Bapi" and "Bieliba". The small field is a simple field performance. It is performed in main streets, intersections, in front of larger units and in crowded places with audiences. The performance is often about quick showing of skills. The big field is a formal field performance. First, performers run around the field collectively, which is called "Dachangzi". Then, they perform in separate performances, which is called "Guodui". All performers run through the field. The team line tricks include "Danhang", "Erlongtuxu", "Jianzigu", "Zhuanbazi", "Zoufangshe", "Longbaiwei" and "Simendou", etc. When they rest, other performers sing songs. In the separate performances, a pair of actors perform in turn and show their different skills. Furthermore, they can interact with audiences sending blessings. The scene is lively with warm atmosphere, and the audiences are immersed in peace and joy.

4.Project apparatus

Stilts are made of 4×6 cm square wood with the height of 80, 100 and 120 cm. The upper part is flat, and the lower part is round with a diameter of 3 to 4 cm.

5.Action parsing

There are "double stilts" and "single stilts" performances. Double stilts are tied on the shanks to show skills. Single stilts are used by the performers who hold the top of the stilts with both hands, which is easy to go up and down. It is dynamic and interesting. They can also be divided into "Wen Stilts" and "Wu Stilts" performances. Wen Stilts pay attention to acting twisting and stepping, while Wu Stilts emphasize personal skills and unique tricks, mainly performing stunts. In the performance, there are such skills as "Jumping the Table", "Jumping over the Head", "Rolling Back", "Jumping on One Leg" and so on. Formation transformation is important in stilts, and the basic transformation forms include "Tajie", "Yitiaolong", "Jianzigu", "Zhuanbazi" and "Qilinsongzi". In the process of stilts performance, performers wear a hat, yellow jacket, and red pants and their feet are tied with wooden rockers. The height of which varies from 1 m to 4.6 m. The formations are different, such as a single line, double line, Z type arrangement, etc. The performance team is mixed with men and women, old, middle and young. In order to enhance the interest of the activity, the performance is also designed with a certain plot, which is lively and interesting.

6.Project inheritor

Qi Yujie, a native of Dezhou, Shandong province, was named the inheritor of stilts. He began to follow Qu Changen to learn the art of stilts at the age of 18. During his many years of stilt performance, he has mastered all the unique skills of stilt art performance. Now there are more than 30 peers and younger apprentices. Qi Yujie once led a team to participate in the folk-art performance of Dezhou in 1979 and 1984 and won Excellent Award. He also won the Excellent Performance Award in 1999 Decheng District Folk Art Show and Special Award in 2007 Decheng District First Folk Culture and Art Festival Folk Art Competition. Led by the older generation such as Qi Yujie, the stilts are not only very famous locally, but also spread to other places, making contributions to the inheritance of the art form.

7.New development

The stilt is a kind of performance with great mobility and relatively free movement. It can be performed in big scenes or walking through streets. In the past, the time of the performance was fixed. But now, the stilt is no longer just a festival entertainment, and people in towns, villages and communities can play it whenever they have free time. The people stepping on stilts are not limited to men. More and more women are participating in this performance. In Ganxian County, Jiangxi Province, there is a stilt performance team composed of young women, which is the only youth stilt performance team in Jiangxi Province. Wang Zhaofu, a folk artist, innovates on the folk performing arts of stilts. He has the new record of magic on stilts, which is not only an innovation on technology and performance, but also a change in the concept of equality between men and women.

The stilt is not only the performance during festivals but also an excellent item of traditional national sports in our country. The forms include racing and art competition. At present, the high-foot racing has been listed as a competition item in the national minority traditional sports meeting. With the spread of the sport and the development of the competitive level, people are stricter with competitive stilts. In terms of apparatus, many bold improvements and innovations have been made from modeling to production technology, which has also played a great role in promoting the development of stilts.

The modern stilt movement is not only widely carried out among folks, but also comes into schools, which has become the content of sports textbooks with national characteristics. Many schools in Miyun area of Beijing have also carried out research on stilt teaching.

第 14 节　聊城杂技

1.项目文化

聊城杂技作为首批国家级非物质文化遗产项目,是山东民族文化的重要品牌,它植根于齐鲁文化沃土,蕴含齐鲁大地特有的英伟与豪气。

2.项目起源

聊城是中国杂技的发源地之一。新石器时代晚期,聊城是东夷人活动的主要区域,当时东夷人的首领蚩尤据说便是一位杂技高手,古代杂技就源于角抵戏即蚩尤戏。聊城杂技现分布于东阿、茌平、阳谷等县及其周边地区。

春秋战国时期,聊城杂技马戏得到初步发展,到汉代已经基本成熟。三国时期,杂技马戏在聊城的东阿一带已很盛行,成为一种以杂技为主兼有其他技艺的表演形式。东阿王曹植曾以"斗鸡东郊道,走马长楸间"的诗句来描述这种状况。历史上黄河经常泛滥成灾,许多农民为了生存不得不弃农学艺,东阿县孟庄、贺庄、张大人集等村就是著名的杂技村。民国初期,仅东阿县就有几十个杂技马戏班。此外,阳谷、茌平、莘县、临清等地还有几十个杂技团,其中有些团体曾到朝鲜、日本、新加坡演出。1955 年,东阿县正式组建马戏团八个;1970 年,聊城杂技团成立。

聊城杂技代表性节目一

Liaocheng Acrobatics representative program 1

3.项目新发展

目前,聊城杂技虽经着力发掘和倡导,但仍有衰落的趋势。这主要是因为随着生活水平的提高,原来作为谋生手段的杂技对现在的年轻人已不具吸引力,由此导致严重的后继无人现象。一些颇有造诣的杂技演员因年事已高逐步退出舞台,有的相继谢世,使得一些绝技面临失传的危险。

1993 年,文化部批准在聊城建立中国少儿杂技基地,并将其列入国务院蒲公英计划。聊城市政府依托中国少儿杂技基地,建立了聊城蒲公英杂技艺术学校,培养杂技后备人才。但这仍然与科学的、立体的、全面的、原生态的保护相距甚远,非物质文化遗产的抢救保护意识和工作力度亟待进一步加强。

3.1　聊城杂技家家练,艺术种子处处传

聊城地处黄河流域的平原地区,黄河的不时溃决与干旱给依靠农耕生存的人们带来严峻的威胁。这就迫使不少人为了生计而闲时学艺,有的则携亲带友一起弃农从艺,当然,也有不少有着怀乡情结的人又返回故里,重新务农。聊城市杂技团常务副团长、聊城杂技非物质文化遗产保护项目的山东省省级代表性传承人王峰认为,这是聊城杂技在历史年轮里得以传承的一个重要原因。

杂技艺术起源于民间，创作于人们的劳动生产过程。而杂技的任何技巧，都是靠常年的汗水以及百折不回的精神换来的。在聊城东阿、茌平等不少自然村中，形成了不怕吃苦练习杂技的传统，形成了以家族式杂技为主的特色地域文化。例如，位于聊城刘集镇一个不足千人的村庄里，就有三人问鼎国际杂技“金小丑”奖，这可视为聊城杂技不断发展的一个佐证。

聊城杂技人还凭借着刚毅与执着，把聊城杂技的种子播撒到全国各地。聊城较知名的近代杂技艺人李禄友(艺名“李半仙”)的儿女李新勇、李凤云带领山东三顺马戏团(又称“山东京剧马戏团”)于1954年进入贵州，三年后和其他兄弟团体组建贵州省工农兵杂技团(次年改组为贵州省杂技团)；20世纪三四十年代，聊城北坝人付茂堂之子付延顺、付延表在上海创办了“花家马戏班”，以后部分人并入上海市杂技团；聊城另一位知名杂技艺人张义成(艺名“张大辫子”)之子张振玉创建的“双盛杂技班”因在青海、新疆一带演出，演员就分别参加了青海省杂技团、新疆杂技团；聊城人田官成(云南省杂技团原团长田海来之父)创建的少林国术杂技团于1949～1956年沿贵、赣、湘、两广地区演出，终落地云南，子女六人分别在昆明军区杂技团、云南省杂技团从事杂技工作。随着时间的推移，他们将聊城杂技的元素与当地文化聚焦融会，成为新中国杂技事业发展道路上的铺路基石。

聊城杂技代表性节目二

Liaocheng Acrobatics representative program 2

3.2　枝枯叶落秋已近，艺苑静待识人来

2006 年，在聊城市政府的大力支持下，经广大文艺工作者深入发掘与系统整理，聊城杂技被批准列入首批国家级非物质文化遗产保护项目。以项目保护单位聊城市杂技团为主体的聊城杂技人为发掘、抢救、继承和弘扬聊城杂技做出了积极的努力，但与生产性的非物质文化遗产项目相比，聊城杂技还普遍存在着剧目创作、理论研究、市场营销等困难，面临着影响传承的诸多问题。

首先，民族文化生态保护亟待改善，本土化的人才断代问题亟待解决。作为根植民间的传统杂技艺术，制约其发展的根本问题是后继人才的匮乏。

东阿县孟庄、贺庄、张大人集村，茌平县城南李庄、广平村等作为孕育杂技文化的自然村落，承载着聊城杂技的历史记忆与文化情感，以此为基础建立杂技文化生态保护村及杂技文化体验中心，具有特殊的文化价值和研究意义。应以这些生态保护村为中心，在周边地区鼓励发展民间杂技表演团体，结合体育和艺术教育，在杂技文化氛围浓厚的村镇中小学开展民间杂技特色课程与普及教学，不断培养青少年对杂技的兴趣，为杂技学校培养后备队伍，解决新形势下民间杂技传承的难题。

其次，传承载体受限于传统思维，严重束缚事业发展。聊城市杂技团作为聊城杂技保护与传承的主要载体，始建于 1955 年，隶属于聊城市文化广电新闻出版局，是副县级差额事业单位。国有事业单位的管理模式，使其在当代市场经济环境中面临着种种尴尬。

一方面，人才培养、作品编创、道具加工、自行营销等小而全的传统剧团功能，使其在竞争日趋激烈的时代渐渐沦为劳动力供应的小作坊营销模式，削弱了团体自身的个性优势，严重束缚了团体的发展。另一方面，传统体制中的人才年龄渐渐偏大，思想相对封闭，专业性单一，创造力有限，舞台作品创新的动力小、周期长。作为处在文化体制改革前沿的杂技院团，财政和编制的年年递减与社会人才的激烈竞争形成强烈对比。新生杂技人才挤不进编制，而面对团体有限的市场竞争力又争不到合同制下编制外的高薪待遇，双向选择致使人才出现高频度的外流。

聊城拥有丰富的杂技资源和发展优势，应鼓励杂技院团结合自身优势整合资源，尽早实现由“小而全”向“精而专”的特色化转型。加强跨地区、跨行业的交流合作，依托 1993 年文化部批准设立的蒲公英聊城少儿杂技培训基地并借

助职业教学机构与演艺团体，从传统技艺保护、人才培养、节目创新等方面入手，培育多样化的传承载体，实现聊城杂技艺术的多元化、全方位发展。

聊城杂技是我国杂技艺术的一片丛林，我们要守望好这片丛林，让它继续繁盛，充满生机。

Liaocheng Acrobatics

1.Project culture

Liaocheng Acrobatics, one of the first National Intangible Cultural Heritage projects, is an important brand of Shandong Province national culture. It is rooted in the fertile soil of Shandong culture and contains the unique heroic spirit of Shandong Province.

2.Project origin

Liaocheng area is one of the cradles of acrobatics in China. In the late Neolithic Age, Liaocheng was the main area of the Dongyi people's activities. Chiyou, the leader of the Dong Yi people at that time, was said to be an acrobatic master, and the ancient acrobatics originated from the corner opera, namely Chiyou Opera. Liaocheng Acrobatics is distributed in the Dong'e, Chiping, Yanggu County and the surrounding areas.

During the Spring and Autumn Period and the Warring States Period, Liaocheng Acrobatics circus developed initially, and it was basically matured in the Han Dynasty. During the Three Kingdoms Period, acrobatic circus was very popular in Dong'e area of Liaocheng, becoming a form of performance mainly based on acrobatics and other skills. Cao Zhi, the King of Dong'e, once described this situation in a poem, "Cockfighting in the east suburbs, horse riding among trees". In history, the Yellow River was often flooded, and many farmers had to give up farming to learn arts in order to survive. Mengzhuang, Hezhuang and Zhangdarenji villages in Dong'e County are famous acrobatic villages at that time. In the early days of the Republic of China, there were dozens of acrobatic circus troupes in Dong'e County alone. In addition, there are also dozens of troops in Yanggu, Chiping, Xinxian and Linqing, and some of troops have performed in Korea, Japan and Singapore. In 1955, Dong'e County formally established eight circuses. In 1970, the Liaocheng Acrobatics Troupe was formed.

3.New development

At present, although Liaocheng Acrobatics has been explored and advocated, there is still a trend of decline. The reason is that with the improvement of living standards, acrobatics, as a means of making a living, is no longer attractive to young people, resulting in a lack of successors. Some accomplished acrobats have gradually retired from the stage as they grow old, and some have even died, making some stunts in danger of being lost.

In 1993, the Ministry of Culture approved the establishment of Chinese Children's Acrobatics Base in Liaocheng and included it in the Dandelion Plan of the State Council. Relying on the Chinese children's acrobatic base, Liaocheng government established Liaocheng Dandelion Acrobatic Art School, training acrobatic reserve talents. However, this is still far from scientific, three-dimensional, comprehensive and original ecological protection, and it is urgent to strengthen the awareness and work of the rescue and protection of intangible heritage.

3.1 Liaocheng Acrobatics' development in the past

Liaocheng is in the plain area of the Yellow River basin. The frequent outburst and drought of the Yellow River have brought severe threats to the people who rely on farming, which forced many people to study acrobatics in their spare time to make a living, and even some people abandoned farming with their relatives and friends. Of course, there were also many people who had a nostalgia complex and returned to hometown and started farming again. Wang Feng, the deputy director of Liaocheng Acrobatic Troupe and the provincial representative inheritor of Liaocheng Acrobatics intangible cultural heritage protection project in Shandong Province, believes that this is an important reason why Liaocheng Acrobatics can be inherited.

Acrobatic art was originated from the folk and created in people's labor process. Its skills rely on sweat over years. In Dong'e, Chiping and other villages in Liaocheng, there formed the tradition of practicing acrobatics hard. There is also regional culture of family-style acrobatics. For example, in Liuji Town, a village with population less than 1,000 in Liaocheng, there are three people winning the international acrobatics "Golden Clown" awards, which can be regarded as a proof of the continuous development of Liaocheng Acrobatics.

With the fortitude and perseverance, Liaocheng acrobats spread the acrobatics throughout the country. Li Xinyong and Li Fengyun, the son and daughter of Li Luyou (stage name "Li Banxian") who is a famous modern acrobatic artist in Liaocheng, led "Shandong Sanshun Circus" (also known as "Shandong Peking Opera Circus") to Guizhou in 1954 and three years later, they organized Guizhou Acrobatic Troupe of Workers, Farmers and Soldiers (the next year it was reorganized as Guizhou Acrobatic Troupe). In the 1930s and 1940s, Fu Yanshun and Fu Yanbiao, sons of Fu Maotang of Beba village, Liaocheng, founded the "Huajia Circus Troupe" in Shanghai and some of them were incorporated into the Shanghai Acrobatic Troupe later. Another famous acrobatic artist Zhang Zhenyu, the son of Zhang Yicheng (stage name "Zhang Dabaizi"), founded the "Shuangsheng Acrobatic Troupe", the actors of which respectively joined in the Qinghai Province Acrobatic Troupe and Xinjiang Autonomous Region Acrobatic Troupe as they once performed in Qinghai and Xinjiang. From 1949 to 1956, "Shaolin National Acrobatic Troupe", founded by Tian Guancheng (the father of Tian Hailai, the former head of Yunnan Province Acrobatic Troupe), performed in Guizhou, Jiangxi, Hunan, Guangxi and Guangdong regions, and finally settled down in Yunnan province. His six children were engaged in acrobatic work in Kunming Military Acrobatic Troupe and Yunnan Province Acrobatic Troupe respectively. With the time went by, they focused on the integration of Liaocheng Acrobatics and local culture, becoming a paving stone on the development of China's acrobatics career.

3.2 Liaocheng acrobatics' promotion nowadays

In 2006, with the strong support of Liaocheng government, through in-depth excavation and systematic arrangement by the vast number of literary and art workers, Liaocheng Acrobatics was approved to be included in the first batch of national intangible cultural heritage protection projects. Liaocheng acrobats, with the project protection unit—Liaocheng Acrobatic Troupe as the main body, have made active efforts to discover, rescue, inherit and promote Liaocheng Acrobatics. However, compared with the production of the Intangible Cultural Heritage projects, there are still many difficulties, such as drama creation, theoretical research, marketing, etc, which affect the inheritance of Liaocheng Acrobatics.

Firstly, the protection of national cultural ecology needs to be improved, and the problem of acrobatics succession needs to be solved. As a traditional art rooted in the folk, the fundamental problem restricting its development is the lack of successors.

Mengzhuang, Hezhuang, Zhangdarenji villages in Dong'e County, and Lizhuang and Guangping Villages in the south of Chiping County nurtured acrobatic culture and they also carried the historical memory and cultural emotion of Liaocheng Acrobatics. On the basis of this, cultural ecological protection villages and acrobatic cultural experience center were established, which have special cultural value and research significance. These ecological protection villages should serve as the center to encourage the development of folk acrobatics group in combination of sports and art education in the surrounding areas, and carry out the teaching of characteristics of folk acrobatics and popularization in rural primary and secondary schools with thick atmosphere of acrobatics culture, and continuously cultivate the interest of young people in acrobatics, train reserve teams for acrobatics schools, and solve the difficult problem of inheriting folk acrobatics under the new situation.

Secondly, the carrier of inheritance is limited by traditional thinking, which seriously restricts the development of acrobatics. Founded in 1955 Liaocheng Acrobatic Troupe is the main carrier of acrobatic protection and inheritance in Liaocheng. It is affiliated to Liaocheng Bureau of Culture, Radio, Film, Press and Publication, and is a public institution at the county level. The management mode of state-owned enterprises is facing various embarrassments in the contemporary market economy environment.

On the one hand, traditional theatre troupes have small but complete functions, such as talent training, creation of works, making of props and self-marketing, but they have gradually become a small workshop for labor supply in the era of increasingly fierce competition, weakening the individual advantages and constraining its development seriously. On the other hand, the talents in the traditional system are gradually getting older, with relatively closed thoughts, single professionalism, limited creativity, and low motivation and long cycle for stage works innovation. As an acrobatic troupe at the forefront of cultural system reform, the annual decline in finance and staffing is in sharp contrast to the fierce competition for social talents. New acrobatic talents cannot be crowded into the organization. Facing the market competitiveness of the limited groups, they cannot compete for the high salary outside the organization under the contract, which leads to the outflow of talents with high frequency.

Liaocheng has rich acrobatic resources and development advantages, and the troupes should be encouraged to integrate resources based on its own advantages and complete the characteristic transformation from "small and comprehensive" to "fine and specialized" functions as soon as possible. Cross-regional, cross-industry exchanges and cooperation can be strengthened for Liaocheng Acrobatics to cultivate diversified inheritance carriers from protecting traditional skills, training talents, innovating programs, and so on. Relying on the Dandelion Liaocheng Children's Acrobatics Training Base approved by the Ministry of Culture in 1993, and with the help of vocational teaching institutions and performing arts groups, Liaocheng Acrobatics is hoped to make a diversified and all-round development.

Liaocheng Acrobatics is like a forest, and we should take care of it so that it will continue to prosper and be full of vitality.

第15节　宁津杂技

1.项目文化

宁津杂技流行于鲁北地区，至明代达到鼎盛，鲁北因此成为全国杂技的汇聚地和活动中心。宁津杂技在漫长的发展过程中逐渐形成各具特色的门类和派别，演出规模和范围日渐扩展，以“惊、险、奇、美、新”的艺术特点闻名遐迩，《蹬板凳》《舞中幡》《小花旦抖空竹》等节目深受国内外观众喜爱。

2.项目起源

宁津县原属古冀州，宁津杂技历史悠久，源远流长。据考证，《汉书》《史记》《述异记》及清光绪年间宁津县志，对冀州的蚩尤角抵戏均有记载：“蚩尤氏头有角，与黄帝斗，以角抵人，今冀州为蚩尤戏。”南朝文学家任昉在《述异记》中写道：“冀州有乐，名蚩尤戏。”

宁津杂技源自宁津县西部以黄家镇为中心的南北八寨，它来自民间、源于生活，是宁津人民敢为人先、勇于探索、精明睿智的结晶。随着京杭大运河的开凿通航，西临运河的宁津更是兼得风气之先，民间杂技艺人南下北上，流布全国，使宁津杂技得以融贯南北，具有了开放性的胸襟和面貌。

唐朝以后宁津杂技在民间广为流传，至明代进入兴盛时期，明景泰年间，中国历史上第一个杂技行业古会——黄家镇杂技古会应运而生，会期从农历九月初开始，历时一月，史称“九月会”。“不赶九月会，不算生意人”这句话，在杂技界耳熟能详。古会期间全国各地的杂技艺人，纷纷云集黄家镇，各显其能，切磋技艺，收徒组班、买卖道具等。

清代宁津杂技活动更加繁荣，出现了半农半艺、或以卖艺为生的演出团体，逐渐形成了南北八寨两大派别。清光绪年间，慈禧太后在京大摆72道皇会，宁津县野猪李村的“艺人张”表演的“顶竹竿过城门”绝技，位列皇会之首，成为当时“名扬紫禁城，声震杂技界”的风云人物。20世纪二三十年代，南北八寨的杂技艺人，纷纷走出家门、国门，行走江湖，当时流传的“宁吴二县、鸡毛变蛋、走南闯北、不捎盘缠”的俗语，就是当时杂技艺人靠卖艺漂泊异乡生活的真实写照。杂技艺人远赴印度、缅甸、尼泊尔、日本、蒙古、苏联以及西欧诸国，形成了中国杂技与世界文化艺术的大规模融汇交流，在国内他们的足迹更是遍布长城内外、大江南北，“没有宁津人难成杂技班”，因此得名并广为流传。

解放后宁津杂技迎来了空前发展繁荣时期，1956～1958 年，在过去杂技艺人班底的基础上，宁津县杂技一、二、三团相继组建，杂技团的演出逐步由城镇农村向大中城市转移，并采取“派出去、请进来”的方式方法，学人之长，补己之短，以提高自身的技艺水平。自此，宁津杂技迎来了一次又一次的发展高潮。

3.动作解析

宁津杂技质朴粗犷、刚柔相济，凸显“惊、险、奇、美、新”五大艺术特色，具有极高的审美价值、观赏价值和文化价值。宁津杂技门类齐全，具有表演类、魔术类、马戏类、驯兽类四个类别，其中表演类有 60 余个节目。“古老中幡”“柔术叼花和滚灯”“空中飞人”“爬竿”“钢丝高车”“叠罗汉”“走钢丝”“蹬技”“地圈”“对口叼花”等十余种节目多次在国内外演出中受到观众喜爱及业内人士赞誉。

叠罗汉

Arhats stacking

4.项目传承人

宁津杂技代表性传承人刘俊昌，目前是省级非遗传承人，至今已培养杂技学员 100 余人。

5.项目新发展

新中国成立之后特别是改革开放以来，在党和政府关怀下，宁津杂技事业得到长足发展，建立了县杂技艺校和杂技团，先后为全国各级艺术团体培养和输送了 2000 余名杂技人才，其中有大批演员、学员成为各地业务骨干，20 余名演员分获国内、国际杂技大奖。宁津杂技团近几年先后赴韩国、沙特、俄罗斯、泰国等多个国家演出，对增进中外文化交流、促进经济发展发挥了重要作用。

近年来，宁津杂技团与全国各大演出团体合作，参与创作了《红色传奇》《徽韵》《盛世梨园》《水浒天风》等大型多媒体文艺演出作品，并进行中韩文化交流演出、中沙文艺交流演出等。

爬竿

Pole climbing

1995 年，宁津县被文化部命名为“中国民间艺术（杂技）之乡”。2005 年，宁津杂技被山东省定为首批申报国家级非物质文化遗产的项目。2008 年，宁津杂技正式入选国家级非物质文化遗产名录。2011 年,宁津县被命名为中国民间文化艺术之乡。2015 年宁津县杂技团选送的节目《吊环》获得泰山文学奖三等奖。2016 年在山东省举办的第十届山东杂技魔术大赛上,宁津县选送的杂技节目《绸操》获得大赛一等奖。2016 年 8 月份举办的泰山文艺奖评选中,宁津选送的《排椅》获得泰山文艺奖二等奖。

宁津杂技艺术学校作为山东省非物质文化遗产传承教育基地,每三年向县杂技团输送 8～10 名演员。尽管如此,仍有越来越多的人不希望自己的孩子到杂技团吃苦,宁津杂技传承人随时有链条断裂的危险,所以亟待保护。

空中飞人

Trapeze Acrobat

Ningjin Acrobatics

1.Project culture

Ningjin Acrobatics was popular in northern Shandong, and reached its peak in the Ming Dynasty, so Northern Shandong became the meeting place and activity center of acrobatics in China. In the long process of development,

Ningjin Acrobatics has gradually formed its own categories and factions, and the scale and scope of its performances have been expanding day by day. It is famous for its artistic characteristics of "surprise, danger, wonder, beauty and novelty". Programs such as *Pedaling the Bench*, *Dancing the Banner* and *Little Huadan Shaking Diabolo* are deeply loved by audiences at home and abroad.

2.Project origin

Ningjin County originally belonged to ancient Jizhou, and Ningjin Acrobatics has a long history. According to textual research, Chiyou's Jiaodi Opera in Jizhou is recorded in *Hen Shu*, *Historical Records*, *Shuyi Ji* and *Ningjin County Annals* in Guangxu period of the Qing Dynasty, "Chiyou fought with the Yellow Emperor with the horns on his head, which is played in Jizhou as Chiyou Opera". Ren Fang, a writer of the Southern Dynasties, wrote in *Shuyi Ji*, "There is an entertainment in Jizhou, which is called Chiyou Opera."

Ningjin Acrobatics originated from the eight villages in the north and south of Huangjia Town in the west of Ningjin County, which came from the folk life, and was the result of Ningjin people's wisdom and courage to be the first and to explore bravely. With the opening of the Beijing-Hangzhou Grand Canal, Ningjin, in the west of the canal, had the advantages of geographical location. Folk acrobats went outside and spread throughout the country, so that Ningjin Acrobatics had a new appearance mixing with other acrobatics.

After the Tang Dynasty, Ningjin Acrobatics was widely spread among the people, and entered a prosperous period in the Ming Dynasty. During the Jingtai period of the Ming Dynasty, Huangjia Town Acrobatics Ancient Fair, the first acrobatics industry ancient fair in Chinese history, came into being. The meeting began in early September of the lunar calendar and lasted for one month. It was called "September Fair" in history. There was a saying, "If you don't go into the September Fair, you are not a real businessman", which was popular in the acrobatic world. During the fair, acrobats from all over the country gathered in Huangjia Town, showing their abilities, discussing skills, taking apprentices to form troupes, buying and selling props, etc.

In the Qing Dynasty, the acrobatics in Ningjin became more prosperous, and the performing groups appeared, which were semi-agriculture and semi-art or made a living by busking, and gradually formed two factions of the eight villages in the north and south. During the reign of Emperor Guangxu of the Qing Dynasty, Empress Dowager Cixi held 72 imperial meetings in Beijing, and the "Artist Zhang" of Yezhuli Village in Ningjin County performed the stunt of "crossing the city gate with a bamboo pole", ranking the first and became a man of the hour in the field of acrobatics, which was famous in the Forbidden City at that time. In the 1920s and 1930s, acrobats from the eight villages in the north and south went out of their hometowns and even went abroad one after another to perform. At that time, the popular saying "Acrobats form Ning or Wu counties can turn chicken feathers into eggs; and it is unnecessary for them to take money when traveling", which was a true portrayal of acrobats' wandering life in a foreign land by busking. They went to India, Myanmar, Nepal, Japan, Mongolia, the Soviet Union and Western European countries, forming a large-scale integration and exchange of Chinese acrobatics with world's culture and art. In China, their footprints were also all over the country. "Without Ningjin people, it is difficult to form an acrobatics troupe" was spread widely, and Nanning acrobats became very famous.

After liberation, Ningjin Acrobatics ushered in an unprecedented period of development and prosperity. From 1956 to 1958, based on the past acrobatic troupe, three Ningjin county acrobatic troupes were set up one after another. The performance of the acrobatic troupe gradually shifted from urban and rural areas to large and medium-sized cities and adopted the ways of "sending out and inviting in" to learn from others to improve skills. Ningjin Acrobatics has a good development from then on.

3.Action parsing

Ningjin Acrobatics is plain and rough, combining hardness with softness, highlighting the five artistic characteristics of "surprise, danger, wonder, beauty and novelty", which has high aesthetic, ornamental and cultural value. Ningjin Acrobatics has a wide range of categories, including performance, magic, circus and animal training types, of which there are more than 60 programs in performance type. More than ten kinds of programs, such as "ancient Zhongfan", "flower-picking by jujitsu", "lamp rolling", "flying man in the air", "pole climbing", "cars on high steel-wires", "arhats stacking", "walking on steel wire", "pedaling skills", "circles on the ground", "flower-picking by mouth" and so on, have been performed many times at home and abroad, which are deeply loved by the audience and praised by the industry.

4.Project inheritor

Liu Junchang, the representative successor of Ningjin Acrobatics, is currently a provincial intangible cultural heritage successor, and has trained more than 100 acrobatics students so far.

5.New development

After the founding of the People's Republic of China, especially since the reform and opening, under the care of the Party and the government, Ningjin Acrobatics has made great progress. Many acrobatics schools and acrobatics troupes were established in the county, and more than 2,000 acrobatic talents were trained for art groups at all levels throughout the country successively, many of whom became the backbones in different places, and more than 20 of them won domestic and international acrobatics awards. In recent years, Ningjin Acrobatic Troupe has performed in Korea, Saudi Arabia, Russia, Thailand and other countries, which plays an important role in promoting cultural exchanges between China and foreign countries and promoting economic development.

In recent years, Ningjin Acrobatic Troupe has cooperated with major performing groups throughout the country, participating in many large-scale artistic performances such as *Red Legend*, *Huiyun*, *Pear Garden in the*

Flourishing Age and *Water Margin Tianfeng*, as well as Sino-Korean and Sino-Saudi cultural exchange performances and so on.

In 1995, Ningjin County was named "the hometown of Chinese folk art (acrobatics)" by the Ministry of Culture. In 2005, Ningjin Acrobatics was designated as the first batch of projects to declare "National Intangible Cultural Heritage" by Shandong Province. In 2008, Ningjin Acrobatics was officially selected into the National Intangible Cultural Heritage List. In 2011, Ningjin County was named "the hometown of Chinese folk culture and art". In 2015, the program *Flying Rings* selected by Ningjin Acrobatic Troupe won the third prize of Taishan Literature Award. In 2016, at the 10th Shandong Acrobatic Magic Competition, the acrobatic program *Silk Exercise* selected by Ningjin County won the first prize in the competition. In August 2016, Ningjin's *Row Chair* won the second prize of Taishan Literature and Art Award.

Ningjin Acrobatic Art School, as the inheritance and education base of intangible cultural heritage in Shandong Province, delivers 8-10 actors to the Ningjin County Acrobatic Troupe every three years. Nevertheless, more and more people do not want their children to suffer hardships in the acrobatic troupe, so Ningjin Acrobatics is in danger of lacking inheritors and needs to be protected urgently.

第 16 节　潍坊风筝

1.项目文化

潍坊市位于山东半岛中部，北濒渤海湾，南临黄海，春天风多雨少，且风向单一，瞬时波动小，风力基本呈正态分布。正是这样特殊的地理环境孕育产生了潍坊风筝，其生产制作集中在寒亭区杨家埠一带和奎文区、潍城区。

潍坊风筝兴于明初的杨家埠村。那时，村民已有木版年画的刻印技术，利用每年春天的空余时间，用印年画的纸张、颜料，绘制出各种图案，扎制风筝。开始时这些风筝仅自娱自乐或馈赠亲朋好友，后逐渐发展为商品，至清乾隆年间，风筝已成为当地重要的手工业。

明代潍坊风筝以板子风筝为主，后逐步形成了以硬翅风筝为主、长串蜈蚣为最(最长可达 360 多米)、软翅风筝为巧、筒子风筝为奇的造型系列，内容有人物故事、鸟兽、鱼虫等。目前，西杨家埠村有风筝扎制专业户近百家，风筝品种达 300 余种，年产近百万只，主要传承人为杨其信、杨其民、杨连敏、杨乃忠、杨学顺等。

潍坊风筝具有起飞平稳、放飞高的特征。无论是软翅、硬翅还是串式、立体式的风筝，除了板子风筝需要坠外，其他不需要任何辅助物都能平稳地直升蓝天。其扎制方法虽简单，少则竹条三根，多不超过七根，但讲究竹条均匀、骨架周正、左右对称、重心拴线、形象简练、色彩鲜艳、对比强烈。但近年来，因考虑制作成本而忽略了传统的文化内涵，变换了材料，使用尼龙布和碳素钢管，丢失了传统技艺，也失去了潍坊风筝的地方特色。

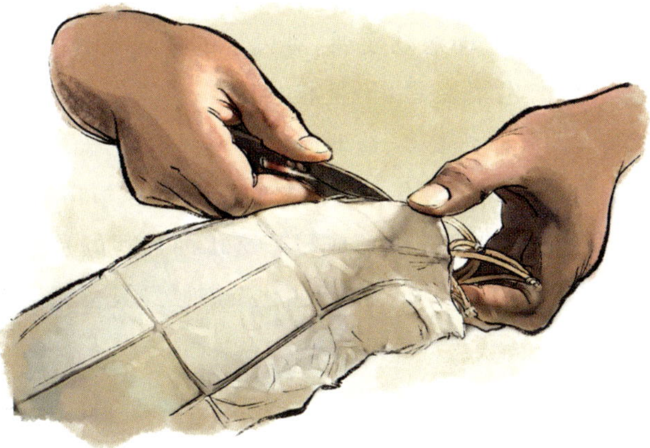

传统风筝制作

Traditional kite making

2.项目起源

风筝起源于齐鲁，放风筝是齐鲁人休闲娱乐的重要方式之一。据说墨子在鲁山“斫木为鹞，三年而成，飞一日而败”(《韩非子・外储说》)，这就是最早的风筝。鲁国人公输般(世人称为鲁班)根据墨子的设计，用竹子做风筝，做成喜鹊的样子，在空中飞翔达三天之久。风筝最初用于传递信息，飞跃险阻等军事需要，后来风筝由木质改由纸糊，逐渐流传到民间，并与清明等民俗节日融合在一起，被赋予了丰富的民俗内涵。放风筝也成为人们清明时节踏青、郊游、娱乐的方式之一。

潍坊风筝兴起于宋代，普及于明代，繁荣于清代。到清朝末期，潍坊风筝经过长期发展，不论在描绘上，还是扎制技术上，都独具特色，成为中国风筝史上的重要流派。潍坊风筝拥有各式各样的人、物形象造型，而且色彩鲜明，形象逼真，据《潍县志》记载：清明时节，少男少女们玩放纸鸢、荡秋千的游戏，所制作的纸鸢各不相同，除了鹤、燕、蝶、蝉各类型外，还有各种人物画像风筝，所制作的风筝都惟妙惟肖，造型独特。潍坊风筝在扎制技术上，相当精细和灵巧，使得风筝的放飞十分平稳。随着扎制技术的发展，潍坊风筝得到新的发展。潍坊风筝艺人根据我国尊龙的传统，同时吸取木板年画中龙的形象，在蜈蚣风筝上安了龙头，制造出了著名的龙头蜈蚣风筝。

伴随着潍坊风筝扎制技术的良好发展，潍坊出现了许多专门扎制风筝的风筝铺。同时，民间放风筝活动蓬勃发展，对风筝的需求量也大幅增加，在供需条件都存在的情况下就产生了交易，于是在古潍县城的白浪河滩上，风筝集市应运而生。在集市上，风筝种类繁多、造型逼真，购买风筝的人络绎不绝，交易频繁，整个市场热闹非凡。清代诗人裴星川有竹枝词为证："风筝市在东城墙，购选游人来去忙，花样翻新招主顾，双双蝴蝶鸢成行。"这首词描写的是白浪河边风筝集市的贸易盛况，反映了该时期潍坊风筝的商业化发展已经具备相当规模。

3.项目内涵

一只看似简单的风筝，人们却赋予了它丰富的意义。风筝既是人们休闲娱乐健身健心的"玩具"，也可以是"故事"（包括神话传说、小说戏曲），进一步提升了这种"玩具"的娱乐性和"可读性"，并内在地表达着人们对真善美的追求和对假恶丑的憎恶的人生态度。风筝还可以是人们对美好生活向往的寄托，乃至表达中华民族文化心理的载体。

潍坊传统风筝的另一个特点，就是善于把一些吉祥图案绘制在风筝上。吉祥图案是一种用具体的事物来表达抽象的意念和感性的手段，这是我们中华文化所特有的一种传统文化形式。从取材上，吉祥图案往往以人物、走兽、花鸟、器物等形象，以及一些吉祥文字、民间谚语、吉语及神话故事为题材；从含义上，吉祥图案则是通过借喻、比拟、双关、寓意、象征及谐音等表现手法，构成"一句吉语一图案"的美术形式，赋予求吉呈祥、消灾免难之意，以寄托和表达人们祈求吉祥、幸福、长寿、喜庆等愿望和对未来美好生活的向往。它因物喻义，将情、景、物融为一体，主题鲜明突出，富有中国独特的文化格调和浓烈的民族色彩。

图案绘制

Patterns drawing

4.设计构思

阳春季节，到郊外放飞风筝，是一项有益身心健康的活动。如果利用休闲假日，举家动手设计制作，更为家庭增添无限乐趣。我国的风筝大体分为三种，一是动物，如沙燕、雄鹰、蝴蝶等；二是人物，如孙悟空、胖娃娃等；三是物品，如扇子、八卦等。风筝的制作必须按照一定规矩，符合物理原理才能升空。一般是用竹篾扎成骨架，上面糊白纸或薄绢，再加以彩绘。

下面以沙燕的制作方法为例进行介绍：第一步要扎好骨架，可以利用旧竹门帘的细竹条，也可选取弹力好的竹子，削成细竹条，扎成风筝骨架；可选取粗细相等的细竹条 5 根，其中 80 厘米的 2 根，做翅膀；85 厘米的 1 根，做头胸，55 厘米的 2 根做双腿尾；将竹条在水中浸泡半日，在文火上慢慢烤，变成圆弧形的膀弯和头弯，要对称；可将一个较理想的圆形膀弯描画在纸上，作为其他三个膀弯的标准，然后用线捆扎，翅膀两端扎成 90°或稍大于 90°，再捆扎头胸和两腿尾；骨架的基本形状像个“大”字，最后在翅膀中间横系一条细线，在腿尾下系两条细线。第二步糊纸要平展，可剪 35 厘米×25 厘米高丽纸两张做翅膀，将纸横向对折，两端剪开 2 厘米的小口，从骨架背后将纸推移至前侧。由于膀线的阻隔而成凹形的迎风面，将骨架平铺桌上，沿翅膀架描绘出轮廓（留出 2 厘米），剪去多余部分；剪 40 厘米×17 厘米的头胸纸及腿尾纸（立档长 12 厘米），留出 2 厘米，描出轮廓；按照描好的图样画好后，先糊翅膀，再糊头胸，最后糊双腿。第三步是绑提线，在两个肩角处及下膀中间系线，将三根线提起，使两肩线等长与风筝平面垂直，将三根线挽结一起即可试放飞。

5.项目传承人

口传心授是民俗文化特有的传承方式，也是潍坊风筝特有的传承方式。由于风筝注重家传，从而形成了著名的十一家，分别是潍坊寒亭区杨家埠村的杨同科、城区的康万香、孙永春、郭乃馨、胡敬珠、牟丹、韩连溪、杨万善、唐洪飞唐洪亮兄弟、陈善庭、张衍禄。从风筝的传承角度看，他们中杨同科、孙永春、牟丹以及唐洪飞唐洪亮兄弟主要是子承父业，陈善庭、胡敬珠、韩连溪、杨万善属于师徒相承，张衍禄、康万香属于师徒相继兼父子相袭，唯有郭乃馨是从画家转化来的风筝艺人。

6.历史变迁

根据历史发展状况，潍坊风筝大致经历了三个阶段：传统社会中的自生自灭，新中国成立后到 1978 年改革开放阶段的逐渐衰微，改革开放后的快速发展。潍坊风筝乃至整个中国风筝的历史发展呈现出波浪式的发展轨迹的原因概括起来无非有两点：一是人们对它的需求程度的改变，二是社会环境变化对它的影响。但从根本上说，社会环境是影响其发展的决定性因素或变量。其实，在任何社会，任何文化现象的兴衰盛亡无不受到来自社会环境外部因素的影响或左右，这是一个无需证明的事实，也是文化自身发展规律之一。在传统社会中，潍坊风筝的发展直接受到社会经济生活条件的制约，人们对风筝需求的程度就会下降，当然也就影响到它的发展。毕竟，只有当最基本的生存条件得到满足以后，像放风筝这样的精神消费才有可能列入人们的日常生活之中，这是符合历史事实的，也正是我们所谓自生自灭的意涵所在。

新中国成立以后，尤其在“大跃进”和“文化大革命”期间，各种社会因素影响了潍坊风筝的发展。“破四旧”运动对风筝民俗以及其他民俗的政治冲击，都对潍坊风筝的发展带来了严重的创伤。但是，即便如此，潍坊风筝还是“没有断线”，清明时节放风筝的习俗虽说受到政治运动的干扰，但传统依然存在。风筝家庭的副业虽说被当时的政治所不容，但在人的生存需要或经济理性面前，政治也不是万能的，所以风筝家庭的副业还是或多或少“在地下”存在着。这正表现出了民间传统文化所固有的草根力量的坚韧性。

7.项目新发展

潍坊风筝选材讲究、造型优美、扎制精巧、形象生动、色彩艳丽，备受世人喜爱。为了将潍坊风筝文化推广到全国乃至全世界，潍坊于 1984 年创办了“国际风筝节”，至今已举办 37 届。一年一度的风筝节为中外风筝专家和爱好者提供了一个观赏、竞技、游览的机会，为风筝文化的传播提供了一个广阔的平台，潍坊被称为“世界风筝之都”，风筝成为其城市名片。

潍坊国际风筝节如同“一块巨大酵母”，引发并推动了一系列有助于风筝文化保护与发展的文化事件。据调查，这些文化事件中比较有影响的大致有十项：举办风筝比赛、风徽的确立、潍坊风筝邮票的发行、评选世界风筝“十绝”、评选“潍坊风筝明星”、成立风筝技工学校、竞选世界风筝都、成立国际风筝联合会并将总部设在潍坊、建造世界风筝博物馆、建造世界风筝都纪念广场。毫无疑问，这十大文化事件对于潍坊风筝文化的保护、传承、发展、传播与弘扬都有着巨大的历史意义和积极的现实意义。

Weifang Kite

1.Project culture

Weifang City is in the middle of Shandong Peninsula, with Bohai Sea in the north and Yellow Sea in the south. It has more wind and less rain in Spring, and the wind direction is single, with little change in a short time. The wind power is normally distributed. This special geographical environment gave birth to Weifang kites, and its production is concentrated in the Yangjiabu, Hanting district, Kuiwen and Weicheng districts.

Weifang kite flourished in Yangjiabu village in the early Ming Dynasty. At that time, the villagers already possessed the technology of engraving and printing wood-block New Year pictures. In their spare time every spring, they took the paper and pigments which used to print New Year pictures to draw various patterns and tie kites. At first, kites were only used for self-amusement or gifts to friends and relatives, and gradually developed into commodities. Until the Qianlong Period (1736-1795), kites became an important local handicraft industry.

Weifang kites in the Ming Dynasty were mainly plate kites, and then gradually formed mainly hard-winged kites, with long strings of centipedes as the longest (up to more than 360 meters), soft-winged kites as ingenious, and tube kites as surprise. These kites are about character stories, birds and beasts, fish, and insects, etc. At present, there are nearly 100 professional kite makers in Xiyangjiabu village and 300 varieties of kites, with an annual output of nearly one million. The main inheritors are Yang Qixin, Yang Qimin, Yang Lianmin, Yang Naizhong, Yang Xueshun and so on.

Weifang kite is characterized by smooth takeoff and high flying. Expect that the plate kite needs tails to fly, other kites, whether it is soft-winged, hard-winged or string-typed, three-dimensional ones can fly to the blue sky smoothly without any auxiliary objects. The kite making only needs three to seven bamboo stripes. Although the method is not difficult, many things should be paid attention, such as uniform bamboo, upright skeleton, concise image, bright color, left and right symmetry and line tied to the center of gravity. However, in recent years, the traditional cultural connotation has been neglected due to the consideration of production cost, and the materials have been changed to use nylon cloth and carbon steel pipe, which has lost the traditional skills and local characteristics of Weifang kite.

2.Project origin

Kites originated from Qilu, and flying kites is one of the important entertainment ways among the people. It is said that Mozi took three years in

Mountain Lu to cut woods to make a wood harrier, but only after flying for one day it didn't work anymore (*Hanfeizi Waichushuo*), which is the earliest kite. Based on Mozi's design, Gongshuban of Lu state (known as "Lu Ban") made a bamboo kite in the shape of magpie, and it could fly in the sky for three days. Kites were originally used for military needs such as conveying information and flying over obstructions. Later, kites changed from wood to paper ones, and gradually spread to the folk and integrated with folk festivals such as Qingming festival. The kite was endowed with rich folk connotations and flying kites also became one of the ways of entertainments for people during the outing in spring in the Qingming festival.

Weifang kites arose in the Song Dynasty, popularized in the Ming Dynasty, and prospered in the Qing Dynasty. After a long period of development, Weifang kites are unique in both depiction and production technology and have become an important genre in the history of Chinese kites until the end of the Qing Dynasty. Weifang kites have a variety of shapes of characters and objects, bright colors, and vivid images. According to *Huai County Annuals*, during the early April, young boys and girls played games of flying paper kites and swinging. The paper kites had kinds of looks, such as cranes, swallows, butterflies, cicadas, and portrait kites, which were exquisite and unique in shape. The production technology of Weifang kite is very delicate and dexterous, which makes the kite fly very smoothly. With the development of kite-making technology, Weifang kite has a new development. According to the tradition of respecting dragons in China, Weifang kite artists absorbed the image of the dragon in the wooden New Year paintings, installed a dragon head on the centipede kite, and created the famous dragon head centipede kite.

With the development of kite-making technology in Weifang, many kite shops specializing in kite making have appeared in Weifang. At the same time, due to the development of folk kite-flying activities, the demand for kites has also increased significantly, therefore transaction emerged based on abundant supply and demand. Thus, the kite market appeared on the Bailang river beach in ancient Wei County. In the market, there are many kinds of kites with realistic shapes, people who buy kites are endless, transactions are frequent, and the whole market is bustling. The Qing Dynasty poet Pei Xingchuan's "Bamboo Song" can be as evidence, "The kite market is in the place of the eastern city wall, and many people come here to buy kites. Kites are renovated to attract patrons, and pairs of butterflies kites are in rows." The poem describes the trade of the kite market by the Bailang river, reflecting that the commercial development of kites in Weifang has reached a considerable scale during that period.

3.Sports connotation

Kites seem so simple, but they have rich meanings laid by people. They are not only people's "toys" for leisure, entertainment and fitness, but also include "stories" (myths and legends, novels and operas), which further enhance the entertainment and "readability" of this "toy", and intrinsically express people's pursuit of truth, goodness and beauty and the attitude of hating fake, evil and ugliness towards life. Kites can also be a carrier for people's longing for a better life and expressing the culture of the Chinese nation.

Another feature of traditional Weifang kites is that people are good at drawing some auspicious patterns on kites. The auspicious pattern is a means of expressing abstract ideas and sensibilities with concrete things, which is a traditional and unique cultural form in our Chinese culture. Auspicious patterns are often based on the images of characters, animals, flowers, birds, utensils and some auspicious characters, folk proverbs, auspicious languages, and mythological stories. In terms of meaning, they express the good luck and reducing disasters by the art form of "one auspicious language and one pattern" using metaphors, analogies, puns, allegories, symbols and harmonics and other expression techniques, which express people's wishes for auspiciousness, happiness, longevity, celebration, and a better life in the future. Because of the metaphor of things, it integrates emotions, scenery, and material things into one, and the theme is clear and prominent, full of China's unique cultural style and strong national color.

4.Design ideas

Flying kites in the countryside is an activity that is beneficial to physical and mental health in the spring season. Family design and production add endless fun to the family during the holidays. There are roughly three kinds of kites in China. The first is animals such as sand swallows, eagles, butterflies, etc. The second is characters such as monkey king and fat dolls, etc. The third is items such as fans and the Eight Trigrams, etc. The kite must be made according to certain specifications and conform to physical principles before it can be lifted off. It is generally made of bamboo to form a skeleton, pasted with white paper or thin silk, and then painted.

The following describes the production method using sand swallow as an example. First, the skeleton should be tied. Use the thin bamboo strips of the old bamboo curtains or the elastic bamboo to cut into thin bamboo strips to make a kite skeleton. Then select 5 similar thin bamboo strips, of which 2 strips of 80 cm are used as wings; 1 strip of 85 cm for the head and thorax; 2 of 55 cm for leg tail. Soak the bamboo stripes in water for half a day. Then, they are slowly roasted over a slow fire to form circular symmetrical bends for wings and heads. You can draw an ideal circular wing on paper as a criterion for the other three wing bends, then tie them with lines, with wings tied at 90 degrees or slightly more than 90 degrees, and then tie the head, chest and legs and tails. The basic shape of the skeleton is like the Chinese character of "大", and finally a thin line is tied horizontally in the middle of the wing and two thin lines are tied under the tail of the leg. The second step of the paper should be flattened, and two pieces of 35 cm × 25 cm Korean paper can be cut to make wings. Fold the paper in half, cut a 2 cm opening at both ends, and push the paper from behind the skeleton to the front. Due to the barrier of the wing line to form a concave windward surface, the skeleton is tiled on the table, and the outline is drawn along the wing frame (leaving 2 cm), and the excess is cut. Cut 40 cm×17 cm of head and chest paper and leg tail paper (stand 12 cm long) to leave 2 cm and draw the outline. After drawing according to the drawn pattern, the wings are pasted first, then the head and chest, and finally the legs. The third step is to tie the lifting line, tie the line at the two shoulder corners and the middle of the lower arm, and lift the three lines, so that the two shoulder lines are equal in length and perpendicular to the kite, and the three lines can be tied together to fly.

5.Project inheritor

Oral transmission and careful teaching of skills are the folk culture and the unique inheritance method of Weifang kite. Because kite-making values inheriting within families, the famous eleven factions have been formed. They are represented by Yang Tongke in Yangjiabu Village, Hanting District, Kang Wanxiang, Sun Yongchun, Guo Naixin, Hu Jingzhu, Mou Dan, Han Lianxi, Yang Wanshan, Tang Hongfei and Tang Hongliang brothers, Chen Shanting, and Zhang Yanlu. From the perspective of kite inheriting, Yang Tongke, Sun Yongchun, Mu Dan and Tang Hongfei, Tang Hongliang brothers are mainly sons' inheriting their father's business, while Chen Shanting, Hu Jingzhu, Han Lianxi, and Yang Wanshan belong to the apprentices' inheriting from masters. Zhang Yanlu and Kang Wanxiang are both, and only Guo Naixin is a kite artist coming from a painter.

6.Historical changes

According to historical development, Weifang kite has roughly gone through three stages: self-perpetuating in traditional society, gradual decline from the founding of the People's Republic of China to the reform and opening up in 1978, and rapid development after reform and opening. Why does the historical development of Weifang kite and even the entire Chinese kite show a wave-like development trajectory? To sum up, there are just two reasons: One is the change of people's different demand for it, and the other is the impact of social environment changes on it. But fundamentally, the social environment is a decisive factor or variable that affects its development. In fact, in any society, the rise and fall of any cultural phenomenon are affected or influenced by external factors from the social environment. This is a fact that does not need to be proven, and it is also one of the laws of the development of culture itself. In a traditional society, the development of Weifang kite is directly limited by social and economic living conditions, and the decline of people's demand for kites affects its development. After all, only when the most basic conditions of survival are met can spiritual consumption such as kite flying be included in people's daily lives. This is in line with historical facts, and it is exactly what we mean by self-sufficiency.

After the founding of the People's Republic of China, especially during the "Great Leap Forward" and the "Cultural Revolution", various social factors influenced the development of Weifang kite and the entire Chinese society at that time. The political impact of the "Breaking the Four Old Traditions" movement on kite folk customs and other folk customs brought serious trauma to the development of Weifang kite. However, even so, the Weifang kite is "alive". The custom of flying kites during the Qingming Festival still exists, even disturbed by political movements. Although the side business of the kite in families is not tolerated at that time, politics was not omnipotent in the face of people's survival needs or economic rationality. Therefore, the side business of kite in families still exists "underground". This shows folk traditional culture's inherent tenacity as the grassroot power.

7.New development

Weifang kite is adored by the world with its excellent material, beautiful shape, exquisite production, vivid image and bright colors. In order to promote the kite culture of Weifang to the whole country and the world, Weifang founded the International Kite Festival in 1984, which has been held for 37 sessions so far. The annual Kite Festival provides an opportunity to watch, compete and visit for Chinese and foreign kite experts and enthusiasts, and provides a broad platform for the spread of kite culture. Weifang is known as the "Kite Capital of the World", and kites have become its name card.

The Weifang International Kite Festival is like "a huge yeast" that triggers and promotes a series of cultural events that are conducive to the protection and development of kite culture. According to the survey, there have been about ten influential cultural events: holding kite competitions, confirming the kite emblem, issuing Weifang "Kite" stamps, selecting the world's "Ten Best Kites", selecting "Weifang Kite Stars", establishing a kite technical school, running for the World Kite Capital, establishing the International Kite Federation and headquartering in Weifang, building the World Kite Museum, and building the World Kite Capital Memorial Square. There is no doubt that ten major cultural events have great historical significance and positive practical significance for the protection, inheritance, development, dissemination and promotion of Weifang kite culture.

文献汇总

一、专著

[1]袁宏.齐鲁体育文化研究[M].济南:山东大学出版社,2016.

[2]刘秉果,赵明奇.中国古代足球[M].济南:齐鲁书社,2008.

[3]解维俊.足球起源地探索[M].上海:中华书局,2004.

[4]解维俊.齐都蹴鞠[M].天津:百花文艺出版社,2006.

[5]解维俊.齐都盛典[M].北京:五洲传播出版社,2004.

[6]舍人亲王.日本书记[M].成都:四川人民出版社,2008.

[7]廖文远,战国策[M].上海:中华书局,2006.

[8]李成银.山东传统武术文化研究[M].北京:北京体育大学出版社,2009.

[9]李成银.齐鲁武术史话[M].济南:山东文艺出版社,2004.

[10]李成银.山东传统武术文化研究[M].北京:北京体育大学出版社,2009.

[11]李群.传统体育与杂技[M].济南:山东友谊出版社,2008.

[12]宋义祥.梁山功夫[M].济南:山东友谊出版社,1994.

[13]刘晓真,胡晶莹.中国国粹艺术读本——秧歌[M],香港:中国文联出版社,2008.

[14]陈学孟.商河鼓子秧歌[M],北京:中国文联出版社,2006.

[15]孙丽.山东胶州秧歌[M],北京:中国文联出版社,2007.

[16]张荫松.山东海阳秧歌[M],上海:上海音乐出版社,2012.

[17]张基振.走进潍坊看风筝[M].济南:山东电子音像出版社,2009.

二、期刊文章

[1]侯雪婷,周建东.论齐鲁体育的文化“性格”——基于“地缘文明”的视角

[J].体育成人教育学刊,2016,32(01):63-65.

[2]牟艳.儒家伦理思想对齐鲁传统体育文化的影响[J].体育文化导刊,2017(04):203-206.

[3]张立天.简议齐鲁文化与齐鲁民间体育游戏[J].运动,2012(21):144-145.

[4]李勇,秀辉.罕见拳种——徐家拳[J].搏击,2014(03):73-74.

[5]闺智惠.探索传统民族体育项目,弘扬民族体育精神——以山东东明佛汉拳的历史演变及发展现状为例[J].武术研究,2017(03),106-109.

[6]李成银.临清肘捶的历史渊源与技法体系研究[J].山东体育学院学报,2011,27(10):37-42.

[7]张雁.商羊舞的非物质文化遗产属性探究[J].名作欣赏,2013(20):171-172.

[8]王庆花.汉族与少数民族鼓舞研究——鼓舞的起源、形制和地位[J].贵州民族研究,2013,34(01):87-90.

[9]邹政.高跷运动的起源、发展与创新[J].池州师专学报,2006(04):86-87+107.

[10]黄文辉."高脚马"与"高跷"的比较研究[J].搏击(武术科学),2011,8(08):91-93.

[11]王伟.聊城杂技的保护与传承[J].杂技与魔术,2017(01):48-49.

[12]郑玉超,刘兵.潍坊国际风筝会的起源与发展[J].体育文化导刊,2013(03):33-36.

[13]秀荣.巧做风筝[J].家庭科技,1999(03):12.

[14]党明德,谢婕.潍坊风筝的传承方式及代表人物[J].民俗研究,2007(03):95-106.

三、学位论文

[1]王艳妮.齐鲁体育文化传承与发展研究[D].山东体育学院,2015.

[2]张志成.非物质文化遗产视角下的山东传统武术研究[D].山东师范大学,2011.

[3]张双建.东明县国家级非物质文化遗产佛汉拳传播研究[D].云南师范大学,2013.

[4]曹海滨.山东菏泽地区传统民间舞蹈文化[D].陕西师范大学,2008.

[5]徐磊. 青州花毽的保护和发展研究[D].山东师范大学,2012.

[6]张基振. 文化视野中民间体育的保护、传承与发展[D].上海体育学院,2008.

[7]翟继萍.临清肘捶的历史传承与保护研究[D].山东体育学院.2016.

后记

《齐鲁传统体育文化》一书耗时四年，现在终于出版了，就好比是看到了自己久久浇灌呵护的植物发芽，又好比刚刚见到新生儿的母亲。久捧书籍，轻闻书香，复杂又激动的心情难以言表。轻抚封面，心中难免激动和欣喜陶醉。于是，想随手一篇后记，用以抒发自己在出书的过程中和见到书之后的欣喜之情。

自从开始研究齐鲁传统体育文化以来，一直在寻找一个契机或者是一个融合点，可以让体育和文化有机融合。齐鲁传统体育不仅仅是中国体育的宝藏，也属世界体育文化的范畴。民族的就是世界的。研究齐鲁传统体育项目的发展不仅仅是对这个传统体育文化的维护和发展，更是赋予了现代体育更悠久的历史长度和厚重的历史内涵。齐鲁本地孕育出来的传统体育项目是世界体育文化的全新的资源。我国正在从体育大国到体育强国的发展方向慢慢迈进，有着五千年历史沉淀的中国孕育出来的体育项目一定能为世界体育项目增添光彩。但齐鲁传统体育文化的传播现状是我们不可忽视的，不论是翻译资源的稀缺还是传播途径的单一都是我们不得不面对的问题，也是我们传播传统项目时必须要解决的问题。传统体育项目的发展短期看依靠国家扶持，继承人主要是通过师徒相传和短期的表演培训来继承，方法单一且效果局限；长期的发展还是要从保护到让群众对项目“有了解、有兴趣、有参与”，这才是让项目长久且蓬勃发展的长久之计。

通过和各位学者的交流与分析，我重新审视了齐鲁传统体育文化发展的必要性，也更加了解了发展和发扬齐鲁体育文化的急迫性，这明晰了我写书的本意也坚定了我成书的决心。希望本书不仅仅可以把体育、文化与外宣有机结合到一起，还可以为齐鲁体育文化的对外输出贡献一份力量。

在此，特别感谢在出书的过程中各位学者给出的富有建设性的意见。感谢山东师范大学李成银教授等专家学者为本书提供文字材料的指导，感谢临淄足球博物馆、孙膑拳国家级代表性传承人刘海港、青州花毽国家级代表性传承人李贤臣、李红及其团队等为本书提供图片。本书在写作过程中曾多次试图联系引用文章作者，但无果，在此向为本书提供文本参考的作者予以感谢，如有问题，欢迎与我们联系。

《齐鲁传统体育文化》一书的完成，只是对外传播齐鲁体育文化的一个开端，还需要更多的专业人士投入更多的精力和时间去研究和发展，为齐鲁传统体育项目的海外宣传做出贡献。

再次感谢为齐鲁传统体育文化传承保护和传播发展而努力的人们！

编者

2022 年 10 月